Also by Jerry Grayson, AFC

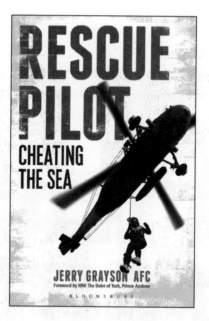

'Interesting to read a different viewpoint of that tragic
Fastnet Race. Grayson's recollection is moving: it reads like
a roll-call of terror.'
Sailing Today

'A grippingly clear insight into sea rescues. Fascinating.'
Yachting Monthly

'You will be disappointed to finish.'
Australian Flying

'There can be no more gripping an account of the highs and
lows of life as a helicapter rescue pilot.'
Pilot Magazine

'Thoroughly recommended.'
Fleet Air Arm Officer's Association

FILM
PILOT

FROM JAMES BOND TO HURRICANE KATRINA

JERRY GRAYSON, AFC

ADLARD COLES NAUTICAL

B L O O M S B U R Y

LONDON · OXFORD · NEW YORK · NEW DELHI · SYDNEY

Adlard Coles Nautical
An imprint of Bloomsbury Publishing Plc

50 Bedford Square
London
WC1B 3DP
UK

1385 Broadway
New York
NY 10018
USA

www.bloomsbury.com
www.adlardcoles.com

ADLARD COLES, ADLARD COLES NAUTICAL and the Buoy logo
are trademarks of Bloomsbury Publishing Plc

First published 2017

British Library Cataloguing-in-Publication Data
A catalogue record for this book is available from the British Library.

Library of Congress Cataloguing-in-Publication data has been applied for.

ISBN: PB: 978-1-4729-4107-7
ePDF: 978-1-4729-4104-6
ePub: 978-1-4729-4106-0

2 4 6 8 10 9 7 5 3 1

Typeset in Haarlemmer MT by Deanta Global Publishing Services, Chennai, India
Printed and bound in Australia by Griffin Press

MIX
Paper from
responsible sources
FSC® C009448

Bloomsbury Publishing Plc makes every effort to ensure that the papers used in the
manufacture of our books are natural, recyclable products made from wood
grown in well-managed forests. Our manufacturing processes conform
to the environmental regulations of the country of origin.

To find out more about our authors and books visit www.bloomsbury.com.
Here you will find extracts, author interviews, details of forthcoming events
and the option to sign up for our newsletters.

To Sara Louise;
the love of my life,
for making it all possible.

And to
Sam and Tips
for making it all worth doing.

www.JerryG.co

Many of the stories in this book relate to sections of films that have made it on to the internet. Visit Jerry Grayson's website for links, more pictures and other bonus material.

CONTENTS

01

CIVILIAN ONCE MORE

'SO WHAT DO YOU DO FOR A LIVING?'

Around forty-five years ago I set out on a journey that would lead to me being able to answer with, 'I'm a film pilot.' The reaction so often became 'What does one of those do?' that I soon modified my answer to 'I fly helicopters on movies.' It serves as a good précis and usually leads to an enthusiastic conversation about the high-profile movies I've worked on.

However, over the years since leaving the Fleet Air Arm I slowly realised that the day-to-day job I was doing was so far outside most people's experience that it shocked them. I was once at the engagement party of an old friend who was working in the City of London, and when a fellow guest enquired which bank I worked at I had to tell him that I wasn't with a bank, I flew helicopters on movies. He didn't come back with any response at all; he just looked quizzically at me and then turned on his heel and went to introduce himself to somebody else. I guess I'd taken him too far outside his

points of reference and he didn't want to deal with this strange creature who'd wandered into his comfort zone.

I never found a neat answer to the question, 'How do you become a film pilot?' Just like anybody who finds themselves in a job they love doing, there has been a bit of luck, a great deal of work and some hard knocks along the way. Most of all there has been a singularity of purpose, which meant that I was unlikely ever to be anything else.

Very few students can have experienced the sort of transformation I went through after a visit to the school assembly hall by a good-looking guy in overalls. He'd left the school himself only a few years earlier and was now returning, in what turned out to be flying overalls, as the holder of the *Daily Mail* prize for their Transatlantic Air Race of 1969. It had been a race that captured the imagination of the nation and made front-page news long before the internet was even thought of. In fact, we had only just installed a black and white television to watch Neil and Buzz walk on the Moon that same year. The swinging sixties had brought Mick Jagger and Marianne Faithful to the steps of our local court house in Chichester, a quiet cathedral town on the south coast of Britain, but I had been too young to understand that the world was rapidly changing.

The Transatlantic Air Race was all about getting a person from the top of the Empire State Building in New York to the top of London's Post Office Tower in the shortest time possible. On the day, Lieutenant Commander Brian Davies AFC RN delivered his observer (the Navy's term for a navigator) Peter Goddard in a time that trounced the RAF by exactly one hour. So it was that Brian made his triumphant way back to Chichester High School for Boys to tell us the story of his race. And so it was that I found myself sitting in the school hall that day asking myself, in incredulity, 'That's a *job*?!'

The concept of being paid to fly a machine captured my attention instantaneously. I now had a reason to concentrate in the classes on Maths, Physics and Geography. I was motivated with a capital 'M'. I was too tall and gangly to ever have a shot at the cutest girls so distractions were minimal as I focused on becoming an aviator; a task I succeeded at in the month of my seventeenth birthday. Very shortly thereafter I became the youngest pilot to be accepted into the Fleet Air Arm. Along the journey to that moment I had nearly lost my way by assuming I'd be better off as an airline pilot, but the closure of the British Airways school for pilots and a kindly careers master had set me back on track.

The next eight years were rich, rewarding and most of all fun, starting with learning which uniform to wear for each occasion, which people to salute and which to expect a salute from. We went to sea in huge aircraft carriers, chased Soviet submarines in Sea King helicopters and relaxed in the fleshpots of exotic European and American ports with sophisticated young ladies whose parents were only too glad to see their daughters on the arm of a British naval officer.

By the age of twenty-five I was a highly decorated 'veteran' on the Wessex helicopter type that had carried Pete Goddard from Brian's Phantom to the Post Office Tower. It's a measure of my enjoyment of those eight years, and particularly of my time flying on Search and Rescue duties, that they warranted a book of their own: *Rescue Pilot – Cheating The Sea.*

It's often said that a man spends his time in the military feeling like a civilian in uniform and the remainder of his life feeling like a military man in civvies. That's pretty much how it's felt for me except that 'civvies' for a helicopter pilot generally still involves uniform, usually with the four rings that denote the same qualifications as an airline captain.

In all other aspects the process of becoming a civilian was a strange and alien task. No longer did 'daily orders' dictate where I should be and at what time; this was now something I had to work out for myself. It was a transition that many of my contemporaries had avoided in favour of joining either Bristow's or Bond's, the two big helicopter companies that fed oil-rig workers out to the North Sea. In those companies, as I heard from time to time, the pilots were still subject to some form of daily orders, with a few differences, such as having a union representative to run to in times of grievance, plus the probability that they would return to sleep in their own beds at the end of their working shift. For the flying part of the job these guys were still working in conditions just as hairy as we'd experienced in the Fleet Air Arm, but with the added responsibility of carrying a full set of passengers who had not signed up to experience daring feats of aviation.

In the sleepy south-west of England my old mate Keith Thompson and I set about establishing a small helicopter charter company under the benign patronage of Roy Flood, a wonderful character who had the reputation of being one of the most successful used-car dealers in the country. You couldn't run a successful business in an area of such sparse population without having a loyal clientele, and that was the first of many good lessons I learned from Roy over the years. Since Roy's car dealership was called Castle Motors we named our new aviation enterprise Castle Air.

The aviation came naturally to us after eight years of the finest training the Queen's purse could provide, but somebody had to pay for each hour of our civilian flying activities and therein lay the challenge. The staple fare for any small start-up helicopter company was pleasure-flying: taking people for what was often their first helicopter experience.

At a good event you could guarantee a queue for most of the day and it was fun to see the delight on each face as they left the earth vertically for the first time in their lives. Even when the greenhouse-like bubble of the cockpit became hot, sweaty and monotonous towards mid-afternoon, I consoled myself with the fact that I was getting to perform a landing every few minutes, whereas contemporaries who had chosen to go to the airlines for employment would only get to do that after about ten hours or more in the seat.

In March 1981 we moved our Bell Longranger helicopter the five short miles from the tiny hangar behind Roy's palatial hillside home, across the top of our rural home town of Liskeard and down to land next to our sparkling new hangar, which nestled in a steep-sided valley alongside Castle Motors. We'd built the new facility quite literally with our own hands. I had learned to drive a JCB backhoe with some success and to weld large chunks of steel together with reasonable confidence.

The new hangar gave us the opportunity to add a Jetranger to what we could now call our 'fleet', plus it gave us a springboard to bigger and better things. High among these was a new contract to provide a weekend shuttle service to the island of Lundy in the Bristol Channel. Not only was that welcome bread-and-butter work, but it also gave me an experience that hugely motivated me towards wanting to do film work from the air.

It was early on a Sunday morning and I was by myself, flying the helicopter to the island. For a sea area that was almost invariably rough it was strange to see flat calm water below and a clear blue sky above. A few miles further out the overnight temperature inversion had created a shallow but dense layer of fog. Through that fog sailed a rusty and unremarkable coaster whose decks were in bright sunshine but whose hull was completely hidden. I marvelled at the ethereal effect created, which could so easily have been from a Pink Floyd or Yes album cover. There was nobody else aboard the helicopter with whom to share the experience and no

camera to hand, so it felt like a very personal moment but at the same time an opportunity lost. More than anything I look back on those few minutes as being the catalyst to my constant quest thereafter to find innovative ways of making the ostensibly ugly look beautiful. There wouldn't always be a helpful layer of fog but there would always be changing light, an interesting perspective or, as a final resort, the ability to use the sun for a stunning silhouette.

The local commercial TV station, Westward Television, was glad to have a helicopter company nearby and began to try us out on a few small jobs. One of the first was filming the start of a transatlantic yacht race. I was entirely at home in the flying environment over the sea and was able to use some of the basic filming techniques I'd learned during my last year in the Navy, when I'd been involved in the fly-on-the-wall BBC series *Rescue Flight*. It had been a ground-breaking project at the time, first shown in ten-minute segments on the national news magazine programme at six o'clock and later assembled into an hour of documentary on its own. Paul Berriff, the producer, had taken time to educate us on how a shot needed to have a beginning, a middle and an end, so I had already learned to keep 10 per cent of my brain thinking like an editor while the other 90 per cent flew the helicopter. As the years passed this proportion would gradually shift until it almost reversed, but for the moment I was happy enough to achieve the job safely and to return with footage that would make the cameraman – we didn't use the term 'camera person' back then – look good at his job and make it into the local evening news. I could not have imagined then that Paul would give my film-flying career another major boost in the fires of Kuwait a decade later.

In the early 1980s 16mm film was still being used for news gathering and the standard of cameraman was, to put it mildly, poor. They all liked to claim years of experience in helicopter work, but the reality was more often that they'd been at the open door of a helicopter on just a couple of occasions in the previous decade. As I ascended out of Plymouth airport one day with an old and bold BBC man in the small cabin behind me, I received a strange call from air traffic control.

'Are you aware that you've got a tail and it's getting longer?'

A quick glance over my right shoulder confirmed that the source of the tail was my assigned compatriot, who was muttering to himself about a jam in the film magazine and was merrily rectifying the problem by discarding about 100 feet of 16mm celluloid into my slipstream. My expletives woke him up enough for him to quickly tear off the ruined material and toss it away before it had the chance to wrap itself around my tail rotor, in what might have been an ignominious end to my fledgling career as a film pilot and an otherwise happy life.

From that day forward my default setting was to assume that any camera operator who didn't specialise in full-time aerial work would probably be overloaded by being airborne and would need constant vigilance. In later years I came to rely on the really good guys as an extra pair of eyes, but for the moment I had to assume that each cameraman had set out that morning specifically to kill us both, and I was often not far off the mark in that assumption.

The quality of footage we were generating in those days would make me blush with embarrassment now. It depended heavily on the ability of the operator to hold a heavy camera on his shoulder in a helicopter that I was keenly manoeuvring over the action beneath us. Most of them settled for a wide and general view (GV) of whatever the event might be as any attempt to zoom in tighter would result in a sequence too wobbly to be of use to the editor. Once I'd seen a few horrible shots make it to air on the local TV news I realised I had to improve the way I communicated with cameramen to give them the best chance of success. If I'd settled

into a steady and smooth descent towards a yacht, then I would make certain the operator was aware of it so he could use a little of the zoom capability of the lens to accelerate the rate at which our shot 'descended'. Conversely I would give him warning of an imminent need to increase power or commence a turn so that he could pull back on the lens to a wide shot and reduce the visual consequence of helicopter movement or vibration.

The opportunity to participate in a day of shooting a local documentary called *The Sheep Walk* gave me an early taste of how my job would take me to places and events I couldn't have dreamt up. For some reason a local farmer had decided to recreate the habit of shepherds in days gone by to walk their sheep to better pastures. In his case he had amplified the issue by setting off from the very top of Britain with his flock some months earlier, periodically accompanied by a documentary crew. We were to shoot the last day of this epic adventure as the sheep arrived back at their home farm on Exmoor. I had been assigned one of the cameramen I respected and on the allocated day we worked well together to find the relevant flock and shoot the last hour of their triumphant march south. This was the first time I'd had to think more broadly than a handful of shots that would each look good in isolation on the evening news. I had to think about how the editor might assemble a sequence of shots to tell a story, and I began to realise it was part of my job to make that process as easy as possible for him.

We started on a high and wide GV to show the context of the barren moorland over which the sheep were travelling and then 'found' them with both the helicopter and the camera, so that the operator and I would simultaneously arrive at the lowest and closest point of our descent to the shepherd. Animals are always a challenge to shoot from a helicopter because you cannot predict how they will react to the excessive noise of the approaching machine. In this case the woolly walkers had presumably become immune to the noise of human toys after an earlier tramp through the large city of Birmingham and more than one long trek down the boundaries of a motorway, so they behaved impeccably and allowed us to get surprisingly close. I was also verging on the conservative side as I didn't feel I would win many friends by scattering the flock to the four winds on the very last day of their adventure.

Having 'established' the location and the subject, we had given the editor a point at which to cut to a ground shot, and of course with the use of film the expression 'to cut' meant the actual use of scissors. We then began to capture other small sequences that might be useful in telling the story visually. For example, we 'revealed' the flock by approaching from low behind a small hill and gently rising up to show the sheep in the foreground. It wasn't an easy shot to capture in the days before forward-looking camera mounts because I had to fly the helicopter sideways in order to allow the side-facing cameraman a clear look at the subject. While a helicopter will certainly fly sideways it doesn't like to do that at any speed and protests by kicking its tail from side to side if it felt it was being stretched. I therefore had to feel the mood of the helicopter through my bottom, my hands and my feet, I guess much like a horseman, and not push the machine to the edge of its capabilities (or mine). Another factor I began to understand in how I flew was the need to match the speed and energy of a shot with the subject matter; the aerials on a documentary about sheep would look horribly out of place if filmed in the way I might shoot a powerboat race, and vice versa. I thoroughly enjoyed the day and realised, with every step on the steep learning curve, that there was more and more to learn.

Looking back on those first tentative days of filming I can see that I'd already begun to go beyond the realm most pilots occupy; I had started to fly the camera instead of flying the helicopter. However

oddly I was making my vehicle behave, it was the elegant progression of the camera that mattered and not the elegant progression of the flying machine.

It was with a wry smile that I set off in 1981 with a photographer to record the first Fastnet yacht race since the disastrous event of 1979, an occasion still known as Britain's worst maritime disaster. The contrast between the mountainous seas I'd done battle with that year, in my previous incarnation as a rescue pilot, and the beautiful summer's day that greeted me in my new role as a film pilot, could not have been more extreme. I spent some of that flight quietly reminiscing to myself about the people lost and the people saved in 1979, but for most of my flight time that day I was occupied with developing a lifetime loathing of carrying stills photographers. Cameramen armed with the ability to capture moving imagery appreciate the smooth sweeping movements that a helicopter performs so naturally and effortlessly. Stills cameramen, on the other hand, like to hover in one place, constantly adjust that position and often ask you to move backwards. This uses maximum power, maximum pilot effort, inputs maximum vibration to the airframe and entices you into positions that can be dangerous. No chopper pilot ever enjoys being at maximum power above about 20 feet in a helicopter with only one engine and a tail wind; the whole thing is a recipe for disaster. I've studiously avoided carrying stills photographers at every opportunity since.

The really good guys are a delight because they understand the platform they're shooting from, allow it to dance from one position to another under the guidance of a creative pilot, then press the shutter to capture the images they like as they pass, but most think they're sitting on a noisy tripod and try to treat it as such. The technique of long hovering periods can also be dangerous for those on the ground or on the water. A hovering helicopter soon builds up a column of rapidly descending air which can knock a standing person or a yacht right over. Racing yachts certainly do not appreciate hovering helicopters (unless they are being rescued by one) and I wasn't about to endanger anybody's race chances, especially given my previous experiences on the Fastnet. I came home grumpy that night, with some below-average photographs.

Two more firsts for me would follow before the end of our second year of operations: my first acting experience on screen, and my first music video, or 'pop promo' as we used to call them.

Although I say 'acting', the expression doesn't exactly apply to the direction notes: 'Pilot helps passenger from helicopter.' Nevertheless an appearance on screen did make Mum wriggle with delight, especially since it was in *To The Manor Born*, one of her favourite TV shows. I flew to Cricket-St-Thomas to participate in an episode where actress Rula Lenska played the part of a predatory cougar. Stalwarts Penelope Keith, Peter Bowles and Angela Thorne turned out to be as delightful in person as they were on screen and it was also my introduction to location catering. I would later realise that the BBC operated at the bottom of the catering ladder but to me the prospect of getting fed with anything during a flying day was a new and wicked treat.

I didn't have to delve too deep to find the motivation for the part – we'd landed and she needed to get out – but there was one small complication. TV producers and editors like continuity and so a landing carried out using a jet engine and two spinning rotor blades would not cut well with a stationary and silent helicopter as 'Pilot helps passenger from helicopter'. I therefore had to leave the cockpit while everything was still running. We had a technique by which we could apply a friction lock to the flying controls and could, furthermore, switch off the hydraulic input to the rotors to help hold them more securely, but it wasn't something we undertook lightly, and if I were to do that on camera today I'd probably be locked up.

At the very least I would, very rightly, suffer severe castigation from my peers. On the day all went well, but I subsequently decided not to do that again when a guy I was sitting next to at a wedding a couple of years later invited me to feel the steel plate in the top of his skull which had replaced the original bone; his helicopter had indeed become a 'chopper'.

My other first that year was for a pop promo by a band called The Teardrop Explodes, to illustrate their new single 'Colours Fly Away'. The director took the title of the song to heart and chose to shoot the film in a factory site near Bristol that was indeed devoid of colour. The probably toxic smoke coming out of the extensive chimney stacks had turned everything to a dull monochrome, including the sheep grazing in the field where I landed. The briefing extended to 'Fly around a bit and then come in to land and to pick up the boys. Might as well take a cameraman with you for the first bit.' I remember the band all dutifully behaving like crazy kids, madly running around the factory as I tried to give the cameraman a clear shot at them, but I'd rather forget the experience after later reading 'The record stalled at number 57 in the UK charts, signalling the end of Teardrops as a popular singles band.' Oops!

By the end of 1981 I'd gained enough experience to be able to assemble a few basic camera moves with confidence and I certainly felt at home with the various types of work expected of us by the local television crews. As we began to look forward to Christmas that year a freak weather event hit Devon and Cornwall. Its impact was so immense that it was to provide us with continuous flying work for the next five months.

Freezing rain is a rare phenomenon but one that terrifies all pilots regardless of whether they fly helicopters or fixed-wing aircraft. We're used to experiencing rain, sleet, snow and hail, especially in Britain, and each has its own effect on a flying machine. Rain doesn't bother us much, the main effect of snow is to reduce visibility, hail can certainly cause serious damage to the engines and to the rotors, but freezing rain is one of the few things that can bring an aircraft down. The mechanism by which freezing rain is generated high in the atmosphere is a complex one. In short, a supercooled droplet of water hits the already freezing airframe and instantaneously turns one-eightieth of itself – for each degree below zero – into clear and solid ice. As you can imagine, this glaze quickly builds up enough to change the shape of a wing or a rotor blade, to the point where it no longer has the ability to generate lift. The problem is aggravated by the weight of the ice sheet on the airframe. If part of the ice sheet detaches from one rotor blade and not the other, it causes an imbalance in both the weight and the lift. The resultant vibration can destroy a helicopter in seconds.

Thankfully I was safely tucked up in bed on the night the ice-storm hit the south-west of the country. I awoke to find a magical and surreal landscape in which every single blade of grass was an individual and very solid stalagmite pointing to the sky. It was a unique sight and extremely beautiful. Less beautiful was the loss of electrical power across the majority of the countryside. As each overhead power cable was hit by a super-cooled droplet, the ice formed so rapidly that the power poles could no longer take the weight and simply collapsed to the ground. The initial result for our business was a couple of days of extra news-gathering work, and of course the local TV stations loved any images we could capture of isolated people, vehicles, farms and animals within this Christmas-card landscape. By around the third day we were beginning to get calls from the South West Electricity Board (SWEB), whose own three full-time helicopters were overwhelmed in their search for line faults. One of their flight observers, Ted Webber, had recently retired from the job and was quickly dragged back into service and assigned to us. We began a crash course in understanding the bare

essentials of an electricity supply network and we took it in turns to fly Ted on emergency line-inspection sorties.

We flew and we flew and we flew until all but the most isolated farms had their power restored. Then the real work began. After an event like that it's essential that every line is visually inspected and faults recorded so that the repair crews on the ground can prioritise their rectification work. In the end it would take several months before SWEB felt able to release us from our temporary contract and allow their own helicopters to complete the task. Those months were hugely enjoyable, provided very welcome income to our fledgling company and of course put us back where we loved to be: airborne.

I would later look back and realise that this job gave me fundamental training that stood me in good stead in my career as a film pilot. For up to seven hours each day I had to fly low, slow and close to a power line so that Ted could see any faults with his naked eye. It didn't matter whether I was pointing the helicopter forwards, backwards or sideways as long as Ted could maintain continuous visual contact with the line as it snaked and swerved over hill and down dale. The only truly dangerous moments were when other lines crossed over the line we were inspecting, and those points were carefully marked on Ted's map in advance of our day's work, in big red circles. Many helicopter pilots have perished over the years by flying into a high-tensile wire that they never even saw before being swatted out of the sky.

In addition to using all my powers as a pilot to achieve a steady progression along the power line, I was also having to think about, and do battle with, the wind coming from all directions. A chopper is always happy to fly towards the wind – it gets extra lift and flies smoothly – but as soon as you start flying sideways or backwards the game changes. On each day of film work I might get ten to fifteen minutes of flying those challenging manoeuvres, but the job of inspecting power lines would give me six or more hours a day refining my ability to feel what the helicopter was about to do and correcting for it before it happened. I shall always be grateful to Ted for his sage advice at that time, and also for his calm trust that I would get him home safely despite occasionally teetering on the edge of losing control. By the end of those months the machine had truly become an extension of myself, and a fine adjustment to the way it flew was less of a control movement than a tiny thought with impetus.

02

A FRENCHMAN AND A STEAM TRAIN

THE OLDER I GET THE MORE I have come to realise how the success of some entire careers or companies are predicated upon the unlikeliest of events. At some point during 1981 a short Frenchman turned up at our office door, without ringing ahead, and asked to talk about a television project. It was called *La Chasse au Trésor* and had either been running in France for some time or was a figment of his imagination: it was really hard to tell through the rapid-fire, thickly accented French, combined with my own schoolboy attempts at his language. He described how it involved two helicopters, which of course we were more than happy to provide, running around the countryside looking for clues.

Once we descended into the finer points of where those clues might be and why there was a need for continuous communication

with a television studio in Paris, I'm pretty sure Keith and I had lost the plot and were searching for clues of our own as to what we might be talking about. Our French friend left with much vigorous handshaking and declarations that he'd soon be back in touch. Keith and I doubted that and we were left rather bemused by the whole event as we returned to our more usual flying work.

Some months passed until we received a phone call from Angela Breheny, who announced herself as a production manager with Chatsworth Television, who had just bought the rights to a French light entertainment programme called *Treasure Hunt* and, furthermore, she understood from the French producer of the programme that we were the experts she should talk to. Within days we were embroiled in meetings, planning sessions and trial flights for what turned out to be a highly successful series that would run for seven years on Channel 4 in the UK and would provide us with two months of work for two helicopters for each of those years.

The concept revolved around a 'Skyrunner' (the ever-enthusiastic Anneka Rice and, towards the end, British champion tennis player Annabel Croft) using a helicopter to search an area of the country for clues that would ultimately lead to the treasure of the week. In what soon became something of a cult, the viewers loved the challenge of trying to work out the clues in advance of the Skyrunner. Annie (and later Annabel) was helped in her task by a host in a studio-based library who would look up facts and figures until the helicopter pilot (Keith) could be dispatched in the right direction. The host was Kenneth Kendall who, as Britain's answer to Walter Cronkite, lent an air of authority and seriousness to the whole business. On arrival at one of the interim destinations our cameraman (Graham Berry) and sound recordist (Frank Meyburgh) would chase after Annie as she dashed around a castle, or perhaps a vineyard, museum or factory, until she found the next clue in the hunt and was able to run back to the helicopter for the next leg of the journey. The fact that the camera was always following behind Annie meant that her own 'behind' became something of a national icon and the literal butt of many comedians' jokes.

We began recording the series in 1982. Annie's helicopter was a Jetranger we'd purchased about a year earlier with the registration G-BHXU (call sign 'X-Ray Uniform') but we needed another helicopter to act as a sound signal relay station between Annie on location and Kenneth in the studio. We purchased another Jetranger, G-SPEY, a very beautiful machine in a dark green and gold livery. Relaying images back and forth with London would have been far too costly and difficult to achieve in those days, and even keeping a good continuous radio signal demanded great technical skill from Nigel Tilbury, the senior communications engineer, and his team. It also required some skillful flying by the comms pilot, who would have to keep a constant and simultaneous line of sight to both Annie and the engineers' truck, often separated by many tens of miles. On one occasion in the mountains of the Lake District, Geoff Newman, in the comms pilot role, found himself with a failing signal and having to climb to levels close to and maybe even above where a pilot should really use oxygen to be sure of remaining conscious. This ability to keep a clear line of sight later came to dominate our activities in broadcasting at the Olympics and other major sporting festivals.

My own role on *Treasure Hunt*, given that my official company title was Operations Manager, was largely confined to an administrative one in the months leading up to initial technical tests and the later shoot period. Working my way through all the rules and laws that our team intended breaking for each series and asking for one-off exemptions meant burning the midnight oil, not to mention taking it in the neck if anything were to go wrong. Nevertheless, persuading our flight operations inspector, John Ramsdale at the Civil Aviation

Authority, to allow the increasingly spectacular stunts that each series demanded was a good professional challenge.

At one of our meetings the dour Yorkshireman complained that he'd 'copped some considerable flak' from his boss for an episode of *Treasure Hunt*, aired the previous evening, in which Keith had flown Annie under a bridge.

'But you authorised that,' I protested.

John responded, 'Yes. As I was watching it I remembered that your application had made it sound as though it would actually be safer to fly under the bridge than over it.'

I decided to take that as a compliment.

Keith had very effectively made the role of Annie's pilot his own, but I usually took a turn at flying as, or with, the comms pilot for at least one of the episodes in each series. This was to keep up with the realities of the production and to keep an eye on the safety aspects. It wasn't something I really needed to do – Keith would always err on the safe side of any decision – but it was a great opportunity to catch up with the team who increasingly became something of a family over the decade of production. There was also a bonus in visiting a *Treasure Hunt* location since they stayed in the finest hotels with exceptional cuisine. The excuse was that they needed to park the two helicopters on the lawn in front of their hotel each night, and any hotel with a lawn like that would just happen to be at the top of the Michelin guide. In any event I was glad that Malcolm Heyworth (owner of Chatsworth TV, series producer and chief gourmet) was footing the bill, and not Castle Air.

The advantage to me in not having to write off a couple of months on the *Treasure Hunt* trail each year was that I got to pick up all the rest of the filming work that came our way and thus extend and broaden my experience. My first television commercial for an insurance company came along in 1982 and although my role was limited to one brief shot of a car plunging over a cliff, which would only be used in the longer sixty-second cinema version, it was a great opportunity to hang out with, and study, how the crew on a commercial worked. Each genre of filming has a different way of approaching the task. Television news gathering was always done in a rush and required about ten seconds of material that encompassed and summarised the subject of the report. Documentaries liked to receive hours of footage which they could cut together to tell a story over extended periods of explanatory voiceover, often for a programme that might last for up to an hour. Pop promos tended to be the poor relation of filming, who wanted anything they could possibly capture from, or of, the helicopter in the shortest time possible; it would be some years before they became a more crafted art form.

By contrast television commercials were already a form of storytelling unto themselves. As the painful renewal of industrial Britain advanced under Maggie Thatcher, a coterie of British directors who would go on to become household names were making their initial mark by directing highly creative and very expensive commercials. Tony Scott, Ridley Scott and Hugh Hudson all cut their creative teeth in this way and produced a decade of exceptional visual feasts. Commercial crews like to polish every single shot until it's exactly how it was envisaged in the script and until all thirty seconds, or sometimes sixty seconds, are as close to perfection as they can possibly be. In the 1980s, 35mm film was still the shooting medium for commercials. In order to assess the previous take it was necessary to view it and review it immediately. To that end the camera operator still looked through a traditional eyepiece but a series of mirrors, known as a video tap, simultaneously sent the image to a tiny and low quality video camera and recorder. The skills of the director of photography (DoP) were still relied upon for the colours, exposure and 'mood' of the eventual celluloid result after the chemical film had been processed, but the tiny black and

white video recording gave the director the opportunity to assess the way the action had been captured and order a reshoot if he deemed it necessary.

One of my favourite commercials from my early years was for British Rail, using the venerable *Flying Scotsman*, a steam engine that set the first 100mph record in 1934. Legendary aerial cinematographer Peter Allwork was the cameraman on what was a technically very difficult job. I say legendary because his CV, even by then, read like a Hollywood Oscars list, encompassing *Superman, James Bond, Aces High, Juggernaut, The Eagle Has Landed* and so on. The director was Ian McMillan, a softly spoken man of very few words who, like a couple of other directors, became very loyal in using me for his helicopter work, regardless of location. In this case we would remain in the UK at a place called Hellifield in the Yorkshire Dales. It was a spot I would return to again and again over the years. Not only did it sit in beautiful countryside but it also featured one of the few lengths of British Rail track that was approved for use by the high speed trains without having any regular services through it. We could close off the track and do whatever we wanted with it.

The script for the commercial called for us to fly very low in formation with the *Flying Scotsman*, then quickly accelerate to keep pace with a modern train along which had been written the words 'Our trains now travel a distance equivalent to going around the world twenty-two times a day'. We would pull back slightly to allow the *Flying Scotsman* to come back into frame, along whose carriages was written 'Well, I'll be blowed!' We would then simultaneously climb and slow down so that Peter could widen the frame for an end shot featuring both trains and the landscape beyond. Apart from the need to transition between these five different flight regimes within exactly thirty-seven seconds, we had the added complication of 'strobing'.

Let me explain that. Classic 35mm film used in the cinema works at twenty-four frames a second, so the human eye is seeing twenty-four still images in a sequence that's fast enough for the brain to run them all together into a smooth movement. However, if I were to move too quickly in relation to the train, or if Peter were to move the camera from one side to the other too quickly, then the change would be too big from one frame to the next. In this case, the brain would cease to see the action as continuous but instead view a series of juddering frames; this is known as strobing. It's an uncomfortable thing to experience on a screen and renders the film unusable. The margin for error between strobing and not strobing can be extremely narrow, especially when you're trying to move quickly enough to fit a long sequence of words into the thirty-seven seconds available.

Peter and I set about rehearsing the move along the track but without the trains. We also asked Ian, the director, to stay in the front seat next to me so the helicopter would be balanced in the same way as it would be when we attempted the shot for real. First we established a smooth speed as if in formation with the first train, then we coordinated a slight deceleration of the helicopter with an equally slight camera move in order to find the *Flying Scotsman*, followed by a tiny acceleration to read the words, then the final big deceleration and climb. When you decelerate a helicopter by pulling the nose up it wants to climb anyway so the last move was the easiest.

Having worked out the technique and the timings, we translated this into the speed we wanted both trains to travel at, then landed to brief the engine drivers. It was rare that I ever got the chance to take the family with me on a shoot but on this occasion my wife had come along with our baby son Sam for a couple of days' break. At eleven months old he didn't know anything of the significance of being photographed on the footplate of the *Flying Scotsman* but

he had been pretty much adopted by every girl on location and was enjoying being passed around and getting all the attention. The art department completed the lettering, the *Flying Scotsman* had built up a head of steam, we'd installed aviation radios into both trains, and we were ready to go.

There are always two teams at work on a commercial. One is the production company who are making the commercial (i.e. doing all the work), with a producer in charge of business affairs and a director in charge of the creative process. The other team comes from the advertising agency for whom the production company is working and whose copywriters came up with the original idea. To a greater or lesser extent there is an us-and-them feel about the proceedings, largely dependent on how 'luvvy' the agency people are being. You could usually judge the degree of luvviness immediately: by their exotic dress, their weird hairdos and the lateness of their arrival on set. A more refined judgment could be made later when they began to express their unique dietary requirements at the catering truck. In the meantime, the two trains, the helicopter and about forty experts in their fields were standing around awaiting the arrival of . . . the agency.

Once their lordships had arrived (lords, not ladies; the gentler sex in those days served only as hand-maidens), we were able to begin. I flashed up the chopper, we cued the trains and everything went like clockwork. Nothing is more likely to produce a good result than planning, planning and a bit more planning, but in a dance sequence involving two trains and a helicopter we needed a bit of luck as well. At the end of the first take I remember all three of us, even the implacable Ian McMillan, whooping for joy in the noisy cockpit at the unbelievable luck we'd had in cracking a hard nut on the first take. The trains reversed down the track to Hellifield and I congratulated them both over the radio; the train drivers had done an amazing job.

I landed the helicopter and Ian triumphantly strode over to the agency people and was able to declare, 'We've got it.'

The agency team were horrified. 'You can't possibly have got it in one take. We've allowed three days.'

'Well, I think you'll find we have,' answered Ian with a confident and polite smile.

The video monitor was duly set up on a picnic table and the agency crew began the familiar process of agonising over every tiny detail of the shot we'd just captured. Was the writing OK? Did the speed work? How was the light? What did anybody think about the landscape? Did the whole idea work? And on and on and on in a dance of self-fulfilling doubt. It was a process I was to become very familiar with over the years and soon learned to accept, but at the time it seemed very strange. Eventually it was agreed that we'd give it another go, so we lined up the trains, took off and shot it again.

My notes show that we stayed for three days and shot it a total of thirty-three times, presumably to justify the huge fee the agency would be charging British Rail. Of course, you can readily imagine the punchline: the shot that went to air was the first one we'd captured.

Along the way to that inevitable conclusion there was a wonderful moment about halfway through the second afternoon. We were hot, tired and more than a little fed up at being strong-armed into continual retakes. Ian asked me to land a little way away from our usual position, actually in the adjacent field, to give him space to relieve himself against a hedge without being bothered by the usual tirade of questions from the agency copywriter. But the chap in question, with his black silk shirt and fashionably shaved head, was not to be denied the opportunity of sharing his opinions by something as mundane as distance. Peter and I could see from our still-running helicopter that Ian's shoulders had dropped at the sight of his nemesis arriving at the trot, straight through the hedge.

We laughed until tears rolled down our faces as the copywriter engaged the still-urinating Ian in fervent conversation. We'd got ourselves back under control by the time Ian had wearily tramped his way back to the helicopter, strapped himself in, donned his headset, then sighed.

Without looking at Ian directly I said, 'When my little boy grows up I think it will be fine if he becomes anything he wants to be, provided it's not an agency copywriter.'

'He won't,' responded Ian emphatically. 'They don't have fathers.'

LENS TO THE FRONT, LENS TO THE SIDE

THE WHEELS SOMEWHAT SPUN on my filming career during late 1982 and most of 1983. I was still getting a good grounding in the basics while working on various documentaries for local TV, and when Westward morphed into Television South West (TSW) these came more and more frequently. I was certainly feeling confident enough to gradually expand my repertoire of moves during the start of the Tall Ships' Race, the Round-Britain Yacht Race and all the other local highlights that came along annually, but it almost always required hand-held camerawork, which was limited by the ability of the camera operator to hold the shot steady. I felt I was becoming a vibration-prevention pilot instead of a film pilot, but it was all good practice and training for the bigger picture. Occasionally I would land another good job on a commercial with

sufficient budget to include a proper camera mount, of which there were two main types: a nose mount and a side mount.

The first nose mount I used was a simple flat plate bolted just under the chin of the helicopter. It was a means of getting the camera outside and looking forward, so it at least dispensed with the need to awkwardly fly sideways. The downside was twofold. In early days there were no usable video taps to enable a view through the lens, so we were effectively flying blind to what we were capturing on film. Before takeoff we would go through the laborious process of getting the camera assistant to hold up pieces of card while the camera operator lay on the ground beneath the helicopter and looked through the eyepiece to determine the edges of the frame. When he called out 'There!' I would sit in my flying position and reach forward to put a chinograph pencil mark on the Perspex windscreen in alignment with my line of sight to the raised card in the distance. In this way I could form a rough framing shape on the windscreen that approximated what the camera was going to see and record. It was primitive, and of course we still didn't know whether we'd got the shot after landing because the chemical film had to be sent away for processing – once the camera operator had first groped around in a black bag to unload the film magazine without exposing it to the light.

The other downside of an external and forward-looking camera was that every insect within 100 miles seemed intent on committing suicide on the flat lens. In one instance we were able to look through a piece of film frame-by-frame and actually see the insect just ahead of us in the final 1/24th of a second before it splattered itself everywhere and rendered the shot useless. When later nose mounts gave us the ability to fully tilt we got into the habit of tilting it through the vertical until the camera was looking backwards and upside down before takeoff. In this way we could at least protect the lens while climbing through the first few hundred feet of atmosphere, where most of the insects hang out. Once we were reasonably sure we'd climbed high enough to avoid the flies rising up from the grass beneath, we could then rotate the camera to the forward position and begin the task. But of course there would always be the odd insect trying to set some sort of height-climb record among its peers and in those instances its flight path would inevitably coincide with our own. It wasn't just an irritating problem: it was expensive and time-consuming because it meant we would have to find somewhere to land to enable the operator to jump out of the co-pilot's seat and wipe the lens clean. We soon got into the habit of attaching a piece of flat optical glass to the front so the really hard-backed insects wouldn't do permanent damage to the valuable lens.

Because these early plate mounts had no ability to tilt up and down, I had to pilot the helicopter accordingly instead if the shot demanded vertical movement. If you raise the nose of a helicopter it immediately decelerates, while, conversely, if you lower the nose you find yourself accelerating towards the ground, and this is not a flight regime that can be continued for long if healthy aircrew are to be preserved. Finally there was the issue of magazine length. On 16mm film we had ten minutes of celluloid on board, but with the 35mm film we were using for cinema and television commercials we only had four minutes of film available. Between magazine changes and fly cleaning I was therefore up and down like a yo-yo on most film jobs and it was always a good idea to organise a nearby landing spot in advance. We didn't have that luxury when we were flying a long way out to sea but thankfully it's rare to find insects wanting to undertake a Channel crossing.

Despite all those problems, I liked flying with a nose mount because I could begin to use the helicopter as a creative tool in itself. Whatever visual results we garnered were entirely down to me, with nobody else to blame since the camera operator was limited to the role of turning the camera on and off when I called 'Turn over' or 'Cut'. When Nick Phillips later engineered the first tilting nose

mount, with all the additional creative opportunities it offered up, we thought we'd died and gone to heaven.

The other main tool in the aerial filming arsenal was the side mount. Three principal manufacturers had designed competing side mounts: Continental, Tyler and Helivision. Peter Allwork made the Continental his weapon of choice throughout his career and the results speak for themselves. Albert Werry designed the Helivision and used it to great effect on a short art film called *The Red Balloon* about the flight of a child's balloon released over Paris. But it was American three-time Academy Award winner Nelson Tyler who married the elegance of design to the skill of his hands to generate some of the most extraordinary aerial sequences you will ever see from those times. My two favourites are both from Barbra Streisand movies. In *Funny Girl* there's a long continuous move that starts wide on the harbour of New York with the Statue of Liberty in the background and a small tugboat in lower foreground. The shot moves down towards the tugboat and smoothly descends to the level of Streisand before reaching the end of the lens on a completely stable head-and-shoulders shot of her singing, just as she hits the high note in the song. It doesn't stop there; it then pulls seamlessly away as the helicopter begins to climb, moves around the front of the boat and continues to circle to an overhead shot, all in one terrific 60-second sequence. It doesn't matter how much expensive gear you've got at your disposal, you need to have a great deal of skill, a little pinch of luck and an almost telepathic relationship between pilot and cameraman to pull that off, but Nelson achieved it right back in the late 1960s with pilot J. David Jones.

A side mount was a monstrosity of metalwork that was either bolted to the rear floor of the helicopter or hung from a framework around the door. It had to be monstrous because of the weight of film cameras back then, especially with the sort of large lenses usually fitted. The camera operator didn't so much sit in it as wear it, since his eye had to be pressed to the eyepiece and he had to have his hands firmly on the handlebar controls, to which were affixed the camera controls such as zoom and focus. His feet were on a rudimentary horizontal bar projecting into the airstream, often with a vertical bar to prevent them slipping off. In any of the light helicopters from that time there was little movement available to the camera operator in either the vertical or lateral plane. When I was training pilots how to film I used to put them in one of those mounts for half an hour, just to give them some idea of how limited the range of movement can be for the camera operator. In that sense the pilot had to present the shot in a way that gave room for small adjustments but didn't require big movements by the operator. Most pilots emerged from that short flight experience wiping their brow and whistling with new respect for their rear 'passenger'.

By 'present the shot' I mean the pilot had to see a composition of relative foreground and background movement that might work, position himself into a flight pattern that would take him to that point, warn the cameraman of what would shortly be appearing in the left of his frame, call 'Turn over' when the time felt right and then develop the move in such a way as to always keep the subject in front of the camera. This might mean a descent to a stop, or a passing shot that became a climbing turn, or some other combination of moves, while always keeping the subject in exactly the same position through the starboard window. If the helicopter was banking during any of these moves, then the side mount would reach the stops at the limit of its upward or downward movement and the sequence would be scrapped. It resulted in some very weird flying techniques, which would make a pilot who was more used to carrying passengers around the sky blanch in disgust.

The result was that the film pilot effectively became the director of the sequence since nobody else could see the multiple changing options of juxtaposition at any given moment, and even if they did they wouldn't have time to verbalise an instruction before those options had all changed again. I came to hate it when a director asked to fly alongside me as there was little he could do to contribute to the process and he was likely to be an active hindrance. Not only that but he would be a couple of hundred pounds of dead weight that could otherwise give greater capability. After a time I found that the best dissuasion was a brief exposition on how a conversation in the air was expensive whereas a conversation on the ground could be long and free. As soon as video taps and decent recorders came along we could therefore plan to land, review the shots we'd captured after a few takes, show and discuss them with the director, revise his requirements, then get airborne once more to fulfil those needs. In this way, and perhaps without fully realising it, I was starting to think like a director.

The other sequence by Nelson Tyler that left me breathless is from another Barbra Streisand film, *Hello Dolly*. It begins tight on Streisand walking in the woods. The camera walks with her and alongside her in a familiar move that's captured from a 'dolly' (no relation that I'm aware of to the title of the film), a camera set on a little travelling cart on rails that have been laid temporarily for the purpose. Except that in this case the camera slowly begins to rise to above head height – no problem there, they obviously had a small crane mounted on the dolly – then climbs further and further to a height that couldn't possibly have been shot from a crane. Only then does the viewer realise that they must be looking at a shot from a helicopter and, if interested in these things, have to re-evaluate all that they've just seen.

Ever since first seeing that move I've maintained the principle that if it never crosses the mind of the audience that they're looking at a shot from a helicopter until late in the piece, then I've done my job well. How did they do it all those years ago? They had a helicopter running on a full-sized rail car pushed along at walking pace by six guys, known in the trade as grips. At the appropriate moment the helicopter gently rose, pulled away and circled so as to obscure the rail car from which it had just lifted, and to capture the railway station full of the cast singing 'Put On Your Sunday Clothes'. I exhort you to watch that movie again, just to appreciate that one move; it's a work of genius.

It's an interesting aside that Nelson Tyler's other long-time obsession has been with human jetpacks. He invented the rocket-powered backpack that wowed the audience at the opening ceremony of the 1984 Los Angeles Olympics, and has been toiling away at that project ever since. At the time of writing it finally looks like it's coming to fruition with the announcement of a production model named the JB-9. I only met the man once and felt privileged to have done so; he is another of those softly spoken and self-deprecating gentlemen, in the old-fashioned sense of the word.

In October 1982 I landed another pop promo. Kim Wilde was an ascending star after the success of 'Kids in America' in January 1981, and her latest single, her sixth, was a dark story called 'Child Come Away'. Cornwall served up a typically stormy day that alternated between blustery sunshine and horizontal rain. The crashing waves against the cliffs added drama to the long opening shot and with the wind behind me I was able to go from open sea to the prostrate artist in double-quick time. Thereafter my helicopter became more of a background prop in the video as Kim was joined by a cast of many local youngsters. My main focus of concern was for the sand and salt the local gale was lifting into the air intake of G-SPEY's engine. For Kim's chaperone, her brother Marty, the prime worry was for the young artist's health as she alternated between lying on wet sand and then singing her heart out, dressed in nothing more than a flimsy white and very wet toga-like dress. For the early 1980s it was a risqué video and it hinted at dark teenage issues I could only guess at.

I could never entirely escape passenger-carrying duties in the early days of film flying, but those duties more often than not led to an

hour or two spent in the company of diverse, interesting and often well-known people. The Red Arrows formation display team, golfer Jack Nicklaus and jockey Lester Piggott all brought their own flying stories along for the brief journeys we spent together. In Lester Piggott's case it was the day of his record ninth and final win at the Derby.

The reputation I was gradually getting for being one of the go-to pilots for film work in the UK meant that I was also called upon to transport film crews around the country in their pursuit of multiple locations within the space of a day. This took me to some strange and mysterious places I would not have otherwise had the chance to visit. A good example of this was the limestone mine in Derbyshire from which much of the interior of the Bank of England had been excavated, together with a good proportion of the headstones for casualties of the two world wars. Hanging out with film crews on the ground also gave me time to appreciate how certain directors liked to work. I was soaking it all up like a sponge.

This was a tough eighteen-month period for helicopter aviators. It started with losing several old mates in the Falklands, then losing Nigel Thornton on an accident while he was filming the movie *High Road to China*, and finally losing a Sikorsky S61 into the sea off the Scilly Isles with multiple fatalities. As the local TV station had my phone number on speed dial I was asked to comment on the nightly news about the last of those accidents – definitely my least favourite television experience. I was glad to resume my own film-flying career at the end of 1983 with a sequence over a lighthouse that became the opening credits to *Fraggle Rock*, a weekly puppet story from *The Muppets* creator Jim Henson.

04

TO THE OLYMPICS

1984 WILL ALWAYS SOUND IN MY HEAD as *osamdeset chetiri*, Serbo-Croatian for the year in which Sarajevo hosted the Winter Olympics. The New Year saw me driving an overladen Range Rover towing an empty 1,000-litre fuel trailer across the mountainous border between northern Italy and Yugoslavia (Slovenia). I had taken a big jump up the international ladder.

Peter Allwork had obviously liked what he saw in my newly formed filming capabilities and invited me to put together a proposal for the Winter Games, for which he had the contract to provide the aerial equipment and team.

Roy Flood and I had taken a Yugoslav Airlines flight to Sarajevo to carry out a recce of the sites I would need to fly from and the event locations I would have to film. I'd then flown to New York with Peter Allwork to present my findings and proposals to the principals of the ABC Sports network. I felt very grown-up when I emerged from that presentation clutching a contract to provide myself as

main pilot, a backup pilot, an engineer, a ground support unit and our Bell Longranger G-LRII. We'd agreed to use the slightly larger Longranger because of its ability to under-sling loads; getting large broadcast cameras into precarious positions on the side of the downhill ski slopes would be one of our tasks.

Suspicious Italian border guards insisted that my engineer, Cliff, and I unload the entire contents of our Range Rover onto the road and spread it out in the pouring rain in the depths of a freezing evening. For about two hours we respectfully awaited an inspection by the senior border guard who had demanded the examination, before being told that he'd gone off watch at midnight and we were free to continue. By contrast, at the crossing into Yugoslavia a solitary soldier sleepily raised a single barrier at his mountainside hut and waved us on our way. Cliff and I wondered if we should be getting him to stamp the extensive international carnet we'd brought with us but by then the soldier had returned to his seat next to a brazier and was already disappearing in my mirrors behind a snow bank, so we pressed on.

Back in the UK another old Navy pal, Geoff Newman, was preparing G-LRII for the 1,200 mile flight that would see him arriving in Sarajevo the day after us. Sarajevo was a straightforward city to navigate around as it lay in a long valley running east-west. I soon found the imposing new broadcast centre that ABC Sports had built in double-quick time after securing the contract to televise the Winter Olympics. Parts of Sarajevo, and on some nights entire Yugoslav states, were on a roster of power cuts in order to get enough electricity into Bosnia-Herzegovina to power the event. For example, the bobsleigh event generally costs around one-third of the construction costs of a Winter Olympics, but even this amount pales alongside the electricity needed to keep the 1.7km track frozen to exactly the right degree regardless of the air temperature.

The imposingly long and empty corridors of the broadcast centre led me to the office of Mike Pithey, who was in overall practical charge and would be my direct boss for the next two months. I presented myself to Mike and to his efficient assistant Melissa Coley, both of whom I'd met during the previous year's recce. Under Melissa's guidance Cliff and I soon had accommodation, accreditation and a ring-binder containing everything we needed to know to participate in broadcasting the event to the world. The next day Geoff Newman arrived with my Longranger and we were ready to go to work.

A veteran ABC aerial camera operator was also assigned to our team when he flew into town with all the other technicians the next day, although the expression 'veteran' hardly covers it. The laconic Bill 'Sully' Sullivan was on his ninth consecutive Olympics and I hung onto every one of the few words he muttered. We soon had both the nose mount and the side mount installed on the helicopter and could begin a few tentative sorties to begin capturing 'bumpers' – the short landscape views that would begin and end all commercial breaks during two weeks of broadcast, often with a sponsor's logo overlaid. We were the only helicopter authorised to film in the country so the list of requirements for all the various broadcast departments was long and varied. Each evening we'd return with our crop of video tapes, put them through an early-version security x-ray, and deliver them while holding our fingers crossed that the x-ray machine hadn't wiped or damaged them.

Seven days before the opening ceremony, we prepared to shoot one of its iconic moments. There was to be a technical rehearsal of lighting the Olympic flame that towered above the huge Zetra stadium at the opposite end of the city from our flight base, and we would be allowed to keep it alight for a couple of extra hours to film John Denver singing just below and in front of it. At around 9pm Sully and I drove to the stadium, presented ourselves at the assigned gate and made our way through the tunnel that led out onto the field of play. As we emerged into the glare of hundreds of huge lamps burning high above our heads, I was bowled over by the scale of the stadium. It was awesome in the true sense of the word. I was playing a very small part in an enormous undertaking. We needed to see the stadium for ourselves both to get a full briefing and as a safety recce. I'd been taken behind closed doors a week earlier to see the demo tape of a thing called Wire-cam, which used ever-changing lengths of wire from the tall lampposts to control a flying camera above the heads of the athletes. It's now in almost universal use but it was the big trade secret back in 1984, and I certainly didn't want to get chopped in half by this giant cheese slicer if it had already been erected.

Sully and I ascended the seemingly never-ending steps through the seating to the top where the Olympic flame was burning bright in the crisp winter's evening. After we were introduced to John Denver, our director for the night briefed us on what he wanted from both artist and helicopter. The idea was that I would descend into the stadium and use the forward-looking nose mount to bring the camera up the long Olympic staircase until we found John, then swoop slowly over his head and climb further, up and over the flame. From the flying perspective it was not a complex shot and would only come unstuck if I slowed to a speed where the tail of the helicopter might kick from side to side in the unpredictable wind eddies within the stadium. I took a careful look around the whole stadium, checking for possible obstructions or wires, before saying yes. The only obstacles were the four enormous posts holding up the lighting arrays in each corner of the stadium, whose radiated power was warming us (while Yugoslavs elsewhere must have been shivering in their powerless homes). There wasn't much chance of forgetting about those lampposts, so Sully and I departed.

'See you in about forty minutes,' I said cheerfully, having given our director one of our hand-held air-band radios.

Back at the airport we reintroduced ourselves to the soldier who manned the security gate next to the helicopter hangar. We had to report to him every evening to list the tasks I'd be undertaking the following day. It was the same soldier every time. Over the two months I spent in Sarajevo, he reacted to me every time as though he had never clapped eyes on me before. I tried greetings in my best Serbo-Croatian, I brought small sweet treats from the broadcast catering facility, I tried humour, but to no avail. Every day we had to explain who we were all over again.

Cliff had the Longranger ready to go and we were soon on our way into one of the blackest nights I'd seen for a long time. I could get a sense of the horizon from the street lamps glowing against the snow drifts. The five-mile flight along the river, followed by a 90-degree left turn, wouldn't stretch even my navigational abilities. Except that when I got to where the stadium should have been, it had gone.

The area we were over was blacker than the rest. We must have wandered into one of the areas of the city that was taking its turn at blackout. Panic can never feature in the vocabulary of a professional aviator, but I began to get the sense of icicles growing down my back – a familiar feeling to pilots when they realise they've made a basic error and are about to pay for it with embarrassment or something worse. I took the only safe course of action and returned to the airfield whose flashing beacon I could identify. I made some pathetic excuse to the air-traffic controller, who was thankfully not interested in whatever strange games I was playing.

Sully, who was sitting alongside me with his video screen on his lap, held up the map for me with a red light on it. Airport – turn right – river – turn left – stadium. Five nautical miles of track along a line feature, with nowhere I could make an error. We set off again,

only this time I flew at a precise 60 knots to be sure that after exactly five minutes I would find the stadium beneath me.

'Sully, please tell me I'm not going mad. It's not here, is it?'

'Nope, can't see it my side,' he said with resignation.

I was now beyond the point of worrying about embarrassment and called the director on the radio. 'Umm, can you hear us yet?'

'Of course,' came back the prompt reply. 'I can see your lights right above us.'

Sully and I looked at each other.

'Have you turned the lights off?' I tentatively asked over the radio.

'Yes, of course.'

'When are you turning them back on again?'

'We're not. We're doing this in the dark. I thought you knew that.'

'For Chrissakes,' muttered Sully, plus a few other colourful phrases, as he set about remotely changing all the camera settings he'd so carefully calculated for a lit shoot during our ground visit.

'Oh, OK, give us a moment,' I replied on the radio before turning back to my cameraman.

'Sully, we're going to have to switch all the lights in this cockpit down to the barest minimum, including your video monitor. If you need to check something, use the red torch. We need to achieve the best night vision we can and then decide between us whether we're happy to do this or not.'

Sully nodded in response and we set about the task.

Our night vision improved quickly and dramatically. Now that I knew what I was looking for, I could see the flame directly beneath us. We orbited a couple more times and with each revolution our eyes adjusted to more and more detail. The flame was faintly shining off the lighting poles, enough to give me the confidence to begin descending. Sure enough, once we were down to almost lamp height in our orbit around the stadium we could see even more of it in relief.

'Happy if you are, Sully,' I declared.

'Sure thing, let's do it,' he responded.

'Ready to run in when you are, guv'nor,' I called on the radio, at which point we were rewarded with a bonus as they flicked the switch on a single spotlight, pointing at John Denver.

I settled down to a filming speed I was happy with and made my turn towards the stadium. As the lip of the seating passed beneath us and the first set of light poles disappeared beyond my peripheral vision, I slightly lowered the collective (the height control) and began our descent to the stadium floor as Sully called, 'Camera running.'

Seconds later I pulled in full power and rose up the opposite banks of seating, found John with the camera (singing his heart out), lingered on him a moment, rose further to the Olympic flame, then climbed rapidly before it could start to singe us.

'Did you get that, Sully?' asked the director over the radio.

Sully, unusually, reached for the transmit button himself.

'Oh yeah, we got it. It's all good. No need to do *that* again.'

'Well done, guys. We'll see you in the bar,' called back our jubilant director.

Once we'd put the helicopter safely to bed, Sully decided it was time he also found a pillow, but I was still firing on about sixteen cylinders so I found the smart hotel in town and high-fived the director. Steak and chips had already been ordered for the four of us: John Denver (singer-songwriter, actor, activist and humanitarian), the director (a delightful man whose name I wish I could find or remember), Kathleen Sullivan (first female anchor at CNN, first American woman to broadcast live from the Soviet Union, first woman to anchor an Olympic telecast), and me. There have been times in my career when I've had to press pause and consider for a moment what on earth a country boy like me, born in a caravan in a forest, thinks he's doing in such a privileged situation. This was surely one of those, but it also felt relaxed, natural and enjoyable. We all needed to come down from the high of achieving a job well

done by sharing our stories of the evening. John, as a keen aviator himself, was fascinated with all the details of the helicopter work and we talked and talked about flying. I later read that his love of flying was second only to his love of music. By the time the night chef had excelled himself with a large bowl of ice cream and a brandy for everybody, John picked up his guitar and started strumming the first bars of 'Annie's Song'. We all joined in with the familiar words. Thank heaven the hotel restaurant was deserted as we belted out 'Rocky Mountain High', 'Take Me Home, Country Roads' and 'Sunshine On My Shoulders'.

I trudged back through the snow to my own pillow just before daylight broke, feeling like I was living somebody else's life. Thirteen years later I was terribly saddened to learn that John had perished by himself in the sea off California while piloting an experimental aircraft, whose fuel gauge and fuel selector had bizarrely been installed behind the pilot's shoulder. He was a genuinely lovely man and I value the memories of that night we sang his compositions until dawn.

Geoff took the seat for most of the ancillary jobs (read that as 'hard work jobs'), such as load-lifting the cameras and moving people around the snow-covered mountains, while Sully and I continued to gather beauty sequences, runs over the city and other shots of the venues for each of the sports disciplines. Every day, provided the tapes survived the x-ray machine, we would submit them to a committee of three Yugoslav colonels, who would review them and delete anything they didn't want to appear on screen. Communication towers and a couple of specific buildings seemed to be their main concern, but as they wouldn't tell us what not to film, it was impossible to avoid a few blanked-out patches on the tapes that were eventually returned to us. With the opening ceremony fast approaching, the colonels asked what arrangements were in place for them to edit the proceedings. Mike Pithey tried explaining to them that a 'live' broadcast meant it couldn't be redacted as the whole world would be watching in real time. This was a concept the colonels couldn't grasp; they dug their heels in. If they couldn't edit all images of the ceremony then the broadcast couldn't go ahead, full stop, no discussion.

After a short period of panic, somebody came up with an idea. A cubicle was erected in a small space in the bowels of the broadcast centre featuring three chairs, a single TV screen, plates of pickled fish, several bottles of Lozavitch, the local firewater, and a large red button. Our colonels settled into their nest for the duration of the opening ceremony and, sure enough, every time they pressed the big red button, *their* screen went blank, while the other one billion or so people watching around the globe enjoyed uninterrupted coverage. I shudder to think what might have happened had the colonels ever discovered the subterfuge.

My memory of the opening ceremony is dominated by two factors. First was the pacing up and down I did for an hour before getting airborne as I tried to wrap my head around the number of people across the globe who would be watching the fruits of my labour. I'd counted sixty-three screens in the main vision control room, each with a label on it, and had been particularly impressed with the screen extreme top left marked 'The World'. What if the helicopter failed to start or I was in the wrong place at the wrong time or the camera froze or I couldn't remember what I was supposed to be doing next or, or, or? I was pretty sure our planning had covered all the bases but it did suddenly seem like a very public way to go to work and, God forbid, screw up.

Second was the moment when despite all our full-dress rehearsals the vision mixer switched to the helicopter camera exactly thirty seconds before the scheduled and practised time. Sully and I were established in an orbit around the stadium which we'd timed to

show the seated crowd holding up coloured cards that together read 'Sarajevo 1984', but the thirty-second difference meant we were still on the wrong side of the stadium so that the gigantic words read upside down. I was mortified until Sully brought me back down to a focused operating level with one of his better one-liners: 'Don't stress it, man, it's only television.'

The city of Sarajevo was unique in the sense that you could stand in one spot and simultaneously see houses of worship for Catholicism, Islam, Judaism and Eastern Orthodoxy in happy co-existence, all without turning your head (of course, that was to change dramatically before another decade had passed). I loved flying in the crisp mountain air (no flies up there!) and I loved being the only film pilot at such a momentous international event. Towards the end of our time in Sarajevo, the pressures reduced on our aerial team to the extent that I was able to secure front-row tickets at the final of the ice-dancing competition when British pair Jayne Torvill and Christopher Dean, performing to *Bolero*, scored a perfect 6 for artistic interpretation from every single judge.

I'd eaten lamb from the spit in dark and smoky bars, and there had been days when the imported McDonald's in the broadcast centre had provided the only sustenance, grabbed on the run. I'd been at a four-person dinner party with one of the ABC producers without even realising until the end of the meal that his charming wife Courtney, with whom I'd been conversing all evening, was Bobby Kennedy's daughter. I returned home firmly and forever addicted to the adrenalin rush of big sporting events, but it was to be another twenty years before I would feel that rush again.

05

BOND, JAMES BOND

THERE MUST HAVE BEEN SOME SORT OF celestial alignment in my favour in 1984. By now we were very much the go-to company for aerial filming and there was no time to rest on my Sarajevo laurels before being thrown back into a full year of commercials, documentaries, and all the usual work that had become our bread and butter. The year also brought me, in quick succession, my first two feature films.

In June I flew Phil Kohn, production manager on a film called *Water*, around North Devon looking for a suitable location for their final sequence. It was a comedy farce, produced by George Harrison, about an American oil company accidentally finding a huge source of natural mineral water on a Caribbean island. They had already spent many weeks on St Lucia, with Michael Caine and Billy Connolly playing hapless British ex-pats batting above their weight in negotiations with the United Nations, when a hurricane had brought the filming to an unscheduled end. The

other commitments of the actors meant the final slates had to be captured in the UK. Good luck with that, I thought, as we selected an appropriate site and Phil set about organising the construction of a Caribbean village, complete with plastic palm trees, in a typically wet English summer.

By the time I returned to the set three weeks later it did indeed look like the village it was supposed to represent and the weather had miraculously changed to a fair imitation of the Caribbean, even if only for a few days. Connolly and Caine turned out to be even funnier in person than they were on screen. I experienced my first sumptuous lunch from proper caterers with them before completing the line in the script that read 'The helicopter takes off and departs to the UN'.

As so often on a movie, I spent most of the day prior to my 'call' poised like a coiled spring with helicopter at the ready. This largely involved hanging around with my hands in the pockets of my flying overalls watching a well-oiled film crew, while remaining sharp enough to produce 100 per cent commitment at a moment's notice when the director shouted, 'Cut. OK, let's shoot the helicopter sequence now.' A couple of hours of intense effort would more often than not result in only two seconds of screen time. For me, it was a valuable lesson in how a role can be both essential and minuscule.

Water was a very British movie, directed by Dick Clement, who had written just about every classic English comedy in the previous decade, as well as being the creator of *The Likely Lads* and Ronnie Barker's sitcom about life in a prison, *Porridge*. George Harrison had brought on board a few old mates, such as Ringo Starr, Eric Clapton and Jon Lord, all very self-effacing and self-deprecating people in the Anglo-Saxon way. So when American actress Valerie Perrine started playing the Hollywood starlet thing and openly criticised Caine and Connolly in front of the crew, Billy Connolly returned the favour by leading the process of 'explanation' that this wasn't how we did it in the UK, in one of the most creative torrents of Glaswegian profanity I've ever witnessed. It was a magical day from beginning to end.

Peter Allwork once again played a pivotal role in my advancement as a film pilot by inviting me to work on the James Bond film *A View To A Kill*. My work in Sarajevo on a contract that really belonged to Peter had resulted in some nice accolades and so I found myself coming in to land at the historic Amberley chalk quarry, which is run as a museum in southern England, not a dozen miles from where I'd been born and educated. As with almost every shot we undertake on a big movie, the real location would become unrecognisable in the finished film. Sometimes the location will be chosen specifically because it's iconic and immediately familiar, such as the Eiffel Tower or the Golden Gate Bridge. In most other cases it will have been selected because it fits with the geographical availability of a key member of the cast or, as in this case, because it has a unique attribute: the entirely white walled cliffs with a distinct and horizontal entrance to a mine. By the time the editors had applied their scissors there would be no clues remaining that the sequence wasn't shot a mile or two outside San Francisco. There would be no starring role for me this time so I was able to concentrate for four days on learning the more refined techniques of flying the camership from a master of the aerial filming trade.

The film pivoted around the evil intent of Christopher Walken as Max Zorin, the head of Zorin Industries, together with his screen girlfriend May Day, played by Grace Jones. Ms Jones had achieved notoriety in the UK three years earlier by punching a chat show host (Russell Harty) on live television in the belief that he was disrespecting her – an incident that BBC viewers voted as the most shocking chat-show moment of all time twenty-five years later and

which she, in her autobiography, put down to having been 'given bad coke'. So the first part of my brief was to give her a wide berth.

It was Roger Moore's era as the quintessential Bond and he was just as charming as his screen persona. Thankfully it would be a long time before I would be exposed to the other end of the scale: actors who believed that life owed them extra courtesies. I had three main tasks, the first of which was to capture close-up images of the Zorin Industries airship. Eventually this would be 'matted' over aerial imagery of San Francisco and the Golden Gate Bridge. The airship pilot and I sat down to work out a plan, then spent a very enjoyable day crossing southern England in close formation. During one sequence I descended towards the spine of the airship using our nose-mounted camera, making the strange flying machine appear huge. I broke off and climbed away when I'd lost sight of the ground on either side of the bulbous white whale: a disconcerting visual effect.

The next day would be more dangerous, requiring much more care in the planning and co-ordination phase as we'd be operating at low levels and in close proximity. Nick Bennett, the highly experienced and competent airship pilot, was to take his machine over the edge and down into the bowels of the quarry in order that Christopher Walken (or rather Bill Weston, his stunt double) could reach out of the gondola to take hold of the heroine, played by Tanya Roberts. First I flew close alongside to capture the beginning of the sequence, then moved far enough away that my downwash wouldn't upset the delicate controls of the airship. Once John Glen, the director, had declared himself happy with the results, the airship and I returned to Goodwood airfield for a break while the ground team used a mock-up gondola suspended on the end of a crane for extreme close-ups of the action.

I took on a drop of fuel from the airfield, but not too much, as my next job would require a high hover for which I'd need all the power I could muster. The scene is a pivotal one, where Grace Jones as May Day exits the mine on a hand-driven rail cart on which sits a powerful bomb designed to unlock the San Andreas fault line. In so doing May Day reveals herself to be less evil than we'd first imagined, saving the city of San Francisco from a catastrophic seismic event at the cost of her own life.

Peter Allwork was sitting in the side door of my machine with his feet hanging over the edge and his shoulders entirely surrounded by the 'Continental' side mount. Unusually the shot called for me to be almost static, as if from a high crane, with just a little forward motion in the initial stages as we prepared to hover. Peter asked me to adjust my hover position until he was happy with the final framing. We backed off by just a few yards, called for 'Action' over the air-ground radio and I initiated a gentle drift forwards to our end position as Ms Jones exited the mine on cue, looking both athletic and dramatic.

As she reached the end of the rail line Peter called to me, 'Hold it, hold it, hold it,' which in the final analysis may have been one hold-it too many. In the intervening seconds the column of downwash beneath me had built up sufficiently to create a small whirlwind of white chalk dust and small stones which set off inexorably towards the extremely dark-skinned actress. As I edged away and set the helicopter moving forwards I realised I was already too late as Ms Jones began coughing, spluttering and wiping white-stained tears from her face.

'Ummm, do you need fuel, Jerry?' asked John Glen gently over the radio.

'No, I'm good if you want to go for it again, thanks, guv'nor,' I answered.

'I think fuel now would be a great idea. Perhaps take a couple of hours about it.'

Thankfully I didn't have to cross the path of Grace Jones over the next couple of days. I did feel honoured the next day to be

invited by John Glen to join him and Roger Moore in a tiny viewing theatre to see the previous day's work, projected for John's approval. Mr Moore was good company on the subject of his work aboard submarines and Sea King helicopters for *The Spy Who Loved Me* a few years earlier, and once we'd reviewed the rushes of May Day's chalk-storm experience I was rewarded with one of his famous raises of the single eyebrow.

The amount of concentrated work that goes into each shot leaves you expecting the finished film to consist almost entirely of your own efforts. Months afterwards the family are gathered in great excitement and ushered to the cinema to feast their eyes upon your great opus. Wives, mothers and young offspring have to be physically restrained from telling patrons in nearby rows that you were intimately involved in the production, while you quietly bathe in reflected glory from James Bond – possibly the most recognised film franchise in the world. By the time the credits roll you have been asked many times over: 'Was that you? Was that your shot? Which bit did you do?' until you're not entirely sure of the answers yourself. Something as recognisable as the bomb clip is easy to identify but for the most part your efforts have been manipulated, surrounded by model shots, overlaid with special effects and moved to another continent.

The final embarrassment comes when you're still in the auditorium awaiting your end credit. This usually appears, for the film pilot at least, around the time that the lights have come up and the cleaners have begun removing popcorn boxes from the floor. Lacking allegiance to any of the unions for movie workers, the film pilot doesn't qualify for a pre-determined position in the credits and is therefore relegated to a spot just after the Assistant Florist's Apprentice. This would perhaps be OK if only the typesetter hadn't lost the will to live at this juncture and applied a random assembly of letters to your name in an approximation that might sound all right if spoken in Portuguese. My own credit on this production reads something like Garry Crayon (one of about twelve variations over the years) – I haven't been back to check because it makes me cringe.

Only one person truly knows how a particular shot is going to appear in the final cut and that's the director. Some of the senior heads of department will have a fair idea of how the shots for which they have personal responsibility will eventually look, but down at the lower end of the food chain it's a matter of trust. The good directors will brief you on the preceding shot, the following shot, and the context for the work you're contributing. The directors who don't take you into their confidence generally miss out on your best work because you are left to operate in a fog of isolation. When I later became more senior among the crew and more confident in my own broader knowledge I would try to be included in the planning stage. At that point it's possible to make suggestions that will both avoid delays in the shooting process and add to the overall value on screen, and I saw this as part of my role. After all, it would be unusual to find a director who knew everything there is to know about aerial filming.

My place on *A View to a Kill* was never going to be a stepping stone to more work on the James Bond franchise because my competitor, and later good friend, Marc Wolff had been well established for many years with franchise-holders the Broccoli family, renowned for loyalty to their regulars. I had only got the gig because Marc was away flying the stunt sequences in Iceland that opened the movie. Nevertheless the film was extremely well received and I was glad of another little gem in life experiences, plus a film credit to die for.

TWINS AND TRAINS

AT THE END OF 1984 WE BOUGHT OUR first helicopter with two engines, known in the trade as a twin. It was an Agusta 109, bearing on her side the nearly perfect registration: G-HELY. She had already had a few starring roles under the ownership of Barratt Homes, who had the habit of letting their helicopters appear in television commercials for the houses they built.

I'm going to beg your indulgence here for a moment to talk about pretty helicopters and ugly helicopters, in a rather Jeremy Clarkson way. If you're not a rotary aviator and the prospect of reading my opinions on this subject fills you with horror, feel free to skip forward a couple of paragraphs. You won't offend me at all.

I am a Bell Helicopter man through and through. If you cut me in half you will find that my veins spell B E L L; just like those sticks of rock we used to get at the fair. This is because Bells are made of metal, which is the material God intended helicopters to be made

of. Whatever your preference, you surely have to agree that the Jetranger was an extremely pretty helicopter when it first came to the market many decades ago and that it does still look like it used to be quite a cool thing. In fact, given the right colour scheme it can still look cool provided it's on high skids and therefore in proportion. The Longranger added just 18 inches to the length and made it look even cooler, but if you look at either of those models on low skids you won't be able to shake the image of something that's been caught out by what it ate in the Kasbah last night and has had to squat behind a tree.

I once had the ultimate pleasure, indeed privilege, of flying a Huey, a properly beaten-up Huey with a few bits missing. Not only did it fly beautifully and handle like a big old lumbering Jetranger, but it also looked how a helicopter is supposed to look and sounded like a helicopter is supposed to sound with its two-bladed *whap-whap* noise. After a good flight a Huey positively loved a slap on the nose in thanks, and actually looked like it was smiling as you strode away with extra testosterone coursing through your veins. Try doing that to a helicopter manufactured in France and there's a good chance your fist will go through the plastic.

We are overdue our regular bicentenary war with the French. Yes, they do produce wonderful cheeses and their champagne is unrivalled, but helicopters? Somebody somewhere is languidly eating a langoustine lunch and washing it down with a glass or two from the local château, proud that he introduced plastic into the design of a helicopter body. Plastic? This is like the old joke about heaven and hell in which heaven was where the French do the cooking . . . Take an American Bell up to a small tree and clip it with your metal blades, and you'll do no more than leave a neat log pile ready for next winter. Do the same with an offering out of France and you'll emerge looking like the road-runner after he's set fire to himself at high speed and has smoke coming out of his ears, while your severed and separated plastic rotor blades should be just about landing on Corsica.

I recognise that 'plastics' have changed over the years and are now high-tech forms of carbon fibre that will probably take more hammering than a piece of sheet metal, but have you ever tried dropping the belly pan off a Squirrel (A-Star, to you Yanks) as it bends first one way and then the other? Would you ever put a Squirrel next to a Jetranger and choose the Squirrel? It got its name because it looks like it's got cheeks stuffed with nuts. Yes, yes, I know the passengers love the extra comfort, the space and the view over the pilot's head, but who cares about passengers? Most of the ones I've carried have barely given me the time of day. They'll tip a doorman but not the helicopter pilot who's just got them safely from A to B. (Other than Elton John, who's a gentleman. Thank you, Mr John.)

All that said I have to confess that I love an Italian Agusta 109 and we can surely all agree that it's the prettiest helicopter ever built. If you told me it was designed by Ferrari I'd believe you. I'll admit I didn't like it when they chopped half of the big shark's fin away on the later models, but apart from that the 109 looks great on the ground and can produce actual sexual tension when hammering towards you at 150 knots with those wheels tucked neatly away in the belly.

The things I liked about the 109 are legion. First, it had wheels instead of skids, which took me back to my Navy days on the Wessex and the Sea King, where you could land on tarmac with a little forward speed and neatly convert flight into ground taxiing without a lot of wobbly hovering (I was never wobbly, of course, but I gather some were). The wheels also meant that, if the right surface to taxi on was available, you could get yourself clear of bystanders before lifting and therefore avoid covering them with small pebbles or blowing their hats off, all of which was a good

thing because the extra weight and the four blades generated considerably more downwash than the smaller Bells I'd been used to. The seat might have looked as though it would put you on the road to the chiropractor after five minutes of flight, but it was truly the most comfortable of helicopter seats and you could sit in it for hours on end without complaint. The speed was also fabulous at a mouth-watering 150 knots, 50 per cent faster than anything I'd flown up to that point. The 109 only had two faults: first, it would sometimes break a thing called the quill shaft on start-up which, although fairly cheap to replace, meant that you weren't going flying that day, and second, when you broke things you had to deal with the Italians, whose responses in those days were always subject to impenetrable delays.

The Civil Aviation Authority (CAA) had the tendency to embrace whatever were the latest and most restrictive practices from around the world. It was all done in the name of safety so it was almost impossible to argue against. We bought the 109 because, among other things, it had been decreed that certain tasks could only be performed from now on if you were using a twin. It left a wry smile on my face that one of these tasks was flight over water, since I'd spent many hours way out over the ocean in the old Wessex Mk1, plucking people out of gale-force seas with just a single engine. Many argued that having two engines only doubled your chance of experiencing an engine failure, and that the other engine would just take you to a revised site for the accident. Whatever, we had to do it.

One of my first jobs with the 109 was to go filming trains. The task didn't need a twin but the two Jetrangers were away on *Treasure Hunt* for a couple of months and the Longranger was under maintenance, so I took G-HELY. That turned out to be a mistake. In fact, it was a mistake to go out on the job at all. The occasion was a once-only run across Britain by an old steam engine, not the *Flying*

Scotsman this time but one whose name I've since forgotten. I joined the fine-looking locomotive as it made its way down through the county of Somerset, swirling clouds of white smoke in the golden afternoon sun. I was astonished at how many steam train enthusiasts filled every conceivable bank and bridge along the route south and was also a bit offended at how many of them angrily shook their fists at me. I was taking great pains not to go low behind the train and ruin their photographs.

At one point the train let go with a steam whistle so loud that I could hear it in the cockpit above the sound of my two jet engines. The herd of cattle grazing in the bright green pasture beside the line stampeded away from the train and towards my helicopter, passing through a sturdy fence along their way. My cameraman had captured the moment on tape and I asked him to jot down the timecode of the incident, in the sure and certain knowledge that I would cop the blame for it. After about an hour of very successful film work along sixty or more miles of people-lined track, we flew home in time for tea. Except that putting the kettle on wasn't the first issue I had to address. The office answerphone was littered with abusive phone calls, plus one very calm one from a CAA inspector who said he'd received a sufficient number of complaints to warrant further investigation and would like to arrange a date to meet with me.

We always studiously avoided disturbing animals with helicopters, not only out of our own natural concern for their welfare but also because a claim for injury to a prize-winning animal could bankrupt a company. I had the taped evidence that any damaged cattle were the fault of the train's whistle and not the noisy 109 I was riding in, so I arranged the meeting with the man from the ministry without worry. He turned up about a week later, and described how he'd interviewed many of the trainspotters, looked at their videos and agreed that the stampede had been the fault of the train.

With no charge he wanted to bring against me, he was about to depart when I remarked: 'The thing I don't get is why there was so much vitriol shown by so many people along the entire route when I was trying so hard to stay out of their photographs.'

The CAA man paused at the door. 'Yes, I couldn't understand that either at first. But when I asked one of these guys to show me his photographs he said he hadn't taken any. He wasn't remotely interested in taking photographs. Then he got out the tape recorder with which he'd been trying to capture the sound of the age of steam but you could only faintly hear the train beneath the clattering sound of your helicopter.'

Sorry, guys! I never did that again.

I need to get another two stories out of the way, even at the risk of you thinking this book is more about trains than about helicopters. In both cases they involve answering the polite questions of English country ladies of a certain age, wearing tweed and stout walking boots. In the first instance I was filming a documentary that told the tale of how painters flock to the Cornish village of St Ives to capture the unique lighting effects offered by the setting sun. A planned segment was to illustrate how they went there by a little train that wound its way along the picturesque coast and were therefore very much in the mood for painting by the time they arrived. The director had a shot in mind: I would hover in a relatively low position behind a headland, the train would come round, and I would then climb and reveal a huge and sandy horseshoe bay with St Ives at the other end of it. This was still in the days of chemical 16mm film; the problem was that we wouldn't know when to start the camera rolling and would be in danger of running out of film if we didn't time it really well.

The solution was to land on the sand and abandon the director with a ground-to-air radio with which he could cue us just before the train arrived. My cameramen and I then hopped away and hid ourselves and our helicopter behind the headland.

It turned out to be some time before the train arrived, during which period our director observed a lady walking her dog towards him from over a mile away across the beach. When she eventually arrived with her panting Labrador alongside she bid our director a very good day and said, 'Excuse me for asking but I couldn't help noticing that you arrived by helicopter, which then left you standing here all by yourself. May I enquire as to what it is you're doing?'

'Madam, I'm waiting for a train–'

'Oh,' gasped his questioner, pulling herself up to her full height and puffing out her chest. 'Well, how very rude. It was a civil enough question. Come along, Winnie.'

She stomped off into the distance, not giving our hapless director any further chance for polite explanation, just at the moment that the train did indeed come around the corner and require our attention.

My last train story involves shooting yet another British Rail commercial up at Hellifield. In this case the intention was to announce the imminent arrival of a new type of high-speed train, the likes of which had never been seen before. The only problem was that none had yet been delivered and the deadline for the commercial to be aired on television was about to pass. The advertising agency came up with the idea of sticking a huge polystyrene shape to the front of an old-style train to make it look like it was the new type, and covering the whole thing in black silk to give the impression that everything would shortly be revealed. From an aerial filming point of view there were a number of small complications, but none so big as the art department suffered in having to drape an entire train in material that was prone to blowing off at the slightest airflow, and having to reset it each time we wanted to do another take.

As you can imagine, the local populace liked to wander down to the bridge next to which I'd parked the chopper and beneath which

was this forbidding apparition of a train, just to see what was going on. British Rail regulations demanded that we always had one of their liaison officers with us; he happened to be a very entertaining man with a dry northern wit. By the time he'd given a sensible answer to the fiftieth person who'd wandered past he was getting tired and felt his answer needed some experimental variations.

Enter two tweedy ladies in sensible walking boots. 'Excuse me, do you mind me asking what's going on?' enquired the first.

The British Rail man looked to one side and then the other before putting his finger to his lips and whispering, 'Please don't tell anybody, but we're rehearsing for the Queen Mother's funeral.'

'Good grief,' exclaimed the second lady. 'I didn't know Her Majesty had died!'

'She hasn't,' responded the British Rail man, 'but she will one day and we just want to be prepared.'

'Oh yes, of course, silly us, don't worry, we won't tell,' answered the ladies before hurrying away, heads bent in animated conversation.

It wasn't more than five minutes before the next posse of rubberneckers came down to the bridge to ask, 'What's all this about a funeral, then?'

07

SPITFIRE

IN 1985 I HAD THE OPPORTUNITY to film a Spitfire, in what would turn out to be a three-part story in my filming life. The Spitfire is probably Britain's best-known fighter aircraft and is largely credited with having saved the country from Nazi domination in the period that became known as the Battle of Britain. By the end of the Second World War over twenty thousand of them had been manufactured in several variants, often built and delivered to their first front-line squadrons by women. ML407 was one of those, destined initially for 485 Squadron of the Royal New Zealand Air Force at Selsey in West Sussex. This aircraft was credited with having shot down the first enemy aircraft on D-Day before later being converted to a two-seater and used for training.

In 1979 the aeroplane was bought by Nick Grace, who was both pilot and engineer. Nick and his wife Carolyn were living in a caravan in Cornwall at the time, on a plot of land on which they were building a new home. Six years later Nick finished lovingly and

painstakingly restoring the beautiful old aircraft and on 16 April 1985 flew her for the first time. Carolyn, as the mother of two young children, took a lot of stick from friends and relatives about going up with Nick that day but as she has said herself, 'There would only ever be one first flight and I wanted to be with him.'

Three months later cameraman Simon Werry and I joined Nick and Carolyn at Land's End aerodrome, at the south-west tip of the country, for a day of air-to-air filming. Our task was to provide footage of Nick flying the venerable lady for a documentary about his ownership and restoration (which, by the way, is still available from the aircraft's own website at www.ml407.co.uk).

I loved the rare occasions when I was given a free hand to capture the best possible material. It meant I could go through the full repertoire of classic shots for the subject, then go on to try to develop new sequences that people might not have seen before. Nick soon demonstrated that he was a pilot I could trust in close formation, not just in the way he flew but in his professional approach to the task. The full set of classic shots, when filming air-to-air, was dictated by the simple chronology of takeoff, flying, and landing, but this could readily be expanded to encompass each flight phase. For example, the takeoff could be preceded by an establishing shot of the airfield from on high, a tighter shot of the aircraft parked among others, the big puff of smoke inevitably ejected from the engine as the propeller begins to turn, the taxi route out to line up on the runway, then the takeoff. Several of these shots were chronological necessities but others had a more specific role to play. In the case of the Spitfire, or indeed any of the fighter planes of the time, the combination of the huge piston engine in front of the pilot, and the way the plane sat down on its tail wheel, meant that the only way the pilot could get a view forward during taxiing was to weave the nose from side to side so that he could look past it. A small detail like this is all part of the story and can most easily be appreciated from above.

For the takeoff itself the most obvious choice is to try to fly alongside as the Spitfire rapidly gathers speed, lifts its tail and becomes airborne. Another option is to follow it from behind, or, if I trust the pilot and we've formed a good understanding at the briefing, then I might choose to loiter in a hover beyond the upwind end of the runway and let the Spitfire climb towards me. Each shot has a role to play for the editor, who, if I'm doing my job properly, should have a wealth of sequences from which to choose. If I've really had a good day, the great shots will get left on the cutting room floor in favour of the superlative ones.

There's another consideration when filming any sort of moving vehicle: 'crossing the line'. The favoured arrangement in the helicopter is for the cameraman to be on the same side as the pilot. Since helicopters are primarily designed to be flown from the right-hand seat, then both of us will be on the right-hand side with the camera facing out to the right. This means that when we're filming in formation, in the finished shot the vehicle we're shooting will always be travelling from right to left of the screen. In some cases, although it doesn't usually apply to something moving as fast as a Spitfire, we are able to film from around the other side. Let's say I give the editor a shot of a car travelling from right to left, then hop across to film it from the other side. If the editor were to cut the two shots together, then the viewer would be asking why the driver had decided to turn around and head back to where they came from. The only way to avoid giving you that confusion – and an editor that headache – is for me to visibly 'cross the line'. I have to execute a move that begins with the subject travelling from right to left, then moves around the back (or front) until the subject is travelling from left to right on your screen. In that way your brain will accept that the car hasn't reversed its direction of travel, and you are simply seeing it from the other side. It then becomes an even bigger editing problem because I've got to provide the editor with an additional shot that crosses the line

back to a right-to-left shot, and they are obliged to use both shots. The solution to all that messy complexity is to decide that the day is going to be a right-to-left day and leave it at that.

When shooting a lot of material that's going to be cut together, it's also a good idea to shoot it as a logical progression from beginning to end. If you were watching the story in which the Spitfire takes off, flies, then lands, it wouldn't make any sense to you if you saw the aircraft take off in a strong midday light, fly for a while with a low sun behind it, then land in full sunshine. So as well as all the basic mechanics and geometry of joining two flying machines and a camera together, there are logic and continuity issues I constantly have to bear in mind.

We were using the Agusta 109 that day because with a top speed of 150 knots we could fly happily in close formation with a slow-flying Spitfire and concentrate on tight shots of the pilot, or perhaps a shot of the undercarriage wheels being raised after takeoff or lowered for landing. Once we'd captured the basic toolbox of shots, we could begin to experiment with more adventurous stuff that's much harder to achieve. For example, a great shot would be one in which the Spitfire comes at us out of the sun. If we get it right it makes a delicious addition to the story and to the look of the final film, but there are a thousand ways to get it wrong. To get it even remotely right, I have to talk to the Spitfire continuously over the radio to guide him into a good position relative to the camera. First I'll choose a good heading for myself that gives my cameraman a clear shot at the sun. We can usually only do this towards evening when the sun is low in the sky, otherwise the camera would be looking up through our own rotor blades. The camera operator then makes his own adjustments to the camera so the image isn't 'blown out' (overexposed). Looking directly at the sun means that everything else is going to be quite dark, but it can produce some interesting effects in any background clouds.

Once we're both settled and comfortable in the helicopter, I begin to talk the Spitfire into a position that puts him somewhere near the sun in our shot before then adjusting that position to put him in complete silhouette. The camera will be running at high speed, which has the effect of slowing the shot down. There will be a shimmering effect around the sun which will look distorted as the engine exhaust of the Spitfire passes in front of it. The aircraft itself will look dark and menacing as it comes towards the camera and the whole shot will be infused with a feeling of power, menace and emotion. You might remember a few classic examples of this from the movies *Apocalypse Now* or Spielberg's *Empire of the Sun*.

By the end of that day Nick and I parted as good friends and with a lot of mutual respect. I'd also enjoyed meeting his beautiful wife Carolyn, who had been so supportive of Nick's passion throughout the rebuild of this lovely old aircraft.

Exactly three years later I got the chance to work with Nick again on a six-part television drama series called *Piece of Cake*. It was based on the book of the same name by Derek Robinson about a squadron of Hurricane fighter aircraft during the first year of the Second World War, but there are so few flying Hurricanes remaining that Spitfires had to be used instead. *Piece of Cake* was a hugely enjoyable series to work on but was certainly not cheap to produce, with each Spitfire flying hour costing around £5,000 and a total budget of £5,000,000. Privately owned Spitfires came from all sorts of places to make up the squadron and some had to be mocked up for the ground sequences. We positioned to various grass airfields around the country during the making of the series and, of course, always attracted a great deal of attention. On one summer's evening the Spitfire boys were alarmed to see two men lying on the grass under one of their machines. When the men were approached and challenged as to what they were up

to, they responded that their hobby was studying and collecting the serial numbers of tyres on vintage aircraft. They were asked to vacate their prone position under the wing, and perhaps to ask permission in future, when one of the enthusiasts burst out that he was sorry to have to break the news but both tyres were inauthentic and probably shouldn't be used in flight at all. The pilot who was supervising their polite removal suggested that if they pulled their attention a little way back from the obscure details they were studying then they might realise that the airframe they'd been lying under was made out of cardboard.

One of the seminal sequences in that drama series told of the day when a member of the squadron establishes the true level of his bravado by flying his Spitfire under a stone-arch bridge. I won't say which bridge was used; it had to have highly illuminated obstructions placed across the river beneath it soon after the episode was broadcast to put a stop to the multiple private pilots who wanted to emulate the stunt and were terrifying the locals. The pilot who performed that impressive feat was legendary aviator Ray Hanna. Ray had been a founder member of the RAF aerobatic display team the Red Arrows more than twenty years earlier, and had led the team for a record four years. Then, in addition to flying a private airliner in the Middle East, he formed the Old Flying Machine Company (OFMC), which he ran together with his son Mark and daughter Sarah. Mark was recently retired from the RAF where he'd flown F4 Phantoms but was now occupied full time with flying the mouth-watering array of vintage aircraft owned and operated by OFMC for air displays and film work on projects such as *Air America* and *Empire of the Sun*.

Ray was an irascible old Kiwi whose word was absolute, but you wouldn't find a pilot in the country who didn't regard him as the consummate fixed-wing aviator (his tombstone bears the single word 'Incomparable'). I remember the exact dimensions of

the Spitfire and the bridge: 36 feet 10 inches for the wingspan of the aircraft and just under 75 feet for the gap at the bottom of the stone arch. Ray was only going to do this stunt once, so it had to be captured from multiple cameras, including mine from above, in order that cuts between the various camera positions could extend the otherwise short sequence. To familiarise myself with the set-up I helped carry the ground camera out to the small stony island in the middle of the river and looked back through the curving arch; it seemed awfully tight.

I got airborne with Simon Werry as my expert cameraman and we waited for Ray to do two practice runs over the bridge. From our view above the bridge we could see the Spitfire drop down to just a few feet above the water; after a couple of seconds Ray pulled up and over the top of the bridge as eddies of wind rippled the surface of the river. He then flew a circuit and positioned himself for the second practice run, which was an inch-perfect repetition of the first. The third run was called 'live' over the radio and if you ever watch the sequence you can see, from the riverbed camera, the moment that Ray committed himself to going through beneath the arch, indicated by the tiniest of nose-down movements that seemed to say, 'This time.' Two seconds later the Spit's wings flashed briefly in the shadow of the bridge and it was through and climbing towards us, executing a perfect roll as it came. It was a spectacular moment and one for which I was glad to have bagged the best seat in the house.

The next day the producer asked if I would perform the same feat with a forward-looking nose mount on the helicopter so the editor could additionally make use of the Spitfire pilot's point of view. I confirmed with Ray that his wingspan was nearly identical to my rotor diameter, although I knew it would be a bit tighter for me as his wings were low and therefore passed through the widest part of the arch, whereas my rotors were on top of my rotor mast and had to pass through the point where the stone arch began to curve

inwards. Nevertheless I was confident that it could be done safely at high speed and told the producer that I'd be happy to perform the same stunt . . . for the same premium as they were paying Ray (he'd already quietly told me exactly how many thousand pounds extra he was charging for the manoeuvre). They rejected it. I never quite understood how they thought it was worth less to have a helicopter with rotating blades fly through the bridge than a pair of non-rotating wings. My two runs at the bridge were therefore broken off at the last moment as I pulled up and over the top. It would almost have been easier to fly through it and certainly would have been more fun but I was damned if I was going to provide something for free that Ray had charged a handsome amount to perform. I think there was also a tiny bit of me that didn't want to in any way diminish the impressive feat of the great man.

We went on our merry way, leaving the bridge and its neighbours in peace, but with footage in the can that has become an aviation legend. *Piece of Cake* received great acclaim when it was first shown on Sunday evenings but had the terribly sad postscript that Nick Grace was killed in a road accident on his way home before it was broadcast. His wife Carolyn decided that she would learn to fly the Spitfire herself in a tribute to the memory of Nick.

So it was that I found myself back in formation with ML407 three years later, flying out of White Waltham airfield with Carolyn at the controls instead of Nick. The occasion was the making of the documentary *Going Solo*, which charted the course of the Grace family's extraordinary relationship with a wonderful old flying machine, and I feel privileged to have had a three-part connection with that story. At the time of writing, all these years later, Carolyn is still thrilling crowds at air displays around Europe with the sweet note of the huge Merlin engine emanating from in front of her as she 'dances the skies on laughter-silvered wings'. She is reputed to be the only woman in the world qualified to fly the Spitfire.

I look back and cherish every minute spent flying in the close company of Ray, Mark and Nick, all exceptional aviators who have sadly now gone. Ray made it to the age of 77 before dying of natural causes – an astonishing achievement for one who lived his flying life so close to the edge. His son Mark, who was an unfeasibly good-looking young man, lived his love life similarly close to the edge and would frequently turn up at our doorstep with a stunning young lady on his arm. We lost Mark in a still-unexplained accident six years before Ray; the suspicion is that a joint cracked in the exhaust pipes of the Spanish-built version of the Messerschmitt 109 he was taking to an air display. Mark turned on to final approach to the airfield but never pulled out of the turn, in all likelihood succumbing to the insidious effects of carbon monoxide poisoning.

08

TRANSATLANTIC VIRGINS

TWO WEEKS AFTER THE FIRST FILMING event with Nick Grace, my two lives of rescue pilot and film pilot came together for one brief moment when I flew out to sea to film the racing yacht *Drum*. She had been taking part in the Fastnet yacht race (which had played such a major role in my earlier rescue career) when she had been dismasted and capsized. Trapped inside was the owner Simon Le Bon, lead singer of Duran Duran. My old diver Larry 'Scouse' Slater was despatched from a Wessex helicopter, dived down under the yacht, found Simon trapped in an air pocket in the cabin and brought him out by sharing the air in his scuba tank. Filming (after the event) what became a high profile national news item brought back a lot of memories and left me feeling a bit strange, like a man stuck between two worlds and times. Just four days later I began another adventure in the Atlantic which again turned out to be a three-part saga stretching over a couple of years as Richard (later

Sir Richard) Branson attempted the first of three record-breaking transatlantic voyages.

I'd been a schoolboy at the time Branson started his Virgin empire at the age of nineteen by selling vinyl records, and I clearly remember the excitement when a schoolmate received *The Who – Live at Leeds* in a brown paper sleeve with the Virgin logo on it. My first (nearly) personal encounter came when I was tasked to film the conclusion of Branson's first attempt at breaking the Blue Riband record for a west-to-east crossing of the Atlantic. Once again my old Navy mates became involved in the story after the *Virgin Atlantic Challenger* sank with little more than an hour to go to reach the lighthouse at Bishop's Rock which demarks the finish line. So my logbook for that day records nothing more than a trip out to St Mary's on the Isles of Scilly at five o'clock in the morning and a return home for breakfast by seven thirty. Ten months later it was a different story as *Virgin Atlantic Challenger II* broke the record by just over two hours and I was able to film her passing the lighthouse at high speed. We rushed back to the airfield and down to the quay in time to greet the successful crew as they came alongside and cracked their first bottle of champagne.

I had the highest regard for how Virgin took on the national might of British Airways and their pompous head Lord King in a bid to conduct landings at London Heathrow and thereby operate across transatlantic air routes on a level playing field. Branson's personal stunts were always fun and usually designed to create maximum PR for his growing airline. When Branson set out on his next attempt to cross the Atlantic, this time by hot-air balloon, he was accompanied by Per Lindstrand, who is probably the best-known balloonist in the world after setting every possible distance, duration and altitude record. I had been tasked to try to intercept and film their balloon's arrival on UK soil by Slim MacDonnell, with whom I'd often worked in his role as an exceptional underwater cameraman. Slim was working for Television South (TVS) as producer on their definitive documentary of the transatlantic balloon attempt. We'd talked through the brief some weeks before as his initial work would be at the launch site in Maine, USA. By the time he'd used one of Virgin Atlantic's more traditional flying machines to return to the UK, Slim would obviously be in a rush, so we all had to know what we'd be doing well in advance.

The mighty balloon had taken off from the USA in some chaos and had accidentally lost one of its exterior-mounted gas tanks in the process but was well on its way across the Pond by the time Slim rang me from Heathrow. We agreed to meet in Blackpool and I set off right away.

The world was about to experience the explosion of communications and GPS tracking capability that we take for granted today, but as Richard and Per caught the upper winds and progressed rapidly that explosion of information was yet to happen. Despite the Virgin team having access to the very latest technology, the probable track of the balloon, deduced from whatever had been their last radioed position, was little more than a guess. Their arrival was not even guaranteed to be anywhere in Britain. As time went on there were fears that slowing winds might delay them until after darkness. With fog forecast for Scotland that night, this would force them to fly over the UK and potentially be over Russia by the time daylight came again and allowed them to land. With little more information than that, we visited the meteorological office at Blackpool airport, applied wind vectors to the last known position, talked with Virgin HQ and tried to narrow down the approach path of the huge balloon.

It transpired that I was flying only one of fourteen helicopters, all trying to do the same thing. A couple of them were in the employ of Virgin and were carrying Richard's family and crew, while most of the others were working for various big television networks. I think all of them were twin-engined machines, as the likelihood of having to fly a good way out to sea was quite high. From Blackpool we took the ten-minute hop down to Liverpool, which seemed to be the best starting point from which to head out to sea, but while I was talking to the Met officer we learned that all the other thirteen helicopters were currently sitting at Carlisle, nearly a hundred miles to the north of us, in a long queue for the refuelling facilities. Slim and I had been betting on a more southerly track for the balloon than everybody else, but as we recalculated we realised that a northerly track was increasingly likely and would take Branson and Lindstrand across the top of Northern Ireland and into either England or Scotland at around the latitude of Carlisle – where all the others were waiting. With a sinking heart, feeling that we had gambled and lost, we set off to the north to join the others. We were pretty sure that the front runners would already be heading towards Ireland and that we were going to join the party about an hour after the Virgin's skirts had been lowered to the ground.

The flight north to Carlisle took forty-five minutes. It later transpired that the other pilots up there had been scratching their heads and asking themselves what on earth it was that Grayson knew and they didn't. The equivalent of a water-cooler meeting for pilots traditionally takes place on the tarmac next to a fuel truck. At just such a meeting they'd decided they should head south and join me in Liverpool. We all passed each other at around 5,000 feet over the highest point of the Lake District and then of course spent the rest of our journeys wondering whether we were doing the right thing or not. By the time we reached Carlisle I was in a combative mood and the refuelling guy was now well used to topping up helicopters in double-quick time. Listening to the Met reports from all the airfields within 200 miles during the flight, I had become increasingly convinced that the balloon was coming in on a more northerly track, so we took off again within minutes of our arrival and headed due west, straight out to sea. Down in Liverpool my thirteen compatriots were forming another orderly queue in line for the fuel truck.

We passed the Mull of Kintyre, a harsh rock towering above the northern end of the Irish Sea, behind which hid the sleepy airfield of Machrihanish, which I knew well. There's only a 12-mile stretch of water from the Mull to the tip of Northern Ireland, with a small island in between called Rathlin. A tiny dot in the sky appeared directly ahead of us and grew and grew until we were sure that we were looking at the Virgin Flyer at the end of her 2,900-mile journey. With growing horror I also realised that we were watching the balloon descend at quite a high rate towards the sea. I had a dilemma and turned to Slim to resolve it.

'She's going to hit the water before I can get there. I can keep going, but I won't make it in time, or I can stop and turn so the cameraman can catch it.'

'Keep going,' he responded in what was probably the best decision of the day, albeit one that means there is no record of that water landing.

It felt as though we were much closer than we actually were when the Virgin Atlantic Flyer hit the water because of the sheer size of the envelope. In circumference the balloon was larger than the Albert Hall and occupied 2.3 million cubic feet – the largest ever built at that point. But she bounced and by the time we reached our target she was climbing rapidly and passing 500 feet.

The problem with filming, or even observing, the gondola of a balloon of that size is that there are guy lines hanging down from all around the envelope so I had to give them a respectful distance; it's a bit like standing several streets away from a very large football stadium and trying to work out what you're looking at in the middle of the pitch. We could see something on top of the gondola that Slim's technical knowledge told him shouldn't be there. It wasn't moving, but it might have been a person, or even two people. With Slim's approval I ducked our helicopter down beneath the hanging ropes and popped up in the shadow of the envelope with the lines to our right and the gondola to our left. In my head I'd moved into full safety mode and didn't care that the camera was now blind to what was happening. I just needed Slim to have a good view of the gondola from his side to be able to assess what was going on. I glanced at the instruments for half a second and noted that we were climbing our way through 2,000 feet towards full cloud cover at 3,000 feet. We were now sure that we were looking at a single person sitting on the side of the gondola roof, but with all the safety gear and other accoutrements we couldn't tell who it was. Slim's best guess was that it was Richard and that Per would still be inside trying to fly the machine and keep it out of the water. His further conclusion was that Richard must be preparing to jettison the heavy roof-mounted generator to lighten the load and give them further flying distance, hopefully to the Scottish shore.

Aware we were about to go into cloud together, I warned Slim that I was going to break away from the balloon and climb through the cloud independently, on a heading that would take us away from the goliath. I dropped my power just as an eerie fog-like effect of the cloud began to appear between the gondola and us. As soon as I was confident that we were clear of the guy lines, I put the helicopter nose down, trading height for speed, and accelerated away. I established myself on my instruments and once I had enough speed I pulled back on the cyclic control to initiate a smooth climb. With that climb established and the knowledge that there was no land this high that I might run into, I could give 10 per cent of my brain to considering the wider picture. On one of the frequencies I was monitoring I could hear that the other helicopters were well on their way and would soon be approaching the area beneath the balloon, but of course they would be unable to see us because we were into the cloud layer by then. As soon as I'd connected the concept of thirteen helicopters beneath a falling generator I had no hesitation in pulling the transmit button and calling 'Mayday' three times. It wasn't strictly the right type of call to make, but it felt as though events were spinning out of control and I wanted to be sure I had everybody's attention. I kept the button pressed and gave a long exposition on what was happening and what might happen next. Just at that moment we broke out on top of the cloud layer into clear blue sunshine and I gingerly began a wide turn back towards where we'd come from, expecting the balloon to appear at any moment.

As luck would have it, there was a Royal Navy frigate in the area called HMS *Argonaut*, who either heard my mayday call or had it relayed to them and quickly launched their own Lynx helicopter in search and rescue mode. So now there were fourteen helicopters all milling around somewhere beneath the cloud bank we were on top of. I circled for what seemed like a very long time but despite our three pairs of eyes being out on stalks for the imminent revelation of a balloon, it never came. We could only surmise that the hot air in the balloon envelope had cooled sufficiently in the cloud for it to level off and begin a slow descent, a supposition that I broadcast over the common frequency we were all using. If that was the case, then I had some quick mental arithmetic to do and some decisions to make. Fuel was getting low and the only airfield within sensible reach was Machrihanish, a sleepy hollow at the best of times but unlikely to be active at seven o'clock on a Friday night. The advantage of Machrihanish was that since I knew it well I'd be able to make an approach out of cloud, with reasonable certainty that I wouldn't run into the tall peak of the Mull of Kintyre; the disadvantage was that there was no way I could contemplate descending into that cloud with a large balloon potentially hidden in it and fourteen helicopters beneath it – that would have been suicide.

In the space of an hour I'd been through the modes of film pilot and rescue pilot, but I now switched into full look-after-yourself-pilot mode and informed both my crewmates that our working day was over. I began the three-dimensional calculations of where I was, where everybody else was and where the hard-centred bit of the cloud was. I must have got it somewhere close to correct because fifteen minutes later we broke out of cloud to find Machrihanish on the nose and the big old Mull clear off to our right.

Not far away the drama was still playing out, as we would later discover. The balloon descended back out of the cloud and the swarm of civilian helicopters was able to stand off at a safe distance and observe the gondola touch the water for the final time as the Navy Lynx moved in to pick up the two intrepid balloonists. Except that there weren't two, there was only one.

Branson's first words to the Lynx crew as he was safely hauled into their machine was, 'Where's Per?' to which he reputedly received the response, 'Who's Per?'

Our own late arrival at the first ditching had hidden from us the fact that Per had leapt 60 feet from the rising craft into the Irish Sea as Richard rode the thing aloft. The plan had been for them to activate the explosive bolts which would release the envelope from above their heads and leave them aboard a new type of yacht, but when the bolts failed and the gondola was relieved of Per's weight it had shot skywards with Richard still sitting on the roof.

This of course had left Per alone in the water for just over two hours. Fortunately for him his Swedish father had made him swim to the other side of their local lake and back again every morning before going to school, and he was therefore much better equipped to deal with the numbing cold than most of us. Nevertheless, when a tiny Irish skiff happened across him he reckoned he was within only minutes of giving up the battle. He was soon transferred to the Lynx and on his way to Prestwick in Scotland along with all the other helicopters, while I went knocking on doors at Machrihanish to find some fuel.

In due course I had full tanks again and was on my own way to Prestwick. I might have found the balloon first but I was going to be the last at the party. When we did eventually arrive, secure our helicopter for the night and make our way to the large hotel that had opened its doors to this plethora of dishevelled aviators, the transatlantic protagonists had already met the media scrum, had a hot bath and gone to bed. An evening in the bar with old flying mates, swapping war stories, was followed by a night of blissful sleep and by the time I awoke in the morning Branson was already on his way south with his family. I made my way home to Cornwall via Carlisle, Blackpool and Southampton.

However, as with so many of these stories that was not to be the end. Only eight days later I was, by pure coincidence, chartered to pick up Branson from a Virgin conference hotel in Torquay and fly him via a fuel stop at Oxford to the British Grand Prix at Silverstone. He was by himself and chose to sit in the co-pilot's seat so we had a good hour alone together to swap stories of how his remarkable trip had ended with us flying in close formation together into cloud. He was only going to be at Silverstone for long enough to be heralded by the crowd for his achievement in being part of the first-ever crew to successfully take a hot-air balloon across the Atlantic, in a time of 33 hours.

As he exited the helicopter he thrust a bunch of notes into my hand and said, 'We're going to Gatwick next because I'm off to the USA to deliver this speech. See what you think.'

He had been personally tasked by Prime Minister Maggie Thatcher to do whatever he could to stop the global advance of AIDS. I therefore found myself sitting in my cockpit at the British Grand Prix reading an astonishing speech about the lifesaving potential of condoms.

We flew down to Gatwick airport together, where there was one more new experience for me. Apparently when you own an airline you don't have to worry about little things like making it to the plane on time – the aircraft waits for you. A fully loaded Virgin 747 had left the gate, taxied out to a clear area, briefly stopped with the engines running and opened the door once more. I was given a special clearance to land right next to the front steps, up which bounded Branson with a small bag and his condom speech in his hand. The airliner doors closed as I wound my rotors up to full speed and got quickly out of the way of the big jumbo jet. By the time I'd settled back down into a more usual parking spot for helicopters, the 747 was already lifting its nose on its way back across the Atlantic.

09

TORNADO, CONCERT, TELETHON AND A BET

OPERATIONAL TECHNIQUES I'D LEARNED in the Navy often turned out to be useful during complex film shoots, particularly when the job required the rapid assimilation of wide-ranging three-dimensional situations. In the anti-submarine role the first asset (by which I mean ship, helicopter or plane) to make contact with a sub-surface threat would generally take charge of shepherding the other assets into a pattern that would give the best chance of success. This was logical, since they were often the only team with enough information to do the job. Over time I'd become used to building a picture in my head of where everybody was, even if they were all many miles beyond the line of sight. In film flying it is a similar 3D chess game of trying to line up your camera with a subject, sometimes more than one subject, together with the background

and the light. Consequently I felt well qualified to take charge of a flight of Tornado multi-role combat aircraft during a wonderful documentary called *White Knights, Fiery Steeds.*

The title came from the 1984 Bonnie Tyler song 'Holding Out For A Hero', and if you'd commissioned a piece of music to go with a film about the men who flew these agile supersonic monsters you could do no better. The song was originally heard in the movie *Footloose* and was iconic by the time we shot *White Knights.* Just one of the YouTube entries for that song has been viewed over 75 million times. The opening line, 'Where have all the good men gone and where are all the gods?' set the tone for the piece from the very start. Much as it pains a Navy man to advocate for the Royal Air Force, I arrived at RAF Honington in August 1988 with great respect already for the guys who earned their living in a flying machine that could change its own shape. At low speed their wings would be swept forward to give maximum lift and the useful ability to take off from relatively short runways, but when penetrating enemy airspace or assigning their sophisticated weaponry to ground targets they would sweep their wings back like a bird of prey to achieve supersonic speeds a diving falcon could only dream of.

By then I was teamed up pretty much permanently with Simon Werry as my cameraman. His size belied his gentle hands on the camera controls and we'd developed an almost telepathic relationship in the air. The teamwork went way beyond the old expression of the whole being greater than the sum of the parts, and we'd begun to achieve a Zen-like state wherein each shoot we did together felt better than the last. Occasionally, although we never voiced it, we'd watch the rushes and think, 'Can't do any better than that, some magic dust was floating in the air that day.' On the ground he would drive everybody nuts by breaking things. Ray Hanna summed it up beautifully the day he declared, 'He's an outstanding aerial operator but it's a bit like having a hyper-active hippopotamus in the cockpit with you. He's usually broken three things before we've even reached the runway.' It didn't matter; I only had to look at the aerial rushes to forgive the chaos that surrounded Simon on the ground.

We spent two days at the RAF base developing mutual respect with the Tornado pilots as we shot them from above in all phases of their flight. Their base lay towards the east coast of the country and they practised their craft out over the North Sea, where they could lock onto targets laid out for them to destroy without disturbing too much of the local peace. It would be another couple of years before the general population became familiar with this type of aircraft from the nightly news bulletins issuing out of the conflict that ultimately became known as Gulf War One. In the meantime Simon and I relished the opportunity to record them at their work and we put together all the techniques we'd employed in shooting Nick Grace's Spitfire, albeit at a rather higher speed. We used a Jetranger as our platform since the additional 50 knots that the Agusta 109 offered would make no difference at all in our air-to-air capabilities with a Tornado. In most cases we simply perched ourselves in a good high-level vantage point and let the speed of the sleek fixed-wing aircraft provide the drama.

I would combine the 3D model in my head with the search-and-rescue technique of translating words heard over the radio into a map of the world around me. In this way I could pick a spot that gave us a nice clean camera frame with some attractive lighting effects off the water, then guide Simon to point the camera at an otherwise unremarkable patch of ocean that would soon be invaded by the incoming Tornadoes. Camera operators are pretty much blind to the events going on around them because their focus is at the micro end of the scale. For them the world exists only in their viewfinder, within which will lie the only record of the day. As the years went on and my experience widened, I came to realise more and more that

my job as a film pilot was to feed that small window with engaging content in whatever way I could.

We didn't leave Bonnie Tyler on the ground either. Listening to songs such as 'Hero' helped us to stay in tune with the pace of other flying machines that truly did create thunder and heat. Pace is an important factor in aerial filming and it has many facets. The most obvious type of high-pace shot is when the helicopter is flying fast and low; the ground is travelling quickly towards or past the lens, depending on whether the nose or side mount is being used, and subjects come into and out of frame quickly. But you can also achieve high pace from a helicopter in the hover if the camera is zoomed quickly in or out, or maybe panned from one place to another. The important thing, as ever, is what's happening in the camera frame, not what's happening to the helicopter. In the case of the Tornadoes they had such speed that a static camera on a hovering helicopter still resulted in a high-paced shot.

Between our two days of daylight shooting we were also able to capture some night shots, although these were confined to takeoffs and landings. With their twin jet engines boosted by afterburner flames for extra departure power, the menacing machines lit up the runway as they accelerated and climbed, but there was little advantage in trying to capture images of them thereafter.

Before bidding our new friends adieu we briefed together for one final sortie that would be carried out over Dartmoor, some 200 miles south-west of Honington, back in our own backyard of Devon and Cornwall. The documentary had been commissioned by Television South West to illustrate how and why the Tornadoes regularly used the deserted moor to practise their low-level work, so the inclusion of Dartmoor was an integral part of the story. The commanding officer of the squadron was happy to oblige, but we would have to fit in with one of their scheduled excursions in that direction and that wasn't due for a couple of months.

When we did eventually meet again over the skies of Devon, we used our mutual respect with the instructor pilots to good effect. Without the earlier brief at their base we wouldn't have achieved much more than short glimpses of black dots in the distance, but the fact that we now trusted each other as aviators meant that we could plan for my helicopter to remain in a constant position while the jets performed around and beneath us. Since light is such a variable factor we had planned for an initial hook-up and visual confirmation by map reference, but that I would thereafter take verbal control of the two-ship Tornado formation in order to vector them in the directions that would best illuminate them for us and provide the widest range of backgrounds. All my military 3D faculties came into play during this fine hour. Inevitably the last pass was their closest as they flashed past no more than 30 feet beneath us; Simon was certain he'd seen the whites of the pilots' eyes through his lens. The net result was an enjoyable television programme featuring many of our shots, most of which we were really proud of. Once again a fabulous opportunity to gain a brief and intense look into other people's jobs.

In between the two Tornado encounters I had my first taste of show business on a grand scale. The French electronic musician Jean-Michel Jarre had already established a name for himself in outdoor performances when he broke the world record with an audience of a million at his free concert in the Place de la Concorde on Bastille Day in 1979. He then became the first western musician to play in China, and seared his name into Texas with his 1986 *Rendez-vous Houston*, a concert that again broke records with an audience of 1.5 million witnessing the music, light, fireworks and laser performance. Imagery was projected onto giant screens reaching up to 1,200 feet on the side of the city's skyscrapers in celebration of Texas's 150th anniversary.

Destination Docklands was scheduled to be a similar spectacle in the derelict Royal Victoria Dock in East London during the last quarter of 1988, where of course Jarre wanted to exceed the visual feasts he'd already achieved in other cities. I received a telephone call from an old producer mate, Alan Morton, who was involved in the show, asking whether I thought it would be possible to bounce lasers off a massive mirror-ball slung beneath a helicopter. And while I was at it, could I look into the viability of getting an entire formation of helicopters together to open the show in the most spectacular way possible? If I hadn't known Alan to be one of those guys who can pull off the ridiculous, and if Jarre hadn't already proved his ability to perform on such a scale, I might have left the request on my desk as one of those things that will go away if you ignore it. But I was excited at the prospect, talked to a few military friends who were similarly inspired, and took some positive steps down the road to pulling off the stunt.

Then, despite having been in negotiations since the early part of the year, Newham Borough Council began to express increasingly petty objections to the event and, in the typical style of British borough councils, delayed their decision until 12 September, the month in which the show was due to take place. Huge investment had already been made in a giant floating stage and all the other paraphernalia that goes along with an open-air concert on this scale. Jarre was distraught when the licence request was rejected and began urgently looking for other locations at which to perform. Two days later I picked up him and his wife, the beautiful actress Charlotte Rampling, in an Agusta 109 from Victoria Docks, which would later become the site of the London City airport. We flew to the docks at Tilbury, to the far east of London, and to the docks in Dover down to the south. I remember it being a rather tense day without much in the way of joie de vivre between us, particularly since Ms Rampling was on crutches from a leg injury and in considerable pain. By the end of our day no firm conclusion had been reached, site preparations were optimistically continuing in the Docklands, and now the local fire authority had climbed on board the general malaise with concerns about access to the venue. The sun had stayed behind the clouds throughout our flight and the whole fiasco felt grey and British in a drizzly sort of way.

Obviously my preparations for a disco laser squadron were curtailed, and by the time the council eventually came through with a grudging and conditional approval on 28 September, it was too late to resurrect them in time for the new concert dates of 8 and 9 October. In the event it's probably just as well that the helicopter plans came to naught. The second night suffered storms on a biblical scale and it's doubtful we would have been able to fly anyway. I still took our mobile office for Alan's production crew to use and I shared a rented suburban house with Alan and his senior managers for the preceding week. After all the effort to get the show on the road there was no way I was going to miss the performance. The concert was fabulous, the fireworks included an effect that gave the impression of a whole factory burning to the ground, and a circle of immensely powerful Second World War searchlights shining up from their positions on a two-mile radius gave the impression that the audience and stage existed within a gigantic waterlogged cathedral. There was nothing significant to record on my credit list but it was still a night to remember.

Many times I've wondered whether I've bitten off more than I can chew. One of those was about sixty seconds into an appearance on *You Bet*, the game show hosted by Bruce Forsyth. To explain to non-Brits, Bruce Forsyth has been a television legend in a career spanning over seventy years and was recently knighted for his work. For many decades, barely a week passed in the UK when he wasn't hosting the most popular game show.

This programme included three celebrity guests, each of whom would introduce their sponsored stunt and invite the live studio audience to 'bet' on whether the stunt could be achieved within a set time period. When I'd been phoned by a producer on the programme to ask if I thought I could use a paintbrush, attached to the helicopter, to paint letters on the roof of a car, I asked how fast the car would be going. The producer was taken aback, as she'd assumed we would use a stationary car, but of course once I'd opened up the possibility of using a moving vehicle she was sold on the idea. The letters to be painted would be 'LWT', the abbreviation for the broadcaster, London Weekend Television.

We changed our Jetranger G-SPEY over from her usual high skids with flotation bags to the low tubular skids that would make it easier for me to lean out of the open doorway and see the paintbrush. I did get to do a couple of evening practices at our base but we were thwarted in our attempt to set up a small oval course in the time available, so I set off for the coast of Lincolnshire on the day of filming without ever having successfully completed the task. We were to shoot it on the sands of Cleethorpes, near the aptly named Grimsby, so that my own stunt could be preceded by one performed by the local lifeguards, which I was to film from the air. As always the schedule fell behind until there was no time left within the available light for me to carry out a practice run.

We quickly affixed the paint brush and before I knew what was happening the car had set off around the sands and somebody had called 'Action.' With a couple of little mini-cams fitted in the cockpit to record my own point of view, I lifted into a low hover, slid sideways to a large tray of paint and dipped the brush. I'd set a stopwatch going on the dashboard but never had a chance to glance at it. The 'L' went on OK in two deft movements but then the car reached the end of its track and began to loop back in the other direction. Three thoughts went through my head in quick succession: one, you need more paint on the brush but you don't have time to collect it; two, you might have to paint the 'W' from the other side of the car but that might make it an 'M'; and three, next time you want to raise the stakes, do it on a horse race, not on your clearly inadequate capabilities.

As the car levelled out for another run down the back straight I could see that I'd got something onto the roof that could loosely be interpreted as a 'W' and went for the last letter, 'T', which should have been as easy as the 'L'. But it wasn't, because my whole forearm and right hand was almost convulsing with the tension that had built up during my previous two attempts at emulating Picasso. Eventually I got the down-stroke of the 'T' applied but two lunges at the cross stroke showed me that I'd gone past the point of no return. Even without time to look at the stopwatch I could tell that I must be within seconds of the limit and was in with a good chance of public humiliation on national television the following Saturday. I stopped trying to paint, pulled slightly back from the car, took a deep breath, consciously relaxed my right hand and put myself in the mindset of doing a precision rescue from all those years previously. One more move towards the car and the crossbar of the 'T' went on perfectly, with about two seconds to spare. I pulled in power and performed a little dance with the helicopter in celebration.

The subsequent appearance on the show was fun to do and I was initiated into a new addition to my job description by having to do a voiceover to the piece, as if I'd been recording it while flying the stunt. In reality I wouldn't have had the spare capacity to speak while flying the thing and, even if I had, it would have sounded like a pilot with severe Tourette syndrome.

There can be events in your life whose effect has a magnitude you never imagined at the time. It's only with the wonderful benefit of hindsight that you're able to identify them as seminal moments and

turning points. The word 'Telethon' in my logbook alludes to just such a moment for me.

The word is a portmanteau of 'television' and 'marathon'. Each year London Weekend Television would allocate an entire day of broadcast to this charity fund-raising event, utilising all the most popular shows from the independent British television stations of the time. *Treasure Hunt* qualified as just such a show. It was decided that we would do five live broadcasts for the special day. The first would be aired the night before, from Edinburgh, at eight o'clock. We would then position south to Castle Howard in Yorkshire, from where we would broadcast for the breakfast television slot, then on to Birmingham in time to make the lunchtime slot. Next would come Shoreham on the south coast for teatime, before returning to London for the final broadcast in prime-time evening viewing. At each stage the *Telethon* audience, and the consequent donations to charity, would increase.

Thankfully, and quite unusually, a good amount of time had been allocated to the planning of the exercise during the preceding twelve months. I guess that since television is so allied to news coverage there is a tendency to assume that most things can be achieved at the drop of a hat, but often they cannot be. Over the years this tendency has become distinctly worse and I've grown increasingly tired of answering phone calls at four o'clock on a Friday enquiring about the possibility of achieving X, Y or Z on Saturday afternoon. Only once did I let my door come off its hinges and hurl back the answer, 'You cannot *possibly* have *suddenly* become aware that you want to achieve this very complex task tomorrow afternoon. Why would you leave it until now to share this little bit of information with me?' All very unprofessional of me but sometimes you've just got to let it out.

Not so with Chatsworth Television, who were always consummate professionals in the way they dealt with the various technical departments that made up the travelling circus for *Treasure*

Hunt. They had allocated enough time for planning, and we were going to need all of it. If you include the practice we would be doing on the reverse legs on our way up to Scotland, then there would be around eighteen hours of flying in just a few days, so every tiny detail needed to be looked at and honed to perfection. The concept of an error or omission on my part resulting in a blank television slot was unthinkable, so in between the events told in other stories in this chapter, I was spending most evenings working out how to crack this task. To help in those endeavours Chatsworth TV allocated a young researcher from the production side of the fence called Sara Hine. I'd never met Sara (pronounced Sarah) but soon grew to know her well down the 200-mile telephone line between her office in London and mine in Cornwall.

Television researchers can often occupy a parallel universe in which everything is absolutely delightful and aesthetically pleasing but bears no relationship to the practicalities of the real world. This one was different. Each evening Sara would ring me at the end of the working day to discuss the new things she'd discovered about the project, the ideas she had for what we'd do during the broadcast, and the practical problems she'd already laid to rest. It was like a breath of fresh air and I increasingly came to look forward to our evening phone call. Very early on in the process it became apparent that the logistics of the task would overwhelm us if we didn't find a really simple and convenient way of transporting several people and a shed-load of technical equipment from one location to another. For the solution I returned to the Royal Navy. I'd been a civilian for nearly a decade but there were still enough good contacts in my address book to validate the theory that it's not what you know but who you know that makes the difference. Within just a few calls (and liberal use of the word 'charity') I was able to surprise Sara with the great news that the Fleet Air Arm had offered us a Commando Sea King for the *Telethon.* From there on things began to fall into place.

I can be accused of remembering past events in simpler terms than the reality, and it's probably fair to say that the expression 'fall into place' does not adequately describe the midnight oil that Sara and I were each burning in the countdown to the technical rehearsal that would precede the main event by six weeks. In increasingly long phone conversations we went through the schedule from end to end in ever more detail. We were only too aware that once the blue touch-paper had been lit there was no stopping the fuse from burning down to dust in a couple of days that would flash past in an instant. There would be no time to stop and think; even the simplest of scenarios had to have a plan B and often a plan C. With each conversation we refined the contents of the operations manual we'd been writing together until it extended to more than two inches thick in the ring-binders that each participant would receive from us at the imminent mass briefing. I was perfectly prepared for the jokes about useful door-stops that would follow dissemination of this document and I knew from experience that we'd be lucky if each crew member read more than 10 per cent of it. But the main point of putting together a document like that is that Sara and I could be confident that we really did have an answer for every possible question, together with a fallback position in the event of problems. We each set off for the London briefing, fully aware of the irony that we'd worked so closely together for nearly a year, grown to have enormous mutual respect, and would be doing an all-day joint presentation, but had never set eyes on each other.

Apart from meeting Sara for the first time, the gathering of the crew felt like a family reunion. It was split pretty much 50/50 down gender lines and almost everybody had been regularly working together for nearly a decade. Sara had returned to her mother's home the night before for a way-overdue family visit of her own; we'd both been concentrating on the *Telethon* task to the exclusion of all others for some weeks previously, and her mum was beginning to get antsy. The story goes that she was caught in a rainstorm, tried to dry her clothes by her mum's open fire, set fire to the clothes, had to choose something from her mother's wardrobe, overslept on the all-important briefing day, didn't have time for hair and makeup, and arrived at the television studios with only thirty seconds to spare. The overall effect of the drab grey dress and the wild hair (and I've said this to her face, but not until several years later) was of a homeless person who had electrocuted herself. I could not have imagined on that day that this would be the girl who would become my second wife.

The briefing went well and, sure enough, one wag actually used the document to prop open a heavy door when the room started to get stuffy. Lieutenant Mike de Winton, Royal Navy, attended as the Sea King pilot and his presence brought a sense of seriousness to the briefing. For many years we'd used our pair of small Jetranger helicopters on the *Treasure Hunt* series, but the distances involved in *Telethon* and the requirement for two engines over central London dictated that this time we would be using our two Agusta 109s. The fact that the usual white van for technical gear had been replaced by 5 tonnes of Sea King seemed to give everybody pause to consider that we'd more-than-slightly raised the bar.

Over the next four days we flew the route in reverse. We tested the flight paths we would use during the live broadcast, we tested all the live video links (still a relatively new thing in British broadcasting), and we tested ourselves. Mick Wright, by then the chief engineer at Castle Air, could regularly be seen grinning from ear to ear as the aircraft performed flawlessly. By the time we reached Edinburgh Sara and I had refined a few details here and there but we'd largely proved the value of detailed planning.

Six weeks later we regrouped to do it all again, only this time for real. As with so many of these high-profile and high-pressure broadcasts my memory of doing the thing itself is blurry in comparison with the memory of the planning process, and I guess that's the way it's supposed to be: polish the planning to somewhere near perfection and the rest will just follow on. The last thing I remember before lighting the fuse is our arrival at the imposing Dalhousie Castle Hotel just to the south of Edinburgh. We had deliberately scheduled a day off after arrival to give everybody a chance to settle down, begin to work as a team, and have the chance to fine-tune their own specialisations. A rest day on location is always a much valued thing, which more often than not results in a raucous team dinner the preceding evening. So it proved to be on this occasion, with our naval contingent performing party tricks more usually reserved for nights at sea, and Sara searing herself into the consciousness of the crew by retiring early to bed and then inadvertently sleep-walking through the reception of the grand hotel wearing little more than a T-shirt, while the entire male contingent of the crew were still swapping war stories in the bar. If you work hard, you play hard; it's a maxim that's worked in team-building throughout my naval and civilian careers.

The *Telethon* itself worked like a dream. Each of the air traffic controllers along our route had been glad of the full and detailed briefing we'd given them long in advance and they went out of their way to facilitate our operation from beginning to end. One group of passengers aboard a holiday jet had to wait a few minutes longer on the runway in Birmingham to allow our strange formation to cross the runway at low level and live on prime-time TV, but apart from that we'd scheduled our activities to cause minimum disruption and the day ran like clockwork. The *Telethon* raised enormous amounts for charity and our final evening together as a team was fuelled by a surfeit of adrenaline. It felt very similar to the Olympic buzz I'd experienced four years earlier and was to serve well as a template for similar operations in the years to come.

10

ONE DOOR CLOSES

AS THE YEAR 1989 DAWNED I HAD NO idea that it would be my last at Castle Air and that by September I would have lost a job and a marriage, and gained my own helicopter filming company.

The first half of the year was unremarkable with the usual mix of film work, pipeline inspections and passenger flights.

My last hurrah in the white and yellow machines that had coloured every aspect of my career for the previous ten years was another TV programme from Chatsworth Television: *Interceptor*. We'd finished making the last of eight series of *Treasure Hunt* in 1989 and, on the strength of that, this new and weird game show had been commissioned. I won't even try to describe the concept in detail except to say that contestants were enthusiastically chased around the country by the Interceptor, an actor by the name of Sean O'Kane, who performed with suitable menace. Still today there is an online account by Clive Harris, one of the contestants in the final show, relating how terrified he was when surprised by the

Interceptor, but for the audience watching the edited show there was somehow a letdown when all that Sean could do was growl at the contestants (since onscreen dismemberment or gory death was still illegal in those days). The show never made it into a second series, but it was fun to make and it felt like a month-long end-of-shoot party for the old *Treasure Hunt* team. Nevertheless it was a joy to watch the delicious Annabel Croft put another professional feather in her cap after her career as an international tennis player and hostess of *Treasure Hunt*, having taken over from Anneka Rice for the final series.

The month of May was also when Sara claims I first voiced the ambition to become a serious and full-time aerial unit director and to leave behind the part-time occupation of flying politicians and blindfolded game-show contestants from one place to another. I don't remember even thinking that at the time, let alone voicing it, but there must have been a spark in there somewhere. One more exciting film job came up on 12 July when I was tasked by ITN (the independent news broadcaster in the UK) to film the first attempt at crossing the English Channel by hang-glider.

The woman who wanted to put her name in the record books was Judy Leden. She'd turned professional the previous year, becoming the only woman to earn a living as a hang-glider and paraglider pilot. She already held more records than I have room to list here by the time we met at Broome Park Golf and Country Club, near the Chaucerian town of Canterbury, on the evening before her cross-Channel attempt. I don't suppose I'd given much thought to how you get a hang-glider up to a sufficient height to cross 20 miles of open sea, and it came as something of a shock to learn that she would be lifted beneath a hot-air balloon, which would climb to 13,000 feet before the balloon pilot would lean over the side of his basket and cut the rope holding Judy with a knife.

The intrepid aviatrix had already explained how an early morning departure was essential to success, both in order to get calm winds for her own activity and dense cold air for the ascent of the balloon. As always, I was wearing two hats. The first hat read 'Pilot', with all the attendant considerations regarding my own rate of climb in order to be at the same height as Judy when she launched, the usual stuff about radio frequencies and fuel, and the extra complication of going into French airspace. The other hat read 'Film', and it was that persona which sat up and listened in detail to the brief about the release point. At the moment the knife was wielded she would, of course, have zero airspeed but she was 'pretty confident' that she would only drop a matter of 100 feet before she'd have enough airspeed to be able to regain control of her flimsy flying wing. If she didn't, then the biggest danger lay in the whole craft turning upside down with her entangled in the fabric, a condition from which she was unlikely to be able to recover. It was important that I stayed a good distance away from her during the critical release sequence and that I hadn't carved up the early morning air anywhere near her with my rotor blades. I was happy to comply with that, not only because I didn't want to introduce any extra risk into an already hazardous undertaking, but also because it would cause us to remain at a good distance with the lens on a wide setting and thus be confident of not losing her out of the bottom of our frame. We retired to bed early and I'm guessing I slept marginally better than the other aviator in the hotel that night.

We were up early in the cold morning air and relieved to find that the weather gods were on our side. Clad only in a lightweight jumpsuit bedecked in Citroën's red sponsorship logos, Judy cut a diminutive figure as she answered questions from the press. In the background the long flames emanating from the balloon's gas burners cast an intermittently eerie yellow light upon the proceedings. They also made a wonderful whooshing sound until I,

with some embarrassment, broke the calm of the early morning with my two noisy jet engines.

I lifted from my helipad long before the balloon and moved well away to a higher vantage point from where we could observe and record the strange vertical train of balloon, basket, rope, hang-glider and Judy tentatively forming an orderly queue just as the horizon began to show the first signs of a new day. Once all the elements were neatly lined up, one beneath the other, the balloon pilot encouraged more gas into his burners and the whole assembly began to climb much more quickly than I'd expected. Thankfully we weren't trying to film the ascent in much detail, so I was able to adopt a heading away from the balloon and concentrate on achieving the best rate of climb I could. Once I'd reached around 6,000 feet I reversed my course and spotted the balloon, now climbing at about the same rate as me and lighting up like a spluttering lamp on a faraway street as more flames generated the hot air that would take it to the planned release height.

As the dial on my altimeter slowly crept up to thirteen I could begin to feel the significant change in air quality. The density had decreased entirely in accordance with predictions, but it's not often that a helicopter pilot finds himself up where the birds fear to tread, and the wobbly flying controls reminded me to treat them with extra sensitivity if we were to avoid going outside acceptable operating parameters. I could only guess at what Judy was thinking as I moved gingerly into an orbit around her at a respectable distance. I couldn't contemplate hovering that high up; there wasn't enough air to support the weight of my chopper. Instead I established a languorous orbit around the strange combination craft on which my cameraman was now focused. The altimeter hit 13,000 feet, the balloon pilot radioed me to say he was about to cut the rope, and suddenly the hang-glider plummeted away from the basket in a manoeuvre that left my heart in my mouth. The thing seemed to drop its nose almost vertically towards the ground and, as Judy later related, her restraining straps went slack as her body hit the fabric of her own wing. Within seconds she was back in control and the sleek fabric of the glider took her almost back up to the balloon from where she'd started.

My flying logbook records it as a flight of exactly one hour from the takeoff in Kent to the landing on the beach at Cap Gris-Nez, just to the west of Calais, but most of that was taken up with the departure and climb. From memory Judy's flight lasted around twenty-five minutes from the moment of release until she alighted gracefully on the sands of France. During that time we'd settled down enough in the helicopter to be able to get alongside her in a close formation position, and even capture a smile and a wave from her before she prepared for her own landing. As with so many film tasks we were back at our start point and eating a fine breakfast before most of the hotel patrons were dressed – at least those who'd managed to sleep through the departure of a balloon, a hang-glider and a very noisy helicopter. It had been another wonderful notch on the totem pole of 'I was there and saw it with my own eyes'.

My final flight with Castle Air featured a sunset landing at our Cornish base following a trip on behalf of the UK transplant organisation, appropriately enough as it would be some time before I could get over the sense of losing my own heart to a company that had been my baby from the start. Ultimately the separation was far more acrimonious than I would have chosen; things were said among old friends that shouldn't have been said by any of us and it's still painful to me that we've not been able to share a beer since then. In the end it boiled down to the fact that the rest of the company wanted to continue to take on any sort of charter work in any area of aviation that would generate income, whereas I wanted to take the company purely in the direction of film, potentially branching out into production and opening us up to all the other forms of earning possibility that go with that. Back in 1984, on completion of the Sarajevo Winter Olympics, I had been offered the temporary job by ABC Sports of organising their entire aerial operation at the Los Angeles Summer Games, but it had been voted down by the Castle Air board as being outside the realms of earning revenue purely through flying hours. It wasn't something that particularly bothered me at the time, but I had now reached a stage where I had to follow the dream. At the end of my time in the Navy I'd already had to make a choice between continuing with helicopters or turning to professional racing. I'd seen one of the drivers I had competed with, during the year in which I had been given the award for 'most promising newcomer' at Silverstone's racing school, go on to become a Formula One driver (Colombian Roberto Guerrero) and I wasn't about to spend the rest of my life wondering 'What if?' when it came to film flying.

So, with the encouragement of Simon Werry, the cameraman with whom I'd built up such a wonderful rapport, I handed in my keys and walked away from the company I'd founded in order to begin a new chapter in my life. I've never regretted that day and I'm proud to have left the company in sufficiently good shape that it's still a powerful force in UK helicopter aviation today.

11

HELIFILMS

PICKING THE NAME FOR OUR NEW company took an entire day of batting around multiple ideas, some of which were trite or clichéd, while others seemed incredibly clever but were obscure beyond access by anyone other than a crossword-puzzle enthusiast. In the end the name Helifilms was so blindingly obvious that it's a wonder we hadn't completed the task by the end of breakfast. In due course some of our clients came to use it as a noun, as in 'I'm ringing because I need a Helifilm.'

Whatever the name, we had our work cut out to put together all the usual paraphernalia required for a new company, including incorporation documents, a logo, notepaper, a small rented mews house in London as a base and some advertising entries to begin attracting work before our meagre funds ran out. We'd decided that London was the only place to base ourselves if we were to have any chance of carving out a slice of the lucrative television commercials industry that would give us the best shot at survival.

To this end the little house in Atherstone Mews, Kensington, served well as permanent accommodation for me, temporary accommodation for Simon during his weekdays away from his family in Cornwall, and as an office for Sara Hine and Sophy Moreland, both of whom joined us direct from the end of their contracts at Chatsworth Television.

Phone calls to just about anybody we'd ever worked with were often met with enthusiasm that the old Jerry-and-Simon team were now available from a more accessible location, and within only two weeks we'd secured our first commission: a Honda car commercial for a visiting Canadian production company. But of course the one thing a company called Helifilms needed rather badly in order to ply its trade was – a helicopter. At the time of our departure it had been made very clear to us that we wouldn't be welcome to use machines from the old firm at Castle Air and, in any event, the whole point of basing ourselves out of a central London location was to avoid any unnecessary flying that would otherwise have to be charged to the customer.

There was a certain irony in holding out a begging bowl and asking for a helicopter. In doing so I was very glad to have subscribed for many years to the old truism: 'Be nice to people on your way up because you might need to call on them on your way down.' I made my first call to old pals at Aeromega Helicopters at Stapleford aerodrome, north-east of London. It's a strange thing that pilots who had retired from the army and air force often ended up flying over the sea to supply oil rigs in their first civilian roles, whereas ex-Navy pilots dominated the inland helicopter companies. So it was at Aeromega, where Kit Pemberton and Mark Barry-Jackson (known to all as BJ) had built a lovely company a couple of years before I started Castle Air. In the subsequent decade we had often traded business between us in mutual respect, but I was still more than relieved when they answered my call in a welcoming way.

I have little recollection of that first film job for the visiting Canadians beyond the unfeasibly large stack of five-pound notes they paid us with at the end, as was often the case with international visitors. Aeromega's pilot Howard Mersey – a lovely man with a great sense of humour who later became a senior inspector at the Civil Aviation Authority – accompanied me during the job as I'd had no time to complete all the usual company tests that are a prerequisite to commercial flying. I soon rectified that omission on our return from the Scottish location and the four of us at Helifilms settled down to explore the directions we wanted to take the company in, secure in the knowledge that finding revenue-paying work was possible. We couldn't have known that the good economic times of Maggie's Britain were about to come to a close with her ousting only two months after we started our little firm.

I had always been inspired by a landmark BBC series way back in 1969 called *Bird's Eye View* in which the future poet laureate Sir John Betjeman read poetry over film images captured entirely from a helicopter; it was a ground-breaking series at the time but had never been emulated since. To try to do so was one of the first projects we undertook under our own steam, and the extensive research carried out by Sara and Sophy resulted in several experimental shoots and edits to contemporary pieces of poetry by writers such as Fleur Adcock and Benjamin Zephaniah. We attended seminars to understand what sort of material the television stations were interested in commissioning and we studied all that we could on the subject of producing our own programmes. It was a good learning curve but in the end it came to naught, as commissioning editors were unconvinced anybody would want to watch continuous aerials of the coast or the countryside. *Bird's Eye View* was regarded as a one-off aberration and *Landshapes,* which I'd worked on a few years earlier, had been pigeonholed as an academic piece of programming on the still-young Channel 4. It was to be another decade before

TV screens were almost flooded with copycat series shot entirely from the air, but by then we would have moved on to other things.

In the meantime Simon was squeezing his address book as hard as he could, with the result that we began working intermittently for big advertising and corporate film production companies such as Rose Hackney and Park Avenue. The first movie we worked on under the Helifilms banner was a controversial feature called *Hidden Agenda*, directed by Ken Loach, who already had a strong reputation for giving voice to those who might otherwise have gone unheard. Ken's anti-establishment dramas in support of the underdogs of British mining, Palestinian outcasts from their own land and the English working class of the industrial north regularly gave politicians the jitters and audiences a fright, not least for the first use of wide-ranging profanity on TV.

Hidden Agenda dealt with the Troubles in Northern Ireland, starred Frances McDormand, and had largely been completed by the time Simon and I met Mr Loach in the little coffee shop at Belfast City airport. We had picked up a helicopter from Dollar Helicopters in Liverpool, crossed the Irish Sea direct to Belfast and met the great man on his arrival by plane from London. His charming and quietly spoken manner belied the angry and revolutionary style of his films. At times he spoke so softly that I had to lean forward to listen. He recounted the tale of his first foray into dealing with an advertising agency on a shoot for a food commercial. He had arrived on set at dawn, shot the required thirty seconds of material and was just about to depart when the agency group exited their limousines and announced they were ready to begin. Ken politely explained that he'd already completed the job, only to be instructed to do it all over again. When he asked why, he was firmly told that it was necessary for the advertising people to observe him at work for him to qualify for his daily rate, and so he meekly did it all over again. The story was in keeping with the all-too-familiar world of advertising, and had the

three of us in tears of mirth. Any number of the characters in Ken's own films would have taken the men from the agency to one side and beaten them to a bloody pulp. The fact that it was told by a perplexed man who exuded the charms of a true gentleman somehow made it even funnier.

The day passed well. Under the director's guidance, in less than two hours of flying we captured some wide establishing shots of Belfast that would pepper the movie. Ken Loach caught his flight back to London while Simon and I packed up our things. We were about to remove the nose mount and camera for the flight back to Liverpool when I happened to glance at the late afternoon sky and notice a strange combination of clouds and the interesting lighting effect as the setting sun hit them. On a hunch I asked Simon to load the last roll of 35mm film into the camera and we departed back across the Irish Sea. Sure enough, just before we reached the Isle of Man, the clouds above us started to glow with an orange iridescence that defied belief. For the four minutes it took to exhaust the available celluloid I turned back towards the setting sun and we flew in a straight line while the heavens put on an exquisite display, the likes of which I had never seen before. As we reluctantly reversed our track again towards Liverpool, Simon remarked that if he ever got around to writing an autobiography he would title it *God Was My Gaffer*, in reference to how the visual effects of the natural world can never be surpassed by the artificial efforts of even the best lighting technicians. It felt good to be a film pilot. At the time the commercial impetus for capturing those clouds on film was unclear but in due course they were to form the genesis of our stock shot library and take us ultimately to Australia, but more on that later.

That was about the only occasion I ever enjoyed a trip to Belfast. I'd lost a couple of military friends and colleagues to the murderous campaigns of the IRA and the place frightened the hell out of me, despite having never served there myself. Once we stayed in the

Europa Hotel, which had been bombed thirty-six times. It's the only time that a hotel check-in clerk has advised me that the curtains should be kept closed – in order to avoid being injured by flying glass. That evening a very drunk and darkly brooding local offered us a drink and then upended the table on my head when we politely declined. The security guards were too frightened of the man's possible connections to contemplate intervening.

On another occasion Simon and I ventured just across the road from our Belfast hotel to enjoy a pint of Guinness in a wooden-beamed pub that was so old it had been adopted by the National Trust. A wizened old man sidled up to us as we took our first sip, proclaimed that our short haircuts told him plainly that we must be squaddies and began a diatribe on the efficacy of the flaming necklace (the favoured technique by which the IRA punished anybody who contravened their rules, involving a tyre filled with petrol and hung around the victim's neck before being set alight). It was odd how just one sip of Guinness caused both Simon and me to need the urinal almost instantaneously, from where we exited through a rear window and scarpered back to the confines, but certainly not safety, of the hotel.

The final straw for me came on another shoot in Belfast when we were in a taxi on our way back from the airport to the hotel. A shiver went down my spine as the taxi driver asked if we'd had a fine day filming over the Mourne Mountains. It indeed was where we'd spent the day, filming a commercial for Bass Bitter, but I knew for certain that we hadn't mentioned that in front of the driver. In the knowledge that there were eyes everywhere, I insisted thereafter that we would always return to the Isle of Man for overnight accommodation and any client who wanted us to film in Belfast could damn well pay for the extra flying time incurred.

While Simon concentrated on finding work for us on movies and commercials, I was also enthusiastically milking my own

contact list among the television stations. This led to an interesting and exciting project for TVS, for whom I'd shot the Branson transatlantic balloon. Their concept was to transmit live segments all day long from Gatwick airport in a fly-on-the-wall look at how the intricate aspects hang together to give the effect of a gigantic and well-oiled machine. Once I'd attended the extensive briefing sessions and applied for all the rather unusual exemptions from the normal rules that I'd need, the day of the shoot offered great opportunity for fun. Although the programme transmitted live, it was constructed more like a magazine with injected pieces that had been edited together from the previous hour of activity. In this way I was spared the need to keep a large proportion of my brain focused on keeping an unbroken line of sight to a remote video receiver and could concentrate on capturing the best possible imagery.

Helicopters are normally highly regulated in everything they do at, or near, an international airport. The arriving and departing airliners are operating to well-established patterns, whereas helicopters are less predictable and have a tendency to briefly stop the hearts of air traffic controllers when they suddenly accelerate from one place to another. In anticipation of this nervousness, I had taken the trouble to meet the controllers I would be working with on the day and to brief them on the toolbox of shots I wanted to achieve. It also gave them the opportunity to reciprocate with the parameters of proximity and position they would like me to keep to. In some cases they indicated that there would be some flexibility, depending on the conditions of the day, while others were set in concrete and not to be transgressed. We devised between us a set of shorthand expressions so that I could request to return to position #3 and the controller could, as a result, inform the next arriving 747 that there would be a helicopter hovering over the grass to the left of his touchdown point and that it would follow him as he decelerated during his landing run. Levels of information and confidence were also helped by the

pre-flight briefing forms that all airline pilots receive at their airport of departure – all of which that day included notes about what they could expect to see me doing when they eventually came in to land at London's second airport.

These levels of mutual understanding and confidence were absolutely key to a safe and successful day of shooting and in the end we had a ball. We hovered between the aircraft parking gates to see a big beast begin its push-back before we accompanied our subject out along the taxiways towards the holding point. As I hovered just outside the wing tips of the airliner, Simon would often be tight enough on the lens to capture a cheery wave from the cockpit or, if I climbed a little, to look down into the windows of the pilots' office and observe their final preparations. We could tell that it was giving the passengers some excitement from the number of noses pressed tight against the glass in the rows of the economy section.

We had pre-authorisation to accompany the big and lumbering machines as they laboriously made the turn onto the runway and carried out their final engine checks. I was careful to avoid getting anywhere remotely near the hot jet efflux which, even at a relatively low idle power, had the capacity to blow me into the distance. With each successive departure we would concentrate on one part of the subject aircraft, such as a single wheel, or perhaps one of the control surfaces, and would keep the camera frame tight until we both felt that the rapidly accelerating airliner was beginning to get ahead of us. At that point Simon would widen the lens to accommodate bits of the airport in the background while I turned gently left to give him room to see along the runway. Simultaneously I would switch from accelerating to decelerating and would transfer all my efforts into keeping the helicopter's as smooth as possible in the flight interest of holding the subject way into the distance and for as long as possible. I found it hard to shake off the idea that the airliner was

like a pelican: big, ungainly and awkward on the ground but beautiful and balletic once up in the medium for which it was designed.

The only other danger to our little rotary machine was the turbulence that occurs behind a landing airliner. With their wheels and flaps down they all generate a good deal of air disturbance during the approach, but in something as big as a Boeing 747 this can extend in hazardous form out to as much as ten miles behind. If I were to cross behind the path of a landing airliner at, say, four miles' separation distance, the turbulence could still be powerful enough to turn my small craft upside down. Nor is this a geographically static phenomenon; the turbulence exists in an expanding cone which, if there is a crosswind blowing, can quickly leave the extended line of the runway and drift across the grass towards me. So, for an exercise such as this, I was allocating the small portion of my brain normally reserved for navigation purposes to assimilating the various invisible wind contours that were happening all around me.

It was a wonderful day of film-flying with plenty of latitude to explore all the creative possibilities, and it was also fascinating to participate in a new form of live documentary television broadcast, which soon went on to become part of the staple diet of small-screen viewing.

My logbook records a diverse range of work throughout the rest of 1990, almost always in the Jetranger helicopters from Aeromega, totalling a little over a hundred hours of revenue generation in the air. We filmed Sealink cross-channel ferries for commercials, launched the BMW 850 series in an air-to-ground shooting fest, returned to Northern Ireland for some low-level work around golf courses, and hovered over Fairoaks aerodrome for hours on end trying to direct a conga line of a thousand people in a commercial for British Gas. Alan Morton, the producer who had invited me onto the Jean-Michel Jarre project, began producing the TV

coverage of the UK offshore powerboat race series, which took us all around the coast of the country, almost always in the rain but requiring a good deal of enthusiastic and dynamic flying. We added a clifftop shot to a pop video for Phil Collins, contributed to another music video for a band called Transformer, and to commercials for Ford, Super-Kings cigarettes and Stansted airport.

In the meantime Sara had been diligently pursuing our independent filmmaking aspirations, which came to fruition late in our first full year with the award of a contract to produce a ten-minute promotional video for a man who wanted to sell his house. The man was Peter de Savary and the house was Littlecote, near Hungerford in the county of Wiltshire. The history of the mansion stretches back to the sixteenth century, being the home where Henry VIII courted Jane Seymour. The extensive grounds, which include the remains of a Roman villa, allowed ample opportunity to use the helicopter as a very tall crane, but we also put our ground-shooting techniques to good use within the large and beautiful interior rooms. Simon made prodigious use of a smoke machine and our learning curve was steep in terms of the end-to-end planning, and execution from initial idea through to delivery of the final film. It was strange but not unsettling for the helicopter work to form a small part of a much bigger whole, but we all fell into our new roles quite naturally and it was a good experience to get under our belts. I was at last becoming a director.

Sometimes my role involved no flying but still resulted in extraordinary experiences, such as the two nights I ended up on stage with the Rolling Stones at Wembley Stadium. I had begun to form a good working relationship with Tim Desbois of the company Flight Logistics, and he had sent regular work in our direction. One involved shooting the opening sequence to the song 'Tumbling Dice' as two huge dice began to revolve on the giant stage in

anticipation of the band's appearance. Just to add a little extra spice to our technical and planning process, I learned that we would be contributing to their IMAX film, *At The Max*.

The IMAX format has a long and fascinating history that I won't attempt to describe here in detail, but which results in the highest possible definition of imagery projected onto screens that are often as tall as a ten-storey building. The associated cameras were so large and heavy that it took at least four men to lift one, so of course the problem of how to mount one on a helicopter became all-absorbing for us. The only man in the world who was worth consulting on the problem was Nick Phillips, who had designed the original tilting nose mount with which we'd had so much success over the years. Nick rummaged around in his workshop at Shepperton Studios and, sure enough, there was an unwieldy contraption buried under piles of ironwork that he'd originally designed for another purpose but which he thought he could convert into a mechanism for supporting an IMAX camera in a helicopter. Quite apart from simply being able to support such a weight, the true black art of any camera-mounting system lies in its ability to isolate the camera lens from the inherent vibrations of the helicopter. Nobody knew more about this than Nick who, despite his boyish looks, had been around throughout the development of helicopter mounts and had made the subject his own. Between Nick Phillips in the UK and Nelson Tyler in the USA, the subject was pretty much wrapped up for a couple of decades.

Secure in the knowledge that we had a technical solution, Tim Desbois and I traipsed off to a pre-production meeting with the IMAX producers at the iconic Wembley venue. They had already shot the majority of the film during the preceding eleven months of the *Urban Jungle* world tour but were lacking aerials, which they felt would add another dimension, however short the shot might have to be. I realised early in the meeting that the job of flying the helicopter

was going to be a simple case of keeping it smooth and travelling at a constant speed in the right direction. This would be easy for any half-competent aviator – the key lay in getting the timing correct down to the last second. Depending on how accurately the Stones timed their arrival on stage, the helicopter would have to be instructed to either speed up or slow down to a precise degree in the latter stages of approach. When I voiced that concern to the assembled company everybody sagely nodded their heads, so I pressed on to enquire how and where the timings were planned and initiated. I learned that it happened at a technical desk on the stage, just behind the drums of Charlie Watts.

'I think that's where I need to be,' I tentatively suggested.

'Oh right,' said one of the production assistants. 'I'll get you stage passes. How many of you will there be?'

I pushed my luck, asked for two, and left the meeting with a pair of the hottest concert tickets I've ever had the pleasure of holding.

On the first of the two concert nights the IMAX camera from the helicopter was going to be needed later in the show in a position atop the scaffolding structure that housed the lighting and sound mixing desks, right out in the middle of the audience. Tim Desbois therefore stayed at the helicopter pad to facilitate the de-rig and repositioning of the camera on completion of the aerial shot, while I set off towards backstage through a maze of security gates. At each step the number of people allowed past the security men became fewer and fewer until finally I found myself walking across a bridge to the back of the stage itself. There were no more than a dozen technicians allowed that far into the inner sanctum and I rather self-consciously set up my ground-to-air radio, and the spare radio, and the spare-spare radio, before peeking around the back of the drum kit to work out whether I could see the already airborne helicopter. I was surprised to note that although the volume of sound confirmed the presence of over 100,000 people who were pumped and ready

for action, it was only possible, through the intense glare of the stage lighting, to make out the faces of the first couple of rows. Presumably this is what a band is accustomed to seeing. I chose a better visual position, nearer to the bridge over which I'd just crossed and shielded from the stage lighting, so that I could properly see the lights of the circling helicopter.

Bang on time, the five principals of the band known and always announced as 'the greatest rock and roll band in the world' made their way across the darkened bridge. They gathered in a thirty-second huddle like a basketball team and then joined hands in the middle of their circle just as the floor manager gave me the thumbs-up that we were going to start right on time. I transferred my attention to the stopwatch, cued the helicopter, confirmed to the pilot that his approach was going to be ideally timed, became momentarily aware that the band were being announced to a wall of sound from the stadium, saw the helicopter pass right overhead, confirmed to him that it was a wrap for the chopper and set off back across the bridge to the landing site. It was all over in a blur and the next hour was spent lugging the immense camera through more security gates, out onto the field, through the crowd and then up the scaffolding. It was a hot night anyway but by the time we'd finished that little exercise I was drenched in sweat.

We all felt it had gone well and I returned home to Sara (with whom by then I was living) in a rapture of heady exuberance. The viewing of the rushes the next day confirmed that there would be no need for a second night shoot so the helicopter was stood down – but I still held two backstage passes. Tim confirmed that he had no desire to spend a second evening in Wembley Stadium just for the sake of it, so Sara and I jumped on my Honda 750, wove our way through the insane volumes of traffic and made our way to the ideal parking spot I had in mind – right where a helicopter had been perched just the night before.

'Just look confident and keep your clipboard firmly in sight,' I advised Sara as we set off through the maze of security gates with which I was now familiar. Most of the security crew were the same as the previous evening and many gave us a hearty greeting along with some quip about not carrying a camera the size of a small car this evening.

We had timed our arrival well, made our way across the bridge and were looking like part of the regular stage crew by the time the Rolling Stones made their way to the rear of the stage, each accompanied this time by their female partners – all of whom, of course, we recognised as well. The team-building routine followed, just as it had the previous evening, and a few minutes later we were watching the crowd go wild from our little spot just behind Charlie's drum kit. It was a rare treat – to be able to really enjoy one of the enormous events that we often get to but are usually too preoccupied with our own task to fully appreciate. We half expected to see backstage drugs flowing like water and at least a little wild behaviour, but by this time in their career we were looking at a totally professional band doing what they do best, and even Keith took his coffee black with no sugar. The only surprise was how poor the sound was. The band performed as flawlessly as ever but of course the entire architecture of Wembley is designed for the audience out front and not for workers who are on-stage under false pretences. So my advice is that if you want to hear the Rolling Stones at their very best you should buy a ticket and stand just under the sound-mixing scaffold, but if you want the buzz of a lifetime, stick with me.

12

LESSONS OF DARKNESS

JUST ELEVEN MONTHS AFTER WE'D started Helifilms, the Iraqi dictator Saddam Hussein decided that he'd like a portion of the Kingdom of Kuwait, so he walked in and took it – all of it. On the night of 2 August 1990, one hundred thousand Iraqi troops crossed the border on their way to Kuwait City, a distance of no more than 70 miles along a black tarmac highway, the single feature of the desert it traversed. By the following January the American General Norman Schwarzkopf had gathered together an extraordinary coalition of international forces whose fragility he only managed by virtue of the sensitivities he'd learned during a childhood upbringing in Iran.

On 17 January, the air war commenced.

One strong memory stands out to me from that time. We had just signed up to a cable TV service and so at any time of the day or night we could see live images coming from the cities from which Operation Desert Storm was about to be launched. This was a new

phenomenon and was in stark contrast to the Falklands War, only eight years earlier, when we had had to rely on verbal reports from a handful of embedded reporters made via satellite phone. When we did get images from the Falklands they were often several days after the event. This new concept of live TV coverage was mesmerising in many ways. The point where it fell down, in my opinion, was in giving a sense of scale. Reportage framing on the correspondent, with the scene of the incident behind them, can be valid from the site of a bus crash but hardly does justice to an entire country being fought over by multiple nations.

The troops were on their way home when Saddam Hussein's parting shot had been to torch 750 oil wells. The photographs of the eerie light beneath a black pall of smoke that turned day into night were hypnotic. I felt that this was a scene that begged to be given scale by means of aerial imagery, but we still weren't seeing any. I had never been to the desert, but one morning at breakfast I said with absolute certainty, 'We're going to Kuwait.'

My relationship with Sara was still relatively new, but she had begun to get used to some of my wild and overly optimistic proclamations, so she sensitively responded with, 'Are you insane? How in God's name are we going to finance that?'

Somewhere in a corner of my head existed the fervent belief that we could do it, and that it needed to be done, so we set about finding a way. The strategic plan we devised was no more sophisticated than telling everybody we could think of that we were going to film from the air in Kuwait. When friends, colleagues and clients asked why we were going to Kuwait, we confidently answered that we were on a big job we couldn't talk about, but we expected to have some spare time while we were there, so if they had anything they needed filming we could probably fit it in at a discounted price.

There were a couple of half-hearted bites but nothing meaty enough to cover the cost of getting there, and certainly nothing that would finance the use of a helicopter in Kuwait, always assuming we could find one. Then one day we got a call from Paul Berriff, the diminutive and highly innovative Yorkshireman who had lived with my Search and Rescue team for six months some twelve years earlier while making *Rescue Flight* for the BBC. I regarded him as a mentor and a catalyst in my filming career.

Paul explained that he was involved in a project with the legendary German director Werner Herzog. Herzog had won Best Director for *Fitzcarraldo* at the Cannes Film Festival in 1982. Each of his films – *Aguirre, Nosferatu* and *Grizzly Man* among others – is a feast for the eyes. I urge anybody unfamiliar with his work to take a look. He began his career by stealing a camera from a Munich film school; an incident about which he later said, 'I didn't consider it theft – it was just a necessity – I had some sort of natural right for a camera, a tool to work with.'

Werner had done a deal with French broadcaster Canal Plus and a brand new German television company called Premiere. He wanted to create an opera and they had agreed to finance it on condition that he made a number of documentaries for them. He then announced that he'd like to make one of the documentaries on another planet but, since that could have been a bit expensive, he thought he would make one in Kuwait while the oil fires were burning instead. The catch was that he was committed to another project and couldn't get to Kuwait for a few weeks, so he had asked Paul Berriff, as a co-producer, to put together a crew who could be trusted to be empathetic to Herzog's aesthetic while delivering significant footage before the oil fires were extinguished. I was almost speechless with excitement.

You would think that 750 oil wells might take a while to extinguish. At that time only three major companies had the capability to extinguish a raging oil-well fire and it came as no surprise that they were all from Texas. When the re-established Kuwaiti government

asked these fire veterans how long it might take them to put out all the fires, they were taken aback to receive the answer: 'Three years.' They put out an 'all-points bulletin' asking any nation, person or company who thought they could put out an oil-well fire to get in touch with them. Soon a number of teams turned up in Kuwait with all sorts of weird and wonderful equipment and started putting out the fires.

Time was running out for us. With Sara in operational overdrive, four of us were soon on a flight to Kuwait: myself, Simon Werry as the cameraman, our camera assistant Steve Brooke Smith, and John Pearson as the sound recordist. Sara was gutted at having to stay behind but the budget was tight and there were many details still to be sorted before our plane touched down in Kuwait City, including the small matter of sourcing a helicopter.

When the engines throttled back and the captain announced our descent, he must have had to struggle with the controls as a cry of 'Oh my God, look at that' from somewhere in the cabin sent all the passengers to the left-hand side with noses pressed to the small glass windows. In the dark desert night, each flame cast light across the sand, more flames than we had time to register before we were firmly invited to resume our seats for landing.

I remember the ambient heat as we filed out of the airliner and across the apron, despite it being midnight, but most of all I remember the smell. If you've ever walked past a construction crew applying hot tarmac to a road, you'll know the smell I'm talking about. In the arrivals hall we retrieved our multiple silver flight cases from the carousel, creating a melee that was probably most annoying for the other passengers. In Kuwait there was no chance of hiring equipment locally so we'd had to bring the whole lot with us. Some gear had to be retrieved from the oversized baggage area: cameras, helicopter mounting hardware, our own domestic bags, and seventy-two cans of super 16mm film, each weighing a couple of kilos.

We were met by our local liaison man, Hashim, whose white flowing beard nicely matched his white flowing robes. If he was in any way surprised by the many overloaded baggage trolleys we were each navigating through the crowd, he didn't show it. He was an elegant and implacable man who indulged our boisterously enthusiastic questions, and in response to any organisational queries said, 'Yes, Sara has asked me about that and I have . . .'

The sandy streets were all but deserted and we were soon at our tall, glass-sided hotel, which smacked of Middle Eastern opulence – or would have had it not been for the sizeable bullet holes in the glass panels, illuminated by the high chandeliers in the foyer. Hashim bid us goodnight after ensuring that our equipment would be safe in the rented four-wheel-drive Pajero he'd secured for us, and we retired to bed in great excitement at what was to come.

There must have been a concerted clean-up effort in the weeks since the city had been vacated by the invading force and more latterly by the allied army. Apart from the holes in the glass frontage, little signified this had recently been a war zone, and the scale of the breakfast buffet had our eyes out on stalks. Hashim waited patiently as we ate like men possessed, then he jumped into his Mercedes to lead our brand new hire vehicle out to the oil wells. We weren't going to try to film on our first day. We just wanted to get out there, see it and wrap our heads around the task. We were slightly self-conscious in the bright orange fireproof overalls we'd purchased for the trip, not knowing what the sartorial etiquette might be in a burning oil field.

The sand that stretched in all directions from the edge of the city was dirty; hardly surprising considering the towering black smoke clouds. The road ran in a straight line with nothing but sand on either side until we arrived at a checkpoint where we were ushered into a small office to have our credentials examined and our faces photographed. We were given three rules. One: don't drive through

any shallow lakes because it isn't water, it's oil, and, as one TV crew had discovered, it tends to ignite once it comes into contact with a hot exhaust pipe. Two: don't walk near the little red flags in the sand because they mark live land mines. Three: always stop and sign in at the gate so that the authorities know who you were if you don't come back.

Before Hashim departed, we asked when and where he thought we would be getting our site and safety briefing, a long procedure required before filming any industrial complex. 'You just had it,' he replied with a smile. 'How much damage do you think you can do to a burning oil well?'

We passed through the raised barrier and headed out into the black desert in excitement and trepidation. It's hard to convey just how devastating each slight rise in the desert road became. We stopped to jump out and take photographs as new and more horrific sights opened up before us. The sky became darker, more and more towering columns of flame appeared on the horizon, vast lakes of what we now knew to be oil came into view on either side of the road and we began to spot the little red flags. The sound of that desert has remained with me ever since: the sound of almost total silence in the immediate vicinity but with the distant beeping of multiple heavy vehicles reversing somewhere out beyond our sight, and the constant but still distant roar of what sounded like an airliner at full power. It was odd how that roaring pervaded everything but seemed somehow muted as if the airliner was sitting in a deep sandy hole.

Before long the tarmac ended abruptly and we were onto a wide sandy track. We knew it was a track because it was white, whereas everything else around us was jet black. The aircon in the vehicle was working well but the gauge showing the outside air temperature must have been malfunctioning as it was only just past eight o'clock in the morning and it was already showing 50°C. We gave a wide berth to the huge yellow trucks and earth movers we occasionally encountered, then decided to follow one just to see where it was going.

We soon found out that all tracks led to a fire. We motored around a long sweeping curve, bounded on both sides by high sand dunes, and found ourselves walking distance from a column of flame so tall that its highest point couldn't be seen through the windows of our vehicle.

We stepped out to come face to face with an oil-well fire. If left alone, it would burn for decades as oil from ancient reservoirs deep within the earth's heart continued to come to the surface at immense pressure. While alight, the only real danger comes from the radiated heat. The gas and the lighter petroleum products burn off, leaving only a river of the heavier tar bubbling away into the sand.

Extinguishing the fire is relatively simple. You literally blow it out with gunpowder. The key is in the preparation. Once you've blown it out, the column of gushing oil contains all the light elements, which will easily ignite again on contact with hot metal. You therefore need to be sure you have sufficient water on site to cool the metal, and the equipment to cap and seal it off before nightfall. To work on it thereafter would be too dangerous.

Huge bulldozers carve a massive depression close to the well head, which is lined with plastic sheeting. The pipelines and pumps that normally carry the oil to the Gulf ports are reversed to bring sea water into the desert. Pumps, carried aboard trucks, are then positioned with multiple high-pressure fire hoses laid out ready to cool things down.

The difficult bit, when a well head has been blown to pieces in an act of war, is to dig down far enough to find an undamaged flange to which a cap can be safely bolted. Until that undamaged flange is discovered there is no point in extinguishing the fire. This digging

has to be performed, of course, within a couple of feet of an inferno blazing at around 800°C. Sheets of corrugated iron are welded to the front of swing-shovel diggers to keep the radiated heat off the driver, who then works through a small slit cut into the iron. If not capped by dusk, the well head must be reignited and left burning again overnight. It's surreal.

This was what greeted us as we stepped from our own vehicle, having been careful to park it out of anybody's way; these Texans did not look like they would suffer fools gladly. It turned out that the vehicle temperature gauge was accurate: the air temperature really was 50°C, only now we also had to contend with the radiated heat from the oil fire. We were glad we had not only brought our fireproof overalls but also white flash-hoods to keep the radiated heat from the face. Now we felt right at home with the firefighters, except that their clothes were covered in oil and we looked like we'd just stepped out of a catalogue.

It was pretty easy to find somebody with spare time to talk to us as many of the crew were sitting around waiting for their colleagues to finish a task before they could undertake their own specialisation, or were taking a heat-break from the open cab of a digger. Perhaps 'talk' isn't quite the right word: we now discovered that the roaring we'd heard in the distance was the noise burning oil makes as it exits the ground, relentlessly and all day long. We resolved to bring ear defenders when we returned.

When Simon said he couldn't understand how they put up with the heat all day, one of the laconic Texans said, 'Go see Alf,' while indicating with his head a guy sitting alone on the sand in a snake-nest of hoses.

'Hi, are you Alf?' shouted Simon.

'Yup, that's me.'

'The guys over there said to come and see you about the heat,' responded Simon at the very top of his lungs.

'Oh, OK,' shouted our new friend Alf. He turned a tap on the huge hose he was idly sitting on and drenched us all from head to toe in salt water. The feeling of being instantly cooled was wonderful, and we soon learned that it was a good idea to go see Alf about every ten to fifteen minutes, by which time our overalls were bone dry again.

We sponged up every bit of information we could from these hardened, blackened, monosyllabic men. They were certainly friendly, but even speaking a couple of sentences would leave your mouth dry and the back of your throat feeling like it was about to crack. Despite this hindrance we asked endless questions about where we could and couldn't go with our camera and we made sure that we fully understood the critical moments that we'd want to capture on film. Steve, the camera assistant, was appalled at the conditions we were going to subject the camera gear and film stock to, but he always managed to find something funny about it, and we were all keen to devise techniques that would help him achieve the task without ruining the gear on day one.

John Pearson, our moustachioed sound recordist, was similarly appalled at the readings he was getting from his sound meter and wondered out loud how he was going to achieve anything other than a continuous track of screaming oil fire. It was clear that this job was going to be a challenge for all of us, and that most of it was going to be conducted in conditions the human body was not ideally designed for.

For my own part I was constantly on the lookout for how I was going to use a helicopter to add to the story, to give scale and perspective to these almost incomprehensible sights, and how I was going to achieve that without writing off the helicopter, or ourselves. This presupposed that Sara was going to be able to find us a helicopter from her lonely desk back in the UK, but I had learned that if anybody could pull off a small miracle then it would be her, so

I assumed she would. While Simon lined up some ground shots with his hands framing a cinema screen out in front of him, as cameramen do, my eyes were constantly drawn back to the skies and the way the enormous jet flame turned into a black column of smoke that rose and rose and rose until it combined with the smoke from a hundred similar fires all around. It was then that I noticed how my eyes were stinging. Drops of black oil were dripping off my eyebrows, a reminder that these were not ordinary smoke clouds; they carried unburnt oil that was drizzling down on us.

By the time we climbed back into the Pajero we were still in awe but also bubbling with enthusiasm at the endless stream of cinematic possibilities the environment presented to us. We couldn't wait to start filming, but the fires weren't about to go away, and since we'd set ourselves the task of familiarisation for the first day, we were keen to see more of this disaster area of biblical proportions. As we slammed the car doors shut against the searing heat and I cranked up the aircon (the pilot always becomes the driver on ground shoots; it's the default task for a temporarily grounded aviator), Steve quietly muttered, 'Oh dear,' looking down at his feet. We followed his line of sight and realised with dawning horror that he, like all of us, had trampled a coagulated mess of sticky black tar and white sand into the carpet of the brand new hire car. It was beyond repair so, like all new realities in this environment, we shrugged and got over it. There was nothing we could do about it now.

While we had been talking with our new Texan friends, another pickup truck had come hurtling into the work area and screamed to a halt. The driver jumped out to ask about a technical part he was short of. Once he'd gratefully received the part and headed back the way he'd come over the black dunes, it was explained to us that he was from the Russian crew, who were working on the next-door fire, about half a mile away from our own position. We resolved then to go for a wider exploration of the operations going on all around us.

As the day progressed, we were to discover the spirit of international cooperation that prevailed throughout this nightmare in Kuwait. Language, culture and broken machines were never a barrier to the common aim of extinguishing the fires and stopping the awful flow of oil. It was almost impossible to tell the nationality of any crew unless you stopped to speak to them. In fact, the only crew you could recognise without getting out of the car was the Iranian team – they were unique in being led by a woman, who wore spectacles and a colourful scarf wrapped tightly around her head. Many years later it dawned on me that I had never again seen such practical and uncompromising international collaboration. Why did it have to take war and unprecedented environmental disaster for human beings to find common purpose? What a very strange animal the human being is.

We had by now spent four hours in this war zone. When we had first driven in, we had stopped to take pictures of the little red flags that denoted live mines. By now we had become so used to them that they barely registered. After a lunch break, we mounted an expedition on foot to take a closer look at a burned-out Iraqi tank on top of the dune we'd arbitrarily parked next to. There were footprints in the tar, presumably of the engineers who had marked the positions of the unexploded ordnance, so we followed their tracks until we got to the tank. We were mesmerised by our objective and ignored the heat as we climbed the low hill. It was only after we'd returned home and re-examined the pictures we took that day that we realised we'd become bomb-happy.

We'd been warned by the firefighters that some vehicles still contained the bodies of dead Iraqi soldiers. Steve, as the youngest, was detailed to climb the side of the large metal killing machine and check inside. Thankfully the corpses had been removed from this one and so we relaxed – none more so than Steve – into taking snaps of the view from the top of the hill, vying for the best photographic composition and framing of tank, oil, smoke and fire. It was also a good vantage point for me to look more closely at the visual opportunities I hoped I would soon be able to record from a helicopter. We were grateful to regain the air-conditioned car after we'd trudged back down the hill.

The afternoon was spent concentrating in a more focused way on the shots we wanted to capture, how we were going to achieve them and how they might coalesce to tell a story. In more normal circumstances we would have had the director with us to guide us on the content, but it was liberating to be autonomous for a change, particularly with such rich pickings. We were confident of generating a wealth of material that we would be proud to offer up to Werner Herzog, if and when he ever arrived. Since Simon, Steve and John had many different technical subjects to address and would each need to concentrate on their craft, my duties needed to expand from pilot-in-waiting and unit driver to include a quasi-second-assistant-deputy-directing role. This was effectively what I did 90 per cent of the time when film-flying, but this would be the first time I had performed the role in earnest on the ground. While Simon looked for the prime shot, I would look for subsidiary shots that would either lead into the prime shot or lead out of it towards another subject. This also gave me more time to think about the aerials I would like to shoot, as they would have to fall into the context of the prime shots we were working towards. Very occasionally I would propose an alternative position for the prime shot, and I was always thrilled if Simon agreed it was better.

On the way out of the oilfield back to the city we continued to refine and prioritise our shopping list of shots. Simon decided that he'd like to make good use of the long 300mm lens we'd judiciously brought with us, which meant our camera positions would be further away from the action than usual. This had nothing to do with safety, although it did have the advantage that we wouldn't be under the feet of the fire workers more than absolutely necessary, but was all about style. On a very long lens the subject looks ethereal and otherworldly, much as Herzog intended. It also does lovely things to the scale of subjects and to the relative positions of foreground and background. In this way, for example, a man standing 20 metres in front of the fire would appear almost to be within the fire, or certainly close enough to touch it.

Hashim joined us in the evening and the planning conversation continued over a fine supper in the hotel, after we had learned how to use petrol to scrub tar off our skin in the shower. We had already learned how to avoid incurring the wrath of the hotel management by carrying a clean (i.e. not covered in tar) set of clothes in the vehicle to change into in the car park. I retired early to pen a long fax to Sara and to receive one in return. She told me there was no sign of a helicopter yet but she had everything else under control and was excited to hear all our news. I had to hold back from phoning as I knew we'd be talking into the night and couldn't afford the cost. The crisp white sheets were in wonderful contrast to the black filth of the day's work and I was instantly asleep.

Days of highly stimulating work followed. As we relished our work in the burning oil fields I began to wonder whether man's ability to adapt to extreme circumstances could be a dangerous thing. How quickly we had learned to accept the city smogs and other pollutions caused by the very vehicles that this black gold was harvested to serve. Being with Sara prompted me to be open to environmental issues some time before they were more generally discussed, and there's no doubt that our time in Kuwait turned me forever into an ardent advocate of clean energy.

With seventy-two rolls of film in our arsenal, each lasting up to ten minutes, we allowed ourselves the luxury of lingering shots, in particular when using the long lens. Simon would focus on the

base of the flame and exclude everything else. We would then wait
patiently and only turn over (let the camera roll) when a huge digger
was about to swing its long arm into shot. We were mesmerised by
how it looked to the naked eye and the effect on-camera was intense
and poetic. From the moment we'd completed our first shot we knew
we were creating something special, perhaps even an important and
unique historical record.

One of the three prime American companies fighting the fires
was the Red Adair Company Inc, still led at that time by its founder
Mr Red Adair himself, at the ripe old age of seventy-five. Red was a
larger-than-life character who had taken up his profession straight
after a career in bomb disposal in the early 1950s. He led from the
front with a rod of iron, a Texan bark and a remarkably pink face
much like the pink of a baby's bottom, the result of the many layers
of facial skin he'd lost and regrown over the years. We were lucky to
encounter Red just as he and his boys were all prepared and ready to
blow out their current objective.

First they welded a 44-gallon oil drum to an extremely long
horizontal arm extending way out in front of a bulldozer, which
also sported a counterweight behind to keep the rear tracks on the
ground. A small hatch was cut into the top of the oil drum and brown
sticks of dynamite were tightly packed within. The site was cleared
with a klaxon and Red himself drove the bulldozer forward towards
the fire in order to position the explosives right into the heart of the
flames, where they would absorb the heat and explode about five
minutes after he'd abandoned the contraption.

We were using the long lens, with the legs of the camera heavily
sandbagged to avoid movement. Simon had chosen a position on
top of a small sand dune about 500 metres away. We'd noticed that
most of the workers had moved a little further on and behind a sand
dune but, hey, we'd never win an Oscar by being faint of heart. We
watched through the long lens as Red Adair jumped down from the

'dozer, climbed into his battered pick-up truck and sped towards us around the long curving white track.

As he drew level with our position he screeched to a halt and hollered, 'Are you guys staying there?'

I hollered back, 'Sure, if that's OK with you, sir?' to which he responded, 'Suit yourself,' and sped off.

Simon called, 'Turn over,' to Steve, who set the camera in motion.

I've often wondered how it is that the brain is able to speed up and register tiny details of dramatic events as they occur, but mine was certainly working overtime. The barrel exploded, the fire went out instantaneously and a doughnut ring of shockwave made its way towards us. I'm pretty sure that I caught the full force of Simon on his way down from his brief aerial excursion but we were both pleased and surprised to find the thin legs of the camera tripod had withstood the blast. We whooped with delight in a scene reminiscent of the movie *Pushing Tin*, where air traffic controllers like to stand behind a 747 Jumbo jet as it revs up for takeoff, just to smell the reality of their job.

After a decent amount of time, to be reasonably confident the fire wasn't going to reignite itself, we returned to the base of the gusher, along with the firefighters, and were just as thrilled as them to see that everything had gone to plan. The 20-foot hole they had dug down into the sand revealed a beautifully intact flange at the bottom of the otherwise twisted steelwork, and the narrow trench they had dug to carry away the (now unburnt) oil to another lake area was flowing nicely.

The tension was palpable and infectious, but the oil-well crew moved quickly and we had to be nimble to get all their actions on film. Three men went down into the hole with gigantic wrenches and spanners to undo the joint and release the damaged metal. The crane operator trundled his machine into place and got ready a contraption known as the Christmas Tree: a thick vertical pipe,

open at the top, with multiple smaller pipes leading out of the main trunk. As soon as the guys labouring in the trench had undone all except one of the bolts at the joint they waved a warning – a shout or a klaxon would have been inaudible in that cacophony of sound – then toppled the damaged metalwork over. The force of the rising oil, at around 3,000 pounds per square inch, took several tons of metal up into the air before releasing it to fall back onto the sand.

Now the crane operator gingerly but precisely manoeuvred the Christmas Tree into position above the gushing column of oil. The open-topped nature of the sculpture allowed the oil to whoosh up through the middle and he was able to the lower it down until the guys in the trench could revolve it by hand and get one of the bolts through to mate with twin holes. Once one bolt was in place it was relatively quick and simple to position the other eleven. The only thing down that hole that wasn't pure jet black was the whites of the men's eyes as they toiled.

With twelve bolts securely in place and torqued down to the required pressure, there was a new flash of white from down in the trench: three sets of teeth in grins from ear to ear. Their job was done and a new crew moved into place to begin turning the wheels on the Christmas Tree. First they shut off the central pipe, after which oil shot out in all directions from the multitude of side pipes. Then they began closing the side pipes in a mysterious sequence that ultimately resulted in silence. Blessed silence. It came as a kind of shock. The well was capped and safe. The drama was over and it now fell to another part of the crew to begin connecting hoses that would pump a slurry mixture of mud down the pipe and further down into the bowels of the earth to plug the well forever. That well could never be used again but another parallel hole could eventually be drilled down to tap the resource once more. That was something for the future – there were still another hundred or more fires to do battle with before the war would finally be over.

The film we were working on became known as *Lessons of Darkness* and there was never a more appropriate name applied to an hour of celluloid. I have described the well we witnessed and filmed being extinguished and made safe by Red Adair's famous crew, but the procedure that ultimately made it into the film was actually performed by Boots and Coots, a rival company formed by Asger 'Boots' Hansen and Ed 'Coots' Matthews, who had been Adair's top lieutenants but had left him in 1978 to form their own company. It's the badge of Boots and Coots that I still wear proudly on the back of my flying overalls.

At the end of every day Steve took the camera to pieces in his bedroom. He took apart every moving element, cleaned it of accumulated tar and sand, laid it back on his crisp linen sheets and reassembled it. There can be no greater tribute to any camera assistant on the planet than the fact that we never lost a roll of exposed film throughout our Kuwait escapade. When Sara rang us one evening to say, 'I've got you a helicopter. You can go fit the gear tomorrow,' Steve breathed a loud sigh of relief. No longer was his beloved camera going to have to subject itself to the tar and sand cocktail he had been coping with every night. It would now have a gloriously cooling airflow across it and would only have to cope with a continuous light shower of oil falling from the skies. It was also time for me to go properly to work.

I felt a sense of how the last twenty years of experience were coming together at one nodal moment. Sara had found a beautiful and almost new Bell Longranger for us to use. The nose-mounting system was basic but effective and was one of the first designs by Nick Phillips. It had no stabilisation like the sophisticated mounts we use these days. It was firmly fixed on a plate that required the

pilot to use his yaw pedals to create the shot. Simon used a primitive video monitor to see the shot I was giving him via the look-through video camera.

Kuwait airport was not exactly a hive of tourist activity and so our takeoff and departure was a simple affair. I'd negotiated that we would first loiter over the city and harbour area and fly close to the iconic Kuwait Towers, which looked for all the world like giant golf balls sitting on their tees, to establish on film where we were. We started a good way out into the Gulf, dropped down low over the water and turned back towards the city. There was no low-level smoke in the vicinity but the sun shining from the south was having to penetrate the intense layers of pollution higher up, turning daylight into something more akin to twilight. As we reached the coast and climbed gently over the built-up area we could see that most lights in the houses and offices were on, and so were the headlights of the few moving cars.

We had set the speed of the camera to about an extra 25 per cent to slow down our flight movements and also the movements of any vehicles in our shots. Not only would this give more of an ethereal feel to the subject matter but it would also smooth out any turbulence. With the first item on our shot list ticked, I called the airport for permission to pass back through their airspace on our way to the oil field to the south.

Most directors like to have several wide and general shots from their aerial crew to use as establishing shots from which they can cut to almost any relevant scene on the ground during the editing process, so I climbed to around 2,000 feet to achieve a wide vista that related the city in the foreground to the blackness in the distance. It was black as far as the eye could see: the sand initially black with the ash of burnt oil, then black with unburnt oil, then black with actual lakes of the stuff. For 99 per cent of my film-flying career I've had to be thoughtful and creative in the way I fly to eliminate irrelevant or distracting subjects. In England, for example, there is almost always a set of power lines somewhere which will hardly add to the ambience of a period costume drama. You would not endear yourself to a director by introducing elements that cost him a fortune to fix. Kuwait was different: everything was relevant. Apocalyptic devastation spread into the distance as far as the eye and the camera could see.

Of the many scenes seared into my memory forever from this time, three stand out. The first was a slow and relatively low pass across one of the burning well heads. I say 'across' but of course it was necessary to stay displaced slightly to one side to avoid the flame and vertically rising smoke. The shot developed well but as we passed near the top of the flame I became aware of intense radiated heat on the side of my face. I was glad to be in a Bell helicopter whose airframe was built of metal, but I did put the back of my hand against the Perspex side window and pulled it away very quickly. Hmm, I don't think I'll do *that* shot again, I decided.

The second was the point at which we climbed as high as we could in order to weave between the towering but distinctly separate columns of smoke. The imagery we captured on camera was magnificent but the rain of oil on our windscreen left me wondering what it was doing to our engine. I doubted that the engineers at Detroit Diesel Allison had ever factored in consideration of an air/oil mixture being fed into the air intake of their jet motor, so I kept a tight eye on all the gauges throughout the exercise. That year *National Geographic* published an extraordinary satellite photograph of the smoke hitting the high level airstream and being carried all the way across India until the cold air of the Himalayas brought it back down to earth. I'm told that there is still a black layer in the snow in those mountains that bears witness to the year one man tried to set fire to the planet.

My third and final flying story from this surreal adventure comes from the lowest of the shots we captured. Whenever regulations and

opportunity permitted, we loved to get as low as we could. With the camera only just above the helicopter skids, we could create a shot that would never prompt the thought in the mind of the viewer that it had been created from a helicopter; something in which we took great pride, if we could do it low and smoothly enough. It had to be flown at slow speed, but still fast enough to leave the wind of our own downwash behind. Something around 15 to 20 knots would usually do the trick.

We wanted to illustrate the way the sand changed colour the closer it came to the core of the fires, so we chose to follow one of the large overland pipes that normally carried the oil product out of the desert. We descended to the pipe and, in keeping with the flavour of the film we'd shot up to that point, we let the film run and run as we followed the line into the blackest heart of the fire zone. In general terms it was our practice to give the director as much useful material as we could, but as soon as air turbulence put any sort of jolt into the camera we would cut straight away. By doing so, we would be sure that we could never be accused of generating wobbly aerials if the director inadvertently used it. But in this case the jolt never came. The Longranger's innovative system for preventing the vibration from the gearbox ever reaching the camera allowed us to keep filming on and on and on above the pipeline across the desert.

After five or more minutes Simon said, 'I think we've probably got enough of that,' but I answered with, 'No, no, don't cut, keep rolling.'

As we crested a small dune I had spotted a gigantic sculptural installation just off to our left-hand side and it was much easier to keep everything flowing smoothly than to cut the camera, climb the helicopter and reposition. When you're in the zone and the gods of the air are on your side, you don't want to stop if you can help it. I gingerly slowed the helicopter to a hover, very gently turned towards the sculpture and revealed it to Simon to be a cylindrical steel storage tank that had melted in the heat of the fires and folded like paper.

The shadow of the helicopter came into shot and our downdraft caught up with us but it didn't matter to me as I had just set us up for a second shot and the editor's scissors would make short work of the brief and unwanted material between the two. In the final cut, and in his own inimitable style, Herzog used the whole thing to make a point in a creative way about the interaction of machinery with the landscape. In his mind the helicopter shadow, normally an absolute no-no that we tried to avoid, added to the otherworldly sense of the piece. I loved the way he used the material we had supplied.

The day after we'd finished filming from the air, producer Paul Berriff and director Werner Herzog arrived together on a flight from Europe. Paul pronounced himself very well pleased with the few processed rolls of film he'd had the brief opportunity to project and view, but Werner hadn't yet seen any of it and had to trust in our verbal descriptions. They had come in person because Paul wanted to do some hand-held ground shots of his own and Werner wanted to conduct an interview. As with all of Werner's undertakings, his interview exceeded all boundaries by being an interview with a mute person; a profound sequence I won't even try to describe, you'll have to watch the film.

That evening it was a privilege to sit down for an evening meal with Werner in the hotel and I defy anybody to find a more interesting, charming and original dinner companion. I was very aware that any student of film would have given several limbs in order to take my place at the table that night. He related, first hand, the well-known story of how he had lost a bet to Klaus Kinski. The forfeit Werner had to pay for was to eat his own shoe, and he described in great detail how he'd visited a famous New York chef and collaborated to make it palatable.

Herzog related, in his wonderfully precise German accent, a short exposition on how he was trying to find a way of filming

unbounded space. He held an empty water glass aloft, told us how easy it was to film the space it contained, but how difficult he was finding it to photograph the same space if it was no longer defined by the shape of the water glass. While I love a bit of the esoteric, this concept stretched me.

The final delight of the evening was when a waiter happened to mention, while pouring the fruit juice, that two Iraqi soldiers had been found just that day hiding beneath the stage of the national theatre, where they had taken refuge months before. Werner's eyes focused into the distance as he commented, 'Just imagine if they didn't know they were in a theatre and believed that the plays they were hearing from the boards above them were, in fact, reality.' At that point he excused himself from the table, declaring he had a few things he wanted to write down.

When *Lessons of Darkness* was released it was either to great acclaim or great anger. The film won the Melbourne International Film Festival but was castigated at the Berlin Film Festival for treating war as an art form. You can't please all of the people all of the time, but for me it still stands, even today, as the work I'm most proud of in a creative sense. Herzog himself remarked that 'the film has not a single frame that can be recognised as our planet, and yet we know it must have been shot here'. The *Los Angeles Times* end-of-year review for 1992 described the film as 'the year's most memorable documentary'. Critic Janet Maslin remarked that the director 'uses his gift for eloquent abstraction to create sobering, obscenely beautiful images of a natural world that has run amok'.

Nearly three decades later if I mention *Lessons* to a group of film people, there is always at least one who will proclaim, 'OMG, that's my absolute favourite film of all time.' My credit simply as 'helicopter pilot' doesn't come close to telling the full story but I am nonetheless very proud of the aerial work and the film has undoubtedly had a profound influence on my own directorial work in later years. The long lens we'd favoured in Kuwait became a long-term preference for me as a result of the way it dramatically shortens the distance between foreground and background. I learned from Werner's editing style that when a shot tells a story, no words are necessary; you can allow the audience to arrive at its own conclusions. The directorial confidence that he exhibited in letting those shots run and run and run was something I was able to take forward into our own IMAX film two decades later, *The Earth Wins*. And finally, of course, it's impossible to experience the shock of an entire country being on fire and not become an ardent environmentalist forever thereafter. I could never again perceive oil as being a good thing in any context.

I tried to buy the out-takes from *Lessons of Darkness* a few years ago, knowing that many important shots of historical significance hadn't made it into the final cut. You can imagine how I felt at hearing the words from the television company who owned the rights, 'Oh no, we had a bit of a clearout a couple of years ago and threw them all in the dumpster.' Apparently nothing lasts forever and we'll probably have to learn those lessons of darkness all over again one day.

HERE, THERE AND EVERYWHERE

AT THE END OF 1990 WE BOUGHT a helicopter. I say 'we' but it was actually purchased and owned by my old friend Barty Smith in an arrangement by which he put up the capital while we financed all the operational and maintenance costs as a result of the good quantity of commercial work we were now doing. Barty's interest lay particularly in being able to get himself to Lundy Island in the Bristol Channel, a very remote spot which would otherwise have been a three-day trip to reach, and where we had shared the dreadful experience of discovering his dead sister. (See 'Emma' in *Rescue Pilot – Cheating the Sea*.)

When you're buying a used car, there is a good chance you can assess the value of it simply by knowing the year of manufacture and the number of miles it has done. To a certain extent that's

true of a helicopter, but there is the added complication that every component on a helicopter has a preassigned life. A rotor blade, for example, is not something you can allow to fail without warning. To prevent that, or at least mitigate against it, a rotor blade is given a life that might, for example, be 3,000 flying hours or ten years, whichever occurs first. Through its life the blade will be inspected at stipulated intervals and if any sign of deterioration in its condition is noted then it will be thrown away and replaced. Through these three parameters – hours, calendar and on-condition – a pilot can have confidence that his machine is in the best possible condition to keep him safe, warm and airborne.

A rotor blade is an obvious, stand-alone item to judge, but there are many much smaller components buried deep within structures such as the engine or the gearbox, each of which has a life of its own, with its own predetermined time for replacement. At any given moment in the existence of a helicopter, some items will be brand new while others may be reaching the end of their life. If you fail to appreciate that an engine is about to require a major overhaul involving multiple part replacements, then you could over-value that helicopter by several hundreds of thousands of dollars. To assess all of that you need a highly qualified and reliable engineer, who will look through the extensive maintenance records to arrive at a conclusion about the value. The only engineer I knew who fitted that description was Mick Wright, the guy I had recruited to Castle Air a decade earlier and who had risen through the ranks to become the chief engineer in my old company.

Mick and his wife Sheena had also become great personal friends over the years so it was natural that I would turn to him for help in assessing G-OJFR, a Bell Jetranger that Barty and I had set our sights on. Not only was Mick the engineer I most trusted with, quite literally, my life, but he had also gained huge amounts of experience over the years in coordinating helicopter activities from the ground. If you needed someone to wear multiple forms of radio communication and run around shepherding people, animals or vehicles into the correct position for the helicopter shot, then Mick was the man. Assessing our proposed new purchase therefore quickly developed into a bigger conversation and Mick joined our fledgling company about a year after we'd started.

G-OJFR was duly given the stamp of approval by Mick and his list of soon-to-be-discarded parts gave us the yardstick by which we could assess and negotiate a fair price for the machine. It was agreed that Mick would spend the first quarter of 1991 stripping down our new baby to bare bones and rebuilding her in the way that we liked to see a helicopter presented, including lots of new parts. I landed her at Barty's farm in Berkshire on 16 January and she emerged like a butterfly from a chrysalis for her first flight three months later, resplendent in a new colour scheme and sporting her new registration letters G-HELE. The single tone of metallic grey had been chosen after an exhaustive search to identify a colour that would best work as a dramatic on-camera character for our film work as well as being non-reflective when we were working in the role of a cameraship. I'm very pleased to tell you that at the time of writing, some twenty-five years later, HELE still flies the skies of Britain today, still flown by Barty, still maintained by Mick and still sporting that paint job.

Around the time that G-HELE was in the manicure department I found myself sitting on an airliner with my nose pressed, as usual, to the window, as we made our approach to Asmara, capital city of Eritrea. The Canadian surgeon who had been my travelling companion on the flight from London had been born and brought up in the country whose thirty-year war with its neighbour, Ethiopia, was only just coming to an end. The tears that rolled down his cheeks were so sad to see as he described to me how the desert

we were looking at had been covered in forest at the time of his departure three decades earlier. It was another lesson in how war annihilates landscapes as well as people.

I bid my new friend farewell and good luck, and the plane set off once again to my destination of Addis Ababa, capital of Ethiopia. I had been employed by Carnival Films – who most recently have produced the worldwide success *Downton Abbey* – to fly the aerial sequences on their five-part mini-series *The Big Battalions*, a story of the interaction between three families, of Christian, Jewish and Muslim backgrounds. On this occasion I would be shooting entirely with a nose-mounted camera so the production company decided they needed only a film pilot to work with their own director of photography (DoP) Chris O'Dell. During pre-production Sara had, once again, picked up the seemingly impossible task of finding a suitable helicopter for me to use in-country and had come up with a beautiful and relatively young Longranger, being used by Helimission, a Swiss Christian charity, which specialised in getting much-needed medical supplies into the heart of this devastated land.

The taxi ride through Addis was a culture shock in itself. Each stop attracted dozens of young children who had been deliberately maimed in order to be able to beg. They were often accompanied by what seemed to be their elder siblings, toting Russian-made Kalashnikov rifles. I was quite affected by the journey and glad to finally meet up with the two delightful Kiwis who operated the Longranger on its essential tasks, both of whom were dual-qualified as pilots and engineers and serving voluntarily. Not only had Sara found a perfect solution to our needs, but she had also arranged that Helimission would make sufficient fuel drums available around the country for the task. In so doing she was establishing our early reputation for being able to independently organise the entire aerial unit without recourse to the client's resources, and this was no mean feat from an office in Central London. Over the years I learned to trust that if Sara said she was going to do it then it was going to get done.

The flight north to our operating base at Gondar was another eye-opener. It lasted for a couple of hours. With two guys who knew the country back to front I had the rare luxury of sitting back and observing the land passing beneath. For my whole adult life I had seen television images of the dustbowl of Ethiopia and the dreadful drought and poverty that dominated a country being devastated by war. It therefore came as a considerable surprise to find pockets of thriving wheat fields illuminated by a light with a golden quality like no other I have ever seen before or since. With each passing mile it was impossible to ignore the fact that this was an extraordinarily beautiful country and nothing like the stereotype I had imagined.

Addis Ababa is situated at 5,000 feet and most of the rest of the country to the north rises to much higher elevations even than that. When we arrived at Gondar it was therefore a shock to see that the world appeared to come to an end in a drop-away to a different land altogether, 8,000 feet below the ancient town.

The flying and filming task was relatively straightforward, mainly involving shooting various vehicles as they transited from one storyline location to another. My only interaction with any of the cast was with the RSC actress Jane Lapotaire, whose very pale and English grace stood in contrast to the beauty of the dark-skinned locals. My all too brief acquaintance with the country of Ethiopia is coloured by two incidents. In the first I was idly watching a ground sequence being recorded when the dreadful noise of an explosion announced the death of a five-year-old girl who had trodden on a land mine just a few hundred metres away. This scourge of the aftermath of warfare apparently took children in this way with monotonous regularity, but was no less shocking for that.

In the second incident I was helping the two New Zealand aviators to transfer some equipment from the main plateau to a very narrow pinnacle of rock perched precariously on the side of the cliff that fell away to the floor of the valley many thousands of feet below. The guys had dropped me off so that I could receive and disconnect the nets containing the underslung film equipment which the ground unit would be using later in the day. I was awaiting the return of the Longranger on its penultimate rotation when two teenage boys appeared out of nowhere. I have no idea how they got themselves into that position; it's not something I would have attempted without a helicopter. The younger one was trying to look as aggressive as his older companion, whose AK47 went off in his hand just as he was hauling himself up on to my ledge. I heard the bullet go past my ear and I just lost it. I delivered a rapid-fire lecture into their faces on the subject of weapon safety, none of which they understood, though I think they got the message all the same. When the elder of the two took umbrage at my telling-off and began lowering his weapon towards my middle bits I did think that perhaps it was time to begin defusing our argument, and indicated that they might like to help me move some of the boxes that had just been flown in. In the end we parted on good terms, after I'd asked them to pose for a photograph that sits on my desk to this day. I hope they survived the tribulations of their country in subsequent years, but I fear that may not have been the case.

It was only on the flight home that I had pause to wonder whether shouting at a teenager who is loosing off rounds from a Kalashnikov might not be the ideal response. I never did work out what the correct etiquette might be in those circumstances.

The rest of 1991 and all of 1992 brought in a great variety of work for our lovely new machine G-HELE. First was a really enjoyable day filming Louise Aitken-Walker, at that time the reigning Ladies World Champion rally driver. The Scottish weather put on a wonderful display of golden light all afternoon as she snaked her way through the forested special stage circuit, hotly pursued by me in the helicopter, often at lower levels than might be strictly legal. At the end of the day Louise beamed with pleasure when I suggested that I'd give her a ride in my toy if she'd give me a ride in hers, and we proceeded to frighten the life out of each other. It's possible to be quite gentle with a Jetranger and still leave your passenger breathless, particularly if you very gently (and it really does have to be *very* gently) climb with the nose to the heavens and then convert that smoothly to a descent with the nose pointing at the ground. By the time you're about 70 per cent through the manoeuvre the front-seat passenger is either silently gripping on to their seat for dear life or screaming in excitement. The latter was true for Louise, who then got her own back very effectively.

Although I am used to fast cars and motor racing, the art of rally driving has always been something of a mystery to me. The rally crew strapped me in very firmly and Louise took off in a spray of gravel and with a burst of acceleration that I would never have believed possible on that slippery surface. Trees went past in an increasing blur until the track ahead ended, or at least seemed to. As we hurtled towards the 90-degree bend in the narrow track I went through several phases. Phase one was astonishment that Louise hadn't yet thought of applying the brakes. Phase two was an absolute certainty that there was no way we could get around the fast-approaching corner without crashing and incurring serious injury. Phase three, with still no sign of brakes and nothing but sturdy pine trunks in front of us, became a conviction that death was imminent and the hope that I'd lived a full life. The concluding phase four was a realisation that some form of black magic had taken us through the right angle and we were accelerating again towards another

impossible turn. It was the ride of a lifetime, and I concluded that perhaps we should all stick to doing what we're good at.

Next up was *Split Second*, a daft tale starring Rutger Hauer and Kim Cattrall in which the participants are pursued by a monster through the drains of a London that's entirely underwater. The only brief to Simon and me from director Tony Maylam was to make the London Docklands area look like it was flooded. We chose to attempt this by getting as much kick off the water from the crimson setting sun as we possibly could, and by slightly under-exposing the image to put the tall buildings into silhouette. When we landed to view the video playback of the rushes it seemed we had indeed made London look flooded and were both surprised and pleased to have achieved the ostensibly impossible for our one shot in the movie.

Emmerdale was the soap opera of choice for many, with over 7 million viewers twice-weekly, but I kept quiet about never having seen it myself when we arrived on set for the occasion of the marriage of the two nationally loved main characters. We had two roles to fulfil: first as an action machine performing to camera during our arrival at the nuptials, then as a cameraship taking the couple away on honeymoon. The word 'cameraship' would normally imply an outward-looking camera but in this case Simon was hand-holding the camera from the co-pilot's seat and looking back to record the first private moment for the newlyweds as they are whisked away. Acting out their first married kiss in the back of my helicopter didn't seem to offer them much of a challenge and in fact seemed to go on rather longer than the script might normally have called for. Simon and I were of course connected by headset but the actors were not. I couldn't see what was going on behind me but Simon kept up a running commentary for me on what they were up to in their endless coupling. As the kiss continued for many more minutes Simon's commentary, still with the viewfinder pressed to his eye, became more and more improbably lewd until I had tears of laugher running down my face while trying to keep us airborne and in a straight line. If I ever needed a little laughter over the next ten years I could simply switch on the television at seven o'clock on a Tuesday or a Thursday evening in order to see G-HELE in the opening titles of the show and be reminded of the kiss that never ended.

We filmed gliders for a water authority commercial in East Anglia and Formula One cars for the Arrows team at Silverstone, pretended to be the eyeline of a dragon for a game show, and made four trips down to the south of France to film car commercials in the magnificent Gorges du Verdon. Then along came a great movie to work on with lots of action sequences to both shoot and appear in.

Wild Justice starred Roy Scheider of *Jaws* fame. It was another of Tim Desbois' gigs so I could concentrate solely on the detail of the flying and we didn't have to get involved in the organisational aspects. To create one short sequence in which Roy's character jumps from my helicopter on to the roof of a car, several individual pieces had to be shot individually then assembled seamlessly. First, there are many points of view (POV) from which the action can be seen. Just some of the POVs that we used in this case were from the car, from the helicopter, from a tracking vehicle behind the car and from beside the road. Then a number of other variations have to be inserted to avoid excessive danger to either the actors or the crew. Insurance companies aren't keen on multi-million-dollar actors throwing themselves from one vehicle to another so stunt men and women are an integral part of an action movie. We then have to consider the flying authorities, who don't like *anybody* throwing themselves out of moving aircraft, so a line in the script that reads 'Roy jumps from the helicopter skids to the roof of the car' probably combines a dozen or more shots,

none of which actually feature that happening. It's only the magic of the editor's scissors that creates the illusion. Often the shots have been captured in wildly different locations and on days that are far apart. For one of those shots I took G-HELE to Pinewood Studios and landed her on a custom-made platform. In that way I could have the engine and rotors turning while close-up shots of Roy standing on the skids, indicating to me where he wanted me to go, then preparing to jump, could be safely captured from the ground. A photograph of us doing that together made the front cover of *Variety*, the Hollywood magazine that tracks all the latest productions being made around the globe.

Each time I worked on a movie such as *Wild Justice* I was filing away knowledge and experience in my head for the day when I might end up directing a sequence, or even an entire film, myself. I don't think I was always consciously aware of doing that but it was definitely happening.

In late September 1992, Sara's tenacity in looking for work for us led to a meeting with the organising committee for Manchester's bid to hold the 2000 Olympic Games. She'd been trying to achieve that meeting for over a year but, as with so many clients, the decision-making process dragged on until there was little point in having a meeting at all. Sara's proposal was that Prime Minister John Major and Princess Anne should not only have photographic imagery in their presentation to the International Olympic Committee (IOC), but would also benefit from a short film of the Manchester venues from above, showing the regeneration of the area that would occur if the city were to win the bid. The main flaw in not deciding to go ahead until late autumn was that the film would have to be finished and delivered in time for a presentation to the IOC on 1 February 1993. The intervening period of course fell in the winter, and a northern English one at that.

We positioned to the Woodford area of Manchester just a few days before Christmas. On the first morning of shooting we awoke to a hard frost on the helicopter and a temperature of minus nine. It's the only time in my entire flying career that an engine has failed to even turn over when I pressed the starter button. It was frozen solid. I insisted we walk away from it for the rest of the morning, but we did the best that we could over the next six days of shooting. Manchester had a wonderful velodrome, built as part of an earlier unsuccessful bid for the 1996 Olympics, but from above it looked like a grey frying pan that had been abandoned on a council tip. One of the intentions of the bid was to build the Olympic Village along the banks of the Manchester Ship Canal, a disused hangover from the coal, iron and steel age of industrial Britain. The idea was that athletes would be able to walk to most of the venues along the tree-lined banks of the waterway, but it took plenty of imagination to embrace that concept and we had to resort to lots of moody sunset reflections off the oily water.

In the final analysis Sydney won the bid for 2000, which was the right decision, and they went on to achieve arguably the finest Olympic Games in living memory.

14

SHOWSCAN

IN 1992 WE PULLED OFF THE BIGGEST independent production contract we had yet achieved. The impetus had come from Mark Hanna at the Old Flying Machine Company (OFMC). Together we had written an ambitious proposal to the Imperial War Museum (IWM) in response to their request for ideas, and a joint presentation to the board had sealed the deal. Our task was to make a simulator ride film for the IWM in the Showscan format. Now that sentence is going to take some explanation, on three counts.

First, the IWM is a British institution that was initially established in order to record and preserve all facets of the First World War, but it's been gradually expanded over the years to encompass all conflicts in which Britain and the Commonwealth have since been involved. The name refers to a grouping of five separate sites: the permanent home of the main museum in Southwark; HMS *Belfast* moored on the Thames; Churchill's cabinet war rooms beneath the streets of London; a northern museum that was established

in Manchester only in 2002; and IWM Duxford. Duxford, sited on an historic airfield near Cambridge, is Britain's largest aircraft museum. It was an RAF base in the First World War and a significant fighter base during the Battle of Britain before becoming a civilian airfield in 1961. Ted Inman served as the director at Duxford for twenty-six years, from 1978, and it was he who gave us the contract to supply two simulator ride films: a form of entertainment whereby the audience is seated on a base that moves in front of a screen to fool their brains into believing they are part of the action.

My fascination with this medium came directly from my flying experience. As a pilot, you have to understand the ways in which the brain can process information and draw the wrong conclusions from it. When you are flying entirely on instruments, this understanding is essential. In the entertainment industry, however, it gives the director a significant extra tool with which to manipulate the emotions of the audience.

The sense of movement is a primary source of information to us. As very small children, when we are learning to walk, we often fall over and hurt ourselves, which teaches us to pay close attention to the relative movements of our body and the world around. If the ceiling is rushing into our field of view from above, then, unless we're in a major earthquake, there's a good chance we're about to find ourselves flat on our back, and our early training tells us this is likely to be painful. Motion is so primary, through our feet, though our bottoms and through the fluid in our ear canals, that once an unusual movement is felt, we use our sense of sight (and to a certain extent sound) only as a secondary sensor to confirm that movement. If confirmation is forthcoming, then we're happy; if the sense of motion and the sense of sight arrive at conflicting conclusions, then we're in trouble and get sick within seconds.

Think about the first time you took off in an airliner. Your motion sensors told you that you were banking but your sight told you that

▲ Mick Wright (right) and Nick Phillips always found new ways to hang cameras from my helicopter, in this case the enormous Megamount.

Nobody believes we shot this from a helicopter. ▲

▼ Search and Rescue flying in the Royal Navy was the best training ground for the precision flying I needed in film work.

▲ Bond, James Bond. Landing in historic Amberlely chalk pits behind the Zorin Industries airship mock-up on *A View to a Kill*.

▼ With Val Kilmer and some of the cast of *Mindhunters* before take off from The Hague, The Netherlands.

VARIETY

FEBRUARY 1, 1993
NEWSPAPER
2ND CLASS P.O. ENTRY
USPS 658-980 02574

$ 4.95
SCS.95/£3.95
FF52/DM25
SA13/Y3000

W I L D
JUSTICE

SILVIO BERLUSCONI
COMMUNICATIONS

▲ Hollywood fame at last as Roy Scheider prepares to leap from the skids of my helicopter while I play the role of... pilot! (Image: *Variety*)

▼ I'm trying so hard to look tough on the set of *Wild Justice*. The reality is that even the simplest of action sequences requires cameras shooting from multiple angles and great planning.

▲ On location for British drama series *The Big Battalions* in Ethiopia, I saw the shocking contrast between the innocence of youth and the dreadful toll of a thirty-year war. This little girl's playmate stepped on a landmine just a few minutes after I took this picture.

▼ Joking with Mark Hanna at the controls of our T33 camera jet on our Showscan film *Dogfight* for the Imperial War Museum, Duxford.

▲ The smoke from the Kuwaiti desert stretched out across the Indian Ocean, all the way to the Himalayas. Each burning well head screamed like a jet aeroplane 24/7.

▲ An eerie silence hung over the desert of Kuwait in the wake of Saddam's retreat.

▼ Two spare minutes to contemplate the magnitude of an ecological disaster – filming *Lessons of Darkness* in Kuwait has influenced my creative direction ever since.

▲ The devastation of the Gulf War overwhelmed us in Kuwait. The combination of war, oil and death confirmed me as a lifelong environmentalist.

▼ Posing with Werner Herzog (centre) and the team in front of one of the 750 burning oil wells of Kuwait for *Lessons of Darkness*.

▲ About the only way baby Sam got to see his dad was to come on location. The wonderful Flying Scotsman before 33 film takes.

▼ A scene from *You Bet*. Let's paint the roof of a car with a helicopter. It seemed like a good idea at the time.

▲ Virgin Flyer drops her skirts into the water for the final time after crossing the Atlantic.

The director asked for a train wrapped in black silk, so that's exactly what the art department provided. ▲

▼ The huge 36-inch-diameter Wescam system hanging from my Huey for *Black Hawk Down*.

▲ A broken levee in New Orleans after Hurricane Katrina hit town. This Chinook helicopter is dropping sandbags to try to fill the breach. It reminded me of the story of the little Dutch boy with his finger in the dyke.

▼ I wrote 'Evacuation Plan?' over this scene from our IMAX film *The Earth Wins*, but even that valid question was deemed too political for audiences in some American states.

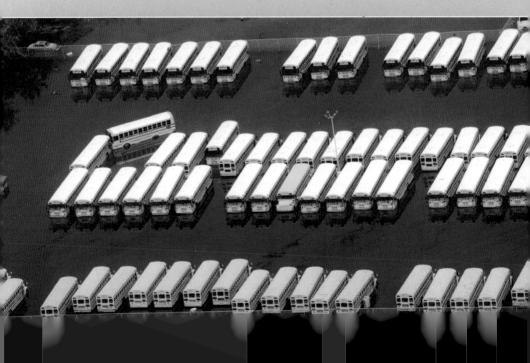

▲ New Orleans – an entire modern city destroyed in a single night by the forces of nature.

▼ My 19 year old daughter Tips found time to learn how to reassemble the rotor head of one of our helicopters at the Athens Olympics, but her true value lay in charming all ten pilots to complete their tedious paperwork promptly.

▲ Preparation plays such an enormous role in any shoot. In this case permission to hover at the end of the runway at LAX contributed significantly to the quality of stock-shot imagery we were able to offer via Getty Images.

▼ So much beauty, so little time to capture it all. One of my favourite sequences from our IMAX film *The Earth Wins*.

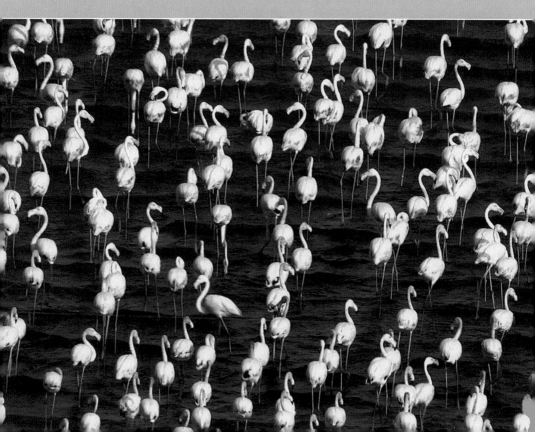

▲ The Earth reclaims a little of her bounty in *The Earth Wins*: wreckage on the east coast of South Africa. Converting real-world ugliness into beauty in-camera proved to be a big part of my job over the years.

▼ It's only from the air that the sheer scale of Australian mining becomes apparent. I used mines to illustrate how the gifts of the Earth don't always come in the colour green.

▲ Shuttle *Atlantis* is already orbiting the Earth every 90 minutes as Sara stands in the flame trench at Kennedy Space Centre's launch pad. We'd filmed at the top of the structure for our *Space Academy* exhibit at the Museum of Arts and Science in Valencia, Spain, earlier in the day.

▲ I always tried to claim the best seat in the house for opening and closing ceremonies and the 2010 Soccer World Cup in South Africa was no exception.

▼ Our ten helicopters and world broadcast aerial team for the 2004 Athens Olympics.

▲ G-HELE all ready to go, with me in my front 'office' and Director of Photography Adam Rodgers nestled into his side mount.

▼ The power of things to come as the drones advance. I had to make a stark choice between continuing in helicopters or embracing these futuristic machines and fully harnessing their potential.

the world (the cabin) was staying in a constant relative position. This conflict between different bodily sensors is upsetting, and indeed sick-making, at first, but it wouldn't happen if you could sit on top of the aircraft in a glass bubble and see the horizon moving at the same time as feeling it happen.

Now, the Showscan format. This camera system won a well-deserved Academy Award the year after we shot the IWM project, because it gave audiences a much more realistic viewing experience. It achieved this in two ways: by having much higher definition than normal film, and by creating a heightened sense of reality through an increased frame rate. The higher definition came about by using 65mm film instead of the more usual 35mm used in cinemas, meaning the human eye sees much less film grain than it would in a movie theatre. We might be unaware of that grain but the brain is still registering it. When the grain is reduced, we are more prepared to accept that we're watching reality.

Frame rate is another way of improving the illusion of reality. In a cinema (at least before the introduction of HD), the film runs through the projector at 24 frames, or static photographs, per second (fps). Our brain runs those still images together and concludes we're watching motion. If the camera and projector ran at a rate that was any slower than 24fps, the images would look jerky and unreal, but if you speed them both up to 60fps, as Showscan does, then the brain concludes it's looking at reality, just as it would if you were looking out of a window. Of course, with an increased frame size and a film-consumption rate that's two and a half times that of a normal movie, the cost of producing in the Showscan format is enormous.

This new technical information was a steep learning curve for us, early on in our existence as an independent film production company. For Simon it meant learning a whole range of new camera settings and lens considerations. For me it meant devising a storyline that could be captured in the air using these monstrous cameras. Sara's role gave her a series of huge mountains to climb, right from the very start. Even sourcing the film stock proved to be a trial. When she rang the Kodak main office in London to order 65mm rolls, she was disdainfully told there was no such thing and that she must mean 16mm, 'love'. It took a call to their office in Hollywood to get the right answer and to have the stock shipped over to us. We really were at the bleeding edge of what was possible and were having to educate Kodak technicians about their own product.

We devised two short storylines for the IWM: one based around a Battle of Britain dogfight between a Spitfire and a Messerschmitt 109, the other based on a Royal Navy helicopter rescue at sea. Around five minutes of motion simulation is all the brain can usefully handle before beginning to suffer motion fatigue, so we kept the storylines short. In partnering with the Old Flying Machine Company we had access to a mouth-watering array of aeroplanes but of course it's the 109 and the Spitfire that are synonymous with the Battle of Britain, so we planned on using two of each. Deciding how to shoot them was not quite so simple, but in the end we chose the Lockheed T33, a two-seat jet trainer that had first flown in 1948 but saw extensive service in over thirty air forces all the way through from the early 1960s to the late 1990s. The advantage of the T33 was that it had a long and voluminous nose, into which we could fit the large and heavy Showscan camera. To do this, the engineers at OFMC had to take the nose right off, take it apart and rebuild it around the camera with special racking for all the ancillary power supplies and so on. It was a big undertaking that also involved interacting with the Civil Aviation Authority for approval, but the rig appeared made for the job by the time they had finished, and the camera lens looked neatly forwards out of a large flat piece of optical glass at the very tip of the nose. They had also managed to feed all the control cables back into the cockpit without destroying the ability of the pilot to pressurise the cockpit for high-level flight. We called it the Jetmount.

At the same time as the fixed-wing engineering was progressing for the first film, *Dogfight*, we also had to find a way of carrying the enormous camera under the nose of a helicopter, preferably our own Jetranger G-HELE, for the second film, *Rescue at Sea*. Back we went to see Nick Phillips and sure enough he scrabbled around in the workshop once again and emerged with a gargantuan yoke arrangement that would not only carry the camera but would even allow us to tilt and roll it during a shot. We named it the Megamount. It was Nick's habit to have an idea, tinker around with it, build a prototype, then shelve it until a commercial role came along, so of course he was delighted when we presented him with just such an opportunity. As with the parallel work on the Jetmount, the Megamount needed test-flying, tweaking and re-flying. To do this we used a mock-up of the camera as the five-figure weekly hire rate put it out of reach for most of this slow technical work. By and large it worked beautifully but the electronics were primitive by today's standards and were often quite sensitive to the helicopter vibrations. By late August we were ready to begin shooting.

For a film pilot it was a whole new experience to sit on the grass at Lydd airfield, near the white cliffs of Dover, and watch five other pilots take to the sky in order to generate footage for which I was ultimately responsible. There was little more I could do than help Simon strap into the confines of the T33 behind Mark Hanna and wish him luck. Even without the cost of the crew and the cameras, the aircraft alone were £25,000 per flying hour, so Sara and I could do no more than glance nervously at each other when Mark called on the radio to tell us he'd murdered a particularly messy fly on the lens during takeoff and instructed the other four machines to

land while we cleaned it off. Thankfully this was a problem we'd foreseen and had taken the trouble to attach a small video camera, no bigger than a lipstick, to the nose of the T33, whose sole purpose in life was to look back at the main Showscan camera lens and give Simon the opportunity to check that the front of the lens was clean before proceeding. Without that precaution, our five-ship formation would have flown their entire sortie without achieving a single useable frame.

Ultimately our pilots and aircraft performed flawlessly, flew the carefully choreographed sequence exactly as we'd designed it and returned with footage that was even better than we had dared hope. The weather and light had been kind to us, the smoke pots had gone off on cue at the critical point in the dogfight and the remaining flies in the county of Kent had heeded the warning dished out to their unfortunate compatriot earlier in the day. Of course, we could only surmise that we'd got the sequence in the can from the hazy black and white video recording through the eyepiece of the big film camera. It wouldn't be until we all met up again at the only viewing theatre in London which could project the 65mm format that our fears would be laid to rest.

Spice was added to that first viewing when the theatre manager asked if we'd mind delaying our assessment of the rushes for twenty minutes as the previous customer, a Mr Stanley Kubrick, was overrunning a little. It was my only encounter with the film director whom I regard as being the greatest ever, and hardly qualifies as an actual encounter since the secretive man was whisked away without us ever setting eyes on him. It did, however, serve to remind us that we'd started playing at a very rarefied level of filmmaking. And when we finally saw what we'd achieved for ourselves, we were knocked out by the giant format, the added reality of the extra frame rate and the jet-flying skill with which Mark Hanna had brought each of our planned sequences to life.

The very next day I was on my way down to the south of France for a week for yet another car commercial in the Gorges du Verdon, before returning to complete preparations for our second Showscan film, *Rescue at Sea*. Mick and Sara had been hard at work making the shell of a wrecked Cessna aeroplane look as though it was brand new, to be the star of our little show. There were still several days of testing to be flown with the Megamount but my phone calls to old colleagues from the Royal Navy meant that we knew we had a good window of opportunity coming up with their helicopter training ship, RFA *Argus*, off the coast of my old hunting ground in Cornwall. Once we arrived down at the Royal Naval Air Station at Culdrose I was overjoyed to be allocated a Sea King from my old rescue squadron 771 to use for our film, and delighted that our pilot would be Lt Cdr Paul Crudgington, with whom I had shared a cabin for our first six months in the Navy.

It's usually Sara's lot either to monitor proceedings from the back of our Jetranger or, if we need to carry a lot of fuel, to be abandoned on the tarmac at our point of takeoff. In this instance she would have some fun of her own supervising the loading, submerging and later recovery of our 'ditched' Cessna aircraft from a boat known as a PAS boat, whose six-man crew more normally supply dockyard assistance using their on-board crane. The preparation, briefing, practice and shoot took no more than three days and went like clockwork. Our camera boxes took up most of the cabin of the huge Sea King on the way to and from RFA *Argus* and the Navy team enjoyed a short diversion from their normal activities. Our script required them to scramble to the ditched aircraft, winch their diver down to recover the pilot and return him safely to the deck of a ship; all in a day's work for the guys on 771 Squadron.

With two films safely in the can and a good volume of raw sound tape it was time to head for Los Angeles, the only place

with the facilities to cut and join 65mm film. I would be lying if I claimed to have taken it in my stride as we parked our hire car outside the edit suite and glanced up to see the Hollywood sign high on the hill at the end of the street. Sara, Simon and I just grinned from ear to ear and performed a little celebration dance right there on the sidewalk. Sadly the actual experience of editing in Hollywood didn't turn out to be quite as professional as we'd imagined. Certainly the mystique was all there, with miles of celluloid hanging from ceiling clips and tumbling into white canvas bins while white-coated technicians manually transferred film from one reel to another, and certainly the atmosphere had all the right ingredients of glue and solvent, but the technicians left something to be desired.

Of course, you don't go to work in Hollywood and immediately start criticising the workers there; you start off with a mindset of awe, respect and an enthusiasm to learn. The process of cutting chemical film involves a pair of scissors and a machine for joining two ends together at a cut point. If you want to transition gently from one scene to another, as we did, then greased white pencil marks are put across the frames that will mix together during the transition from the outgoing scene to the incoming scene. This goes off to another part of the process, and another and another, until you finally get to see the fruits of your labours projected for approval. The old boy allocated to us gave us considerable concern that he might not live long enough to complete the process, for which we'd budgeted a single day. The whole point of a ride-film is that it shouldn't have many cuts or transitions in order not to break the illusion of looking through a window and experiencing the ride. To that end we had only scripted three transitions, quite possibly setting some sort of record.

As the morning wore on and the aged editing technician made a great show of unpacking our reels, putting on his white gloves, sharpening his grease pencil and peering at obscure markings on the film stock, we began to get a bit itchy. By mid-morning he had delighted us by actually making his first white mark on the film and by the time the lunch bell sounded and everybody immediately started to pull off their gloves to depart he declared himself well pleased with our morning's work together. All we could do was glance nervously at each other, not feeling that we could voice our anxiety that he had disregarded every request we'd put to him, spent the whole period telling us all the films he'd contributed to, then put his white marks in what we were certain were not the right places. We declined the kind offer of lunch in the works canteen and held a short board meeting in the edit room. Unanimity was reached in under thirty seconds and so, while Sara watched the door and I wound the film from reel to reel, Simon erased the whole morning's work, inscribed new pencil marks where we actually wanted them, then set about putting everything back where we'd found it. By the time our highly paid pensioner returned from lunch, he was delighted to find that his clients were much more relaxed then they had been before the break. The many compliments thrown in his direction convinced him that we were well-satisfied with his efforts and that there was nothing more to do other than to pack up the reels back into their cans and despatch them to the processing laboratory, which he proceeded to spend the entire afternoon doing.

The sound edit, in direct contrast, was everything that Hollywood should be. A darkened cinema lined in red velvet welcomed our arrival and our jaws dropped at the size of the screen at the front. The only clue that it wasn't actually a public cinema came from the array of wide black desks, each featuring more than five hundred knobs, switches, sliders and dials, and each glowing with a radiance that pulsed. The young and keen team who manned this homage to the end of the analogue editing era danced their fingers across

their work stations as if they were possessed. They had listened attentively to our briefing, watched each of our two films, injected our raw sound into the bowels of their mysterious engine, made a few creative suggestions to us and to each other, then set about making planes and helicopters fly aurally over our heads and across the room. There is a joy and a delight in watching somebody else's team perform magic tricks at the highest world standard, and it was a privilege to have had the experience of creating something in the very room where the early *Star Wars* films had been given their sound effects.

There then came a surprise at the end of the post-production period when a suggestion by Sara that our Megamount might be of interest to George Lucas' Industrial Light and Magic (ILM) elicited an invitation to visit their San Francisco headquarters. ILM specialised in the use of large-format film to capture huge action sequences, but prior to our development of the Megamount it hadn't been possible to mount their big cameras on a helicopter. Even cranes and tracking vehicles were difficult platforms for the large-format cameras, so they were keen to hear about the new capability. If I was a little overwhelmed by all the original *Star Wars* creatures and space battleships that lined their corridors, it was as nothing compared to the pronouncement by our host that he hoped we didn't mind but he'd gathered together *eighty* of their available staff, who were hugely looking forward to my presentation. Thinking that we were going to a one-to-one meeting I didn't exactly have a presentation under my arm but soon invented one in the men's room under the pretext of a sudden gastric attack.

We departed for the UK with a glow of satisfaction at what we were about to present to the client. The timing of our editing coincided nicely with the installation of the motion base at Duxford from which the audience would experience our two films. The

process of programming the movements of the base was almost as overwhelming as the sound edit. Some technicians were responsible for the physical things going on while others were pure software engineers who would spend many hours smoothing out the rates and extents of movement through each individual second of our film. We learned all about programming the six axes of movement: pitch, roll, yaw, surge, sway and heave. Then, since you can't actually perform a real barrel roll in a simulator, we learned how to trick the brain into thinking that each of those movements had occurred, but to a much greater extent than they had. Most of those tricks involve fooling the fluid in the ear canals by very gradually moving the audience seat in one direction and then sharply moving it in the other direction. When allied to imagery and sound there are no clues left for the brain to conclude anything other than what the director wants you to believe. It was the start of what was to be a major part of our work in years to come.

We'd carried out the initial programming at the manufacturer's base in southern California where a tour of the facility by the Duke of Kent was scheduled during our time there. He came in his capacity as president of the Board of Trustees for the Imperial War Museum, so we had concentrated on smoothing out the motion on one small part of the film in an effort to avoid making the Queen's first cousin ill from motion sickness. Thankfully that worked, as did Sara's suggestion that our American colleagues bring in their best china tea service from home, rather than offer refreshment in their more usual Styrofoam cups.

I had chosen to use German voices and words for parts of the dogfight script but this was the one area in which we were at odds with our client, Ted Inman. Eventually the German had to be dropped but in all other respects the production was greeted with great enthusiasm by the IWM and by the thousands of visitors who were soon screaming with delight at the experience it gave them.

Now that we've moved on so far into an era of continual digital magic, I'm excited to have found, while writing this, that the museum still plays *Dogfight* to this day. I can also happily report that the Megamount went on to have a career of its own in Hollywood, on movies such as *Braveheart*, where it was not only used on helicopters but often on cranes as well.

15

ROCK GOD, ROCK STRIKE

THE SHOWSCAN PROJECT TURNED OUT to be the last major project that Simon would work on at Helifilms. Our creative relationship in the air was terrific but we were starting to drift apart in how we saw the company progressing. Simon's natural business environment was to take on a filming commission, execute a good result, earn the associated daily rate, then move on to the next job. This had been the business model throughout his working life and had been carried forward from his father's identical career trajectory. I certainly couldn't knock it but it didn't serve well in the lean times, which turned out to be the first half of 1993. The weekly commute to London from the far south-west of the country became less appetising to Simon, particularly when there wasn't any flying to be done, and the draw of his young family understandably led to us seeing less and less of him in the office.

By the end of the year we had formally severed our business relationship and Helifilms settled into being the core threesome of

me in the pilot and film-directing role, Sara as producer on all our own productions, and Mick Wright as head of all things technical and practical. We knuckled down in the determination that we could make our original vision work. That vision broadly involved continuing to provide the sort of aerial services we were used to, but striving at the same time to explore other avenues by which we might generate income that could continue beyond the moment we landed and disconnected the camera from the helicopter. First, we needed to find another camera operator with whom I could begin to build an airborne relationship. As luck would have it, our very next commission achieved exactly that.

In my opinion, three genuine rock gods still walk this hallowed Earth and I can die happy in the knowledge that I have served at their tables, albeit for only one day in each case. The gentlemen I'm talking about are the 'Glimmer Twins', Mick Jagger and Keith Richards of the Rolling Stones, and Robert Plant, the golden-haired voice of Led Zeppelin.

They say that if you can remember the sixties then you weren't there, but having moved into my teens only in the second half of that decade I can claim with confidence that I was both there and remember it. By the time I first donned a flying helmet the Stones had already been together for ten years but Led Zep were relatively new on the scene. A little over twenty years later the guy who became one of my all-time favourite aerial cameramen, Adam Rodgers, had me whooping for joy at the prospect of spending a day with Robert Plant on the production of a music video for his solo single 'I Believe'.

Adam is one of those guys who not only has the sort of eye needed to create images that will remain with you forever, but also has the wealth of technical knowledge needed to back up those visions. In addition to that, he has great hands on a camera in the air, can feel through the seat of his pants exactly what the helicopter is about to do next, and can clearly communicate what he's trying to achieve. Our mutual respect in the air gave us a frisson of excitement every time we flew together, and one of the few regrets I have in my career is not having flown with him more often. Adam's best ground work can be seen in Peter Greenaway's film *Drowning By Numbers*, and I'd like to think that his best aerial work was done in my cockpit. He related happily to me as the aerial director, a mantle I was wearing quite naturally by now. So many of my favourite productions over the subsequent years were made with Adam's eye pressed to the camera.

Adam came from great theatrical stock as the son of Anton Rodgers, but it was Adam's long-time partner Annie whose job as the producer of music videos provided us with our first job together and the opportunity to film one of the gods of rock and roll. Arriving on the set of any production in a helicopter ensures that both the cast and the crew know who you are. When your role also includes flight in very close proximity to the star, then you can be sure that at some point in the day you're going to have a meaningful conversation with him or her and that you will have their full attention. Our day with Mr Plant dawned cold but bright at our location on top of the dramatic cliffs of North Devon, cold enough for him to be wearing a long dark overcoat that almost trailed in the early morning dew. In keeping with the legend of his excesses, a pocket in the overcoat held a half bottle of scotch, which would make the occasional appearance throughout the day.

Music videos were often the poorest of cousins in the film hierarchy, but when you get the chance to work on something special with people who know what they're doing, it's a privilege and a challenge. The director and of the director of photography must stay faithful to the artist and their vision. As a film pilot, there are many ways in which you can contribute. The lighting contributes to the mood and the helicopter has to be positioned according to

the light. Music with a warm feeling to it might be best front-lit in the golden hour of the day, for example; music with a suggestion of menace could be shot at the same time but from the other side in silhouette. Pace is another element to consider: this is created not just by the speed at which the helicopter is flown but also by the rate at which the lens is moving.

I was hugely taken with the melody and the lyrics of 'I Believe' when I first heard it but it wasn't until many years later that I understood the significance of it in relation to Robert Plant's personal journey and the ultimate demise of Led Zeppelin. The story has been told many times of how Robert had to leave the 1977 American tour on the day that his young son Karac succumbed to illness and died in England. At the time we were shooting 'I Believe' I was certainly aware that it related to his lost child but it was only much later that I looked more closely at aspects of the lyrics such as 'neighbour, neighbour, don't be so cold. There's so much glory in the story untold' and came to believe that the line defined Robert's heartfelt cry of regret that his musical partner, Jimmy Page, couldn't bring himself to be there for Plant when he most needed him. From everything that I've ever read about Led Zeppelin's inability to effectively reform it has been this, and not the death of drummer John 'Bonzo' Bonham, which has been the insurmountable hurdle.

Adam and I initially worked by ourselves to create some textures: some fast and low material with the forward-looking nose mount, which the editor could use as linking shots. Since the video was being shot on the coast, we concentrated on the unusually calm ocean, the cliffs, the wide sandy beach and the surf line. Despite it being our first time working together, we were already developing our own shorthand. For example, 'Let's do a *Miami Vice*' meant a fast run towards the coast across a stretch of water with the camera looking down, followed by a gradual tilt-up to reveal something on the horizon – named after the opening titles of the television programme. The lyrics of 'I Believe' included 'Tears, tears at the water's edge', so for this we concentrated on the gentle surf line. For 'Say brothers, sister, see your brother's in the sky' we'd do a modified *Miami Vice* move in the direction of the open sea, which continued the camera tilt-up as I simultaneously raised the nose of the helicopter to accentuate the climb into the infinite blue. In the final cut I was mesmerised by the way the post-production team had turned the water texture shot on its side and created a mirror image to left and right of frame. Once the image of Robert, lying on his back in a pool, had been superimposed over this, the effect was pacey, ethereal and highly original.

On any film shoot, the 'talent' tends to be left disrespectfully to one side until required to instantaneously perform a very specific move, like a trained monkey. This can lead to much frustration as the star struggles to understand what they are supposed to do while we circle above until the issue is resolved. In the case of Robert Plant we were dealing with a consummate professional who naturally moved gracefully and energetically on a stage, so we simply asked him to take a walk across the wet sands and to behave in whatever way felt natural to him each time we came near in our helicopter. The results saw Adam and I in euphoric mood. Each shot came together even better than the last. At one point Robert stuck a sword he was carrying – it seemed entirely natural that he should be carrying a sword – firmly into the wet sand and continued along the shore. I circled back, waited for him to clear the shot and then descended steadily from on high with the sword growing bigger from the centre of the frame. When you're on a roll on a day like this you become invincible; we could do no wrong. The sword grew and grew, the helicopter stayed smooth and focused and I simply continued the descent until our skids kissed the sand and our camera came to rest just a few inches away from the sword. On

any other day that landing would have caused the camera to either wobble from side to side or to tilt down as the skids decelerated the forward motion of the helicopter. But when you're on a roll you're on a roll so, of course, the shot stayed entirely smooth to the very end and even the seagull feather that our downwash lifted into the air at the conclusion of the shot seemed choreographed. In the final cut that sequence became the end shot with a short piece of poetry superimposed. We always dreaded the superimposition of words across one of our shots because when you give a viewer a visual reference point, any imperfections in the flight path are amplified exponentially. In this case, despite being long before the days of gyro-stabilised camera mounts, it worked just beautifully.

As the sun dipped towards the exceptionally clear horizon, the crew lit a bonfire on top of the hill to give it time to generate some heat and light before sunset. They then headed back down the hill for a cuppa while we waited. I had shut down and exited the helicopter to await the golden hour of light and Robert happened to climb the hill just as I was staring into the flames, working out the various moves I could fly around the bonfire. He did no more than smile, seat himself upon a log and begin very quietly to strum, on the guitar he would be using in the upcoming shot, the first few bars to 'Stairway To Heaven' in the falling light with the Atlantic ocean stretching into infinity behind him. Knowing every word I first began to hum and then to sing beneath my breath: 'There's a lady who's sure all that glitters is gold . . .' Within minutes it was time to get airborne again and I swear I could have done it at that point without the encumbrance of a helicopter. My later claim to have sung the iconic piece with Robert Plant may be a slight stretching of the reality but it is nevertheless true that I've sung 'Stairway To Heaven' alongside the rock god who made it his own . . . on a hilltop . . . next to a bonfire . . . with nobody else around. If King Arthur himself had risen from the waves at that moment, it would not have been a surprise.

We got airborne, the sun dipped towards the horizon, Robert performed perfectly as we circled him and the gods smiled down upon us as the light just got better and better. Of such things dreams are made.

Nightmares, on the other hand, are largely composed (at least in my sleeping hours) of fast-moving helicopter parts suddenly coming into contact with an immovable object. For this reason I find myself still unable to climb into a Subaru car without a cold shiver going down my spine, as if somebody has just walked across my grave.

It happened in the summer of 1993. From an extremely slow start we had progressed into a very busy summer. The day after working with Robert Plant I was off to northern England at the crack of dawn to shoot a promotional video for one of the first new wetland sanctuaries that were cropping up out of the industrial wastelands. The next day, my thirty-eighth birthday, I found myself flying players into a polo match in Cirencester. I flew passengers into the British Grand Prix (I never minded that job), then came more work on a commercial for the British Sugar Corporation, followed by a production of our own (more on that later). Next up: a flight into the Scottish mountains to find a film location and to contribute to a documentary about Hadrian's Wall. This was a sobering experience as it took us right over the small town of Lockerbie into which the New York-bound 747 of Pan Am Flight 103 had fallen five years earlier, following a Libyan terrorist bombing. The grass had regrown but the crater was still there and half of a row of houses was clearly missing. At around 2,000 feet over Lockerbie I was suddenly and acutely aware of being in the airspace in which 259 people had spent the last seconds of their lives together.

Two days later, already quite tired, I set out to shoot a big commercial for the Japanese car manufacturer Subaru. The first day was spent filming the 'hero' – as an inanimate subject is known to filmmakers – at Birling Gap, right at the south coast spot over which we had shot our *Dogfight* simulator ride. The second and third day were spent doing the same thing. On the fourth day we moved from the far east of the country to the far west, and on the fifth day we moved all the way back again. This dance continued from one side of the country to the other for a total of nine days, with two days off in the middle to accommodate the legal requirement for rest. I have no idea why the schedule had been so badly put together but the result was a very tired crew, including me.

The final location was a desolate spot on the side of a Welsh hill in the Black Mountains. It wasn't actually raining but it felt like it might do so at any moment. Tim Desbois, having again secured this extensive piece of work for us, was in attendance to coordinate the aerial proceedings, and Mick Wright had been with me throughout the exhausting task in order to keep G-HELE fuelled and in tiptop form. Apart from being a genius with a helicopter, Mick is also one of the finest aerial camera technicians on the planet, but was getting pretty tired himself after so many days of changing from nose mount to side mount and back again. Our task was ostensibly over by eleven o'clock in the morning with a final side mount shot of the hero car, but we were asked to stick around just in case any more shots came to mind. After nine days on the road I really didn't think there was another car shot that could be found in the southern half of the United Kingdom, so I began to settle into going-home mode as we counted down the hours to the end of the shoot.

I had timed my fuel to be just right for a quick hop down to Swansea for a top-up before heading back home (mistake #1), the cameras were all off the helicopter (mistake #2) and our bags were all packed and ready to go (that makes three mistakes in a row). Just before five o'clock in the afternoon, the tracking vehicle with which the ground camera team were filming the Subaru became unserviceable, leaving the director short of his last important sequence. Summon the helicopter.

After the initial groan I shook myself down from the end-of-shoot reverie I'd fallen into, which was greatly amplified by the fact that it was a Friday, and set off to Swansea in a hurry to catch them before the fuel man went home for the night. I was back on location in under thirty minutes and Mick had the nose mount and camera fitted in double-quick time. Just like all of us he was looking forward to the weekend but he bent to the task with consummate professionalism. The Japanese director briefed me, through an interpreter, that he would like a long and continuous shot from the front of the helicopter looking forwards at the rear of the Subaru as it wound its way up the tortuous mountain road. There were no trees lining the road, just shale and rock and the occasional tuft of hardy grass on the steep hillside.

With a Japanese camera operator in the seat alongside me, we set off for a practice run. The Subaru hit a constant and comfortable speed and I settled into a position with the camera just behind the rear window of the car. To the right of us a safety barrier prevented any unwary motorist from bouncing down the long and steep slope to where sheep grazed in the valley far below. It wasn't a vertical drop but with no vegetation beyond a light covering of grass there would have been many bounces and rolls before surprising the herd with a noisy arrival. To our left a similarly steep slope climbed into the sky from the edge of the tarmac. The road itself featured only the briefest of straight sections but otherwise rolled nicely from sweeping left-hand curve into sweeping right-hand curve and back again. It was the sort of road that would have been a joy to negotiate on my Honda 750 but involved quite a dynamic piece of flying in the Jetranger.

At one point during the practice run I allowed the helicopter to drift just a little too far out to the right and as we crossed the crash barrier I made a quick mental note to myself that I would have to tighten up the bank angle on that corner if the shot was to succeed. Back we went to the start line at the bottom of the road's incline and I declared myself happy on the air-to-ground radio. The car arrived at the start point, executed a neat three-point turn and set off back up the climb, with me in hot pursuit. Bank right, bank left, bank right; I was immediately into a nice rhythm and the car was keeping up a constant pace at exactly the speed we'd agreed. The checklist in my head told me that the next left-hander was the one at which I needed another degree or two of bank angle if I were to stay within the confines of the road. What a mistake that turned out to be.

An almighty double bang ricocheted through G-HELE and I can clearly remember thinking that I must have hit a road sign I hadn't seen. Our beautiful Jetranger immediately conveyed to me that she'd done quite enough flying for that day and had no further interest in participating. Survival mode kicked in as I rolled level, flared the nose upward to reduce my speed, shut down the engine, pushed the nose forward again to level the skids and raised my left arm to cushion our imminent reacquaintance with Mother Earth. My feet were also working overtime to keep us pointing straight and, even though I say it myself, we touched down gently with very little forward speed and our nose still facing in the direction of travel. Quite frankly it was enough for me that we were still upright; a function of luck that I'd found the sole widened passing point along the entire stretch of road. Only the *whish-whish* of the slowing rotors remained. They normally rotate at around 400rpm, which dictates that the rotor tips are travelling at about 765kmph (the speed of sound is just over 1,200kmph). As they slowed to the point where I could make out each of the two blades individually it was very clear that neither would be doing that speed again; both were bent like bananas.

As soon as I applied the rotor rake and the blades came to a rest my new Japanese friend exited the co-pilot's position and ran away, shouting something in his native language that I'm pretty sure wasn't about either cars or sheep. I was simultaneously mortified that I'd done such horrific damage in a nanosecond and grateful that I was around to tell the tale. By the time Tim and Mick arrived on the scene, both looking as pale as ghosts, I was out of the cockpit and straining to look back along our route to find the road sign that had done the damage. According to them I had transmitted over the radio just three words 'HELE going down' (of which I have no memory), and they had no idea what sort of carnage they were going to find until they rounded the bend.

In response to the query, 'What on earth did you hit?' I had no answer beyond, 'I have absolutely no idea.'

Together we set off back down the road on foot to try to find something that would bear witness to HELE's decision to terminate proceedings for the day. Right on the apex of the corner there was no road sign, just two thin and sequential gouges in the hillside, each about 20cm long, where each blade had dug into the shallow grass covering the rock of the mountain. The expletives we exhaled paid tribute to the knowledge that if either blade had impacted for a second time I would now be sharing a valley with a herd of sheep, probably for evermore.

There is a regular monthly magazine article entitled 'I learned about flying from that'. Thankfully, with no members of the public to witness the event, it wasn't something I ever had to openly contribute to, but I took the lesson to heart all the same. *Never ever go flying if you're not in tiptop form.* It will kill you.

16

SPACE – PART ONE

I'VE ALWAYS BEEN FASCINATED BY spaceflight but I suppose that's hardly surprising for a kid who grew up in the 1960s, in the time of JFK's wonderful adventures: Mercury, Gemini and finally Apollo. It saddens me that school leavers can often quote the names of dusty politicians from centuries ago, half the English World Cup soccer team from 1966, or the name of an internet cat phenomenon and yet very few people can quote even two names from the Apollo programme, let alone all the men who were the first humans to set foot on a celestial body other than Earth. Try even asking how many men have walked on the Moon, perhaps over your family meal table ~~t~~. If anybody gives the correct answer of twelve, then you can ~~ly~~ as being exceptional.

~~en~~ three main strands of spaceflight within my ~~ne~~ Moon-landing programme described above, the ~~ding~~ and operation of the International Space Station (ISS) by means of the shuttle fleet, and the unmanned probes that have now

visited all the planets in our solar system. It's been an exciting part of my career to have been involved in two out of three from that list, albeit peripherally. I do at least claim to be the only helicopter film pilot who has ever had a hand in capturing film from another planet, although I couldn't have envisaged that as the outcome when the project was first mooted.

As was so often the case for us in the 1990s, it was the Flight Logistics team of Tim Desbois and Andy Clayton who kindly brought us into their conversation with Martin Baker Aviation (MBA). MBA was originally formed as a small family firm of aircraft manufacturers in 1934 but after supplying armoured seats for the Spitfire throughout the Second World War they quickly established themselves a unique reputation for knowing how to extract a healthy pilot from a sick aeroplane. James (later Sir James) Martin was deeply affected by the death of his partner, Valentine Baker, in a flight testing accident in 1942; after this, the company dedicated itself to the production of rocket-powered ejection seats. To this day they continue as a privately owned company, manufacturing just about every ejection seat in the world for military planes. As you enter their unassuming reception area you cannot help but be impressed with the ever-changing plaque on the wall that records the number of lives saved by an MBA seat. At the time of writing, that number exceeds 7,500.

Once a cockpit canopy has been blown away by explosive bolts and the pilot has been shot clear of his stricken craft, there is, of course, an urgent need to arrest his descent. MBA have a wealth of knowledge associated with the deployment of a sequence of parachutes of increasing size, until the largest of these results in the pilot being gently deposited on land. As a result of this expertise, MBA have occasionally provided services to both NASA and the European Space Agency (ESA). In the Cassini Huygens project, for example, the two space agencies were collaborating to send a mission to Saturn. Cassini was the responsibility of NASA, with the main objective being to establish an orbit around Saturn and thus be able to fly through the planet's spectacular rings and understand more about the way they were formed.

In the meantime, ESA had charge of Huygens, a separate spacecraft that would make the eight-year voyage while still joined to Cassini and then be released to make a descent to one of Saturn's moons, Titan. Nobody had ever seen the surface of Titan as it is constantly covered in an extremely thick layer of clouds. Since clouds indicate the presence of liquid and life needs liquid to begin, it was postulated that Titan might hold the clue to the origins of life. Distant analysis had suggested the liquid might be methane but until scientists could take a look beneath the clouds, no one could be sure. To make its descent to the surface of Titan, the Huygens craft had to be arrested from its trans-solar-system speed, and this is where Martin Baker came into the story.

The initial process by which Huygens would slow down would be through the use of a convex heat shield, much in the same way as the Apollo spacecraft had re-entered the atmosphere on their journeys back to Earth. Thereafter, again in a mirror of the Apollo technique, a small, thin drogue parachute would be deployed, then a slightly bigger single parachute, and finally an array of three much bigger parachutes, which would give the craft the chance to use its on-board sensors to sniff the components of the new atmosphere through which it would be floating. Each successive parachute arrangement was explosively discarded as part of the deployment process of its successor.

Our task was to provide MBA with the helicopter platform from which they would drop their experimental parachute designs over a period of about two years. Each drop would be recorded using ultra-high-speed cameras so the designers could analyse every micro-second of the inflation procedure and modify their designs

accordingly. Initially they would use a capsule that resembled a bomb to achieve high velocity after release from my helicopter. Towards the end of the two-year period they would begin using the full shape of the Huygens capsule, before ultimately despatching it to the far north of Scandinavia to conduct drops from very high-altitude balloons.

The first problem we had to address was how to use our underslung hook to pick up the capsule in a way that would avoid tangling lines, and would leave it suspended below G-HELE in an attitude that would allow a clean release when Mick pulled the red trigger from his rear seat position. Our 'bomb' was only a little bigger than a large person but many times heavier. For a couple of days Mick and I experimented with differing lengths of scaffolding pole, counterbalances and bearings until we had perfected the structure we wanted. A forklift could now lift the capsule into an upright position supported by two scaffold arms. We could start the helicopter, move over the top of the structure while being careful not to tangle the various cables, and as soon as we took the weight of the capsule beneath the helicopter, the supporting arms would fall away and allow us a clean lift. We were rather pleased with ourselves. It seemed to mimic something along the lines of the launch tower for a Russian Soyuz rocket.

The two parameters most important to a successful drop would be speed and position. We could determine the latter by using the brand new GPS screen we had just installed into G-HELE. It was certainly nothing like the sophisticated applications that we're all used to on our smartphones these days, but it did give a reasonably accurate position on its crude monochrome display, which simplified the job when trying to hover at 3,000 feet. We were using Martin Baker's own airfield at Chalgrove, just to the west of London. We simply needed to be in the middle of the airfield in order to avoid generating embarrassing headlines (or worse) by dropping anything onto the nearby M40 motorway. Immediately before conducting a live drop we would climb up to the drop height, drift slowly into the drop co-ordinates and chuck a small lead weight attached to a Day-Glo streamer out of the open rear door. The amount by which the telltale streamer drifted from the centre of the airfield told us how far we had to offset the drop in order to avoid the Huygens parachute from drifting too far towards the perimeter of our safety zone.

I put all these procedures down on paper and soon received the permissions we needed from the Civil Aviation Authority to drop the things from our helicopter. However, wind speed was always going to be an issue. Even from only 3,000 feet a parachute can drift quite a long way in only a light wind. As a result, we always tried to be ready for our first drop at around first light when the winds are at their calmest. Anything more than 5 knots would write us off for the day. For many months it became my habit to check the forecast winds each evening and then ring the MBA project manager, Hugh Pickerin, if it seemed like we would be in with a chance. When you observe the weather in that amount of detail, you realise how rare zero wind speed at dawn is. Even if it's zero on the ground, as it often is in the winter, it's usually blowing at more than 5 knots above 1,000 feet.

The final part of the jigsaw was to achieve zero airspeed at the moment of drop, as any forward airspeed had the potential to skew the technical results with the parachute. There are few things a helicopter pilot hates more than being asked to hover at height. The airspeed indicator is of no use below about 25 knots so we rely on outside visual references to achieve a smooth hover, and of course there aren't any up at that height. I therefore adopted the flying technique of gradually washing off my speed as we approached the GPS release point, and tried to time it so that we were at zero airspeed as we arrived at the co-ordinates. I finally relied on the

helicopter movements I could sense through my bottom to tell me when to give Mick the command to release; a helicopter will soon tell you when it's reaching the hover by the amount of increased power it demands to stay there. If you continue to decelerate and begin going backwards there is a horrible wallowing effect, which can be dangerous if you don't recognise what's going on and quickly take action to get back into forward flight.

The ultra-high speed cameras provided the film footage of everything that happened to the parachutes. Normally a great deal of our attention would have been focused on camera technicalities, but in this case there was little we could do beyond activating the downward-facing camera at the moment of drop and letting it run until it ran out of film.

Our first drop went extremely well, except that the parachute didn't open. The rest of the morning was spent digging our little bomb out of the airfield grass. There was then a break for a few weeks while the components of the parachute ejector were redesigned and rebuilt. With each successful drop, and with each different parachute design, we became more and more confident. Since there were to be three different types of parachute deployed during the descent to the surface of Titan, each one of them had to be extensively tested, and the months of trying soon stretched out to beyond a year. Occasionally the conditions would be a little too perfect and the dummy capsule would destroy itself on the tarmac of the intersecting runways. More often than not it was the increasing wind that caused us to curtail our activities, none more so than the day we dropped our streamer into the back garden of a small cottage. We drew lots for who was going to knock on the door to ask for our streamer back, but thankfully the little old lady who answered the door was more than happy to let us across her lawn, and there was palpable relief on our part that the lead weight hadn't gone through the roof of a greenhouse. We didn't feel there was any need to bother the authorities with a report on such a trifling matter.

Eventually the three types of parachute were combined into a single sequence that worked like clockwork. The first thin 'chute deployed perfectly, dragged out the bigger single canopy, then the explosives fired on cue to reveal a neat trio of large parachutes that took the capsule gently to the ground. The whole team was overjoyed. It had been a long journey to get us to this point and we were all keen to repeat the exercise. Unusually we had registered this success during a low-wind evening slot, and the conditions for the following dawn looked just as good. After a small celebratory drink we all retired home in anticipation. Our team included highly skilled packers, whose technique had much to do with how well a parachute left its enclosure and inflated. They would need half an hour or less to repack the following morning, while we prepared the helicopter.

Everybody arrived pumped and ready to go at dawn but we were dismayed when the project manager announced that we wouldn't be doing another drop after all. He looked rather sheepish and mumbled quite a bit before admitting that he'd lost the parachute assembly. Our incredulity prompted the fuller explanation that he'd put it away in a large black plastic bag overnight ready for repacking in the morning. He'd left the bag next to his office desk and the cleaners had been in overnight and thrown it away.

In the ensuing weeks, while they stitched together some new parachutes, we all kept our eyes out for any tramps wandering along the local highways and byways wrapped in billowing white parachute silk.

In due course our efforts were declared to be at a successful end, and we followed news of the similarly successful high-level tests in Scandinavia. On 15 October 1997, Cassini Huygens launched from Kennedy Space Centre and set off towards Saturn. Actually, it set off in the opposite direction in a complex routing that enabled it to use the gravitational pulls of the Sun, the Earth, Venus and Jupiter to continue accelerating throughout the first part of its long journey. I couldn't quite wrap my head around the fact that this led to the spacecraft flying past the Earth again, although at much increased speed, some months after launch. Nevertheless, it seemed to work, as the twin craft settled into orbit around Saturn in mid-2004, having taken 26,000 individual photographs of Jupiter along the way. Other en-route achievements included the first accurate measurement and proof of Einstein's theory of relativity, and the discovery of three previously unseen moons of Saturn (a further four were discovered later in the solo flight of Cassini). The new moons were named Methone, Pallene and Polydeuces.

On Christmas Eve 2004 'our' Huygens separated from her partner of eight years and began her own final journey alone. Twenty days later she began the two and a half hour plummet and the parachutes we had so lovingly created worked entirely according to plan. As she fell slowly through the thick clouds she began transmitting data back to Cassini, who obligingly forwarded that data to planet Earth. Excitement mounted as the camera indicated a successful initiation, although of course we were viewing the data many hours after it had been captured. At around 10,000 feet the gently swaying Huygens broke clear out of the cloud layer and we became the first humans ever to see the beautiful landscape of Titan, featuring land, sea and lakes, the latter two formed from liquid methane and ethane. This was the first discovery of lakes on any celestial body other than Earth.

At the end of her drop, Huygens landed on solid ground, completed the last of her 350 images and then died on that spot. I was so proud to have played a very tiny part in this magical mission. Cassini continues to fly around Saturn and her moons, gathering ever more interesting data, including downward-looking radar imagery of the cold place where her mate expired. In the same way as the Apollo programme gave us the iconic first image of our entire planet seen from above in a single photograph, Cassini gave us a special selfie on 19 July 2013, with our arm held out to 898 million miles. It's called *The Day The Earth Smiled*. The Cassini project team asked that everybody on our planet that day turn their faces to the sky and wave as the spacecraft was revolved to look back at us with Saturn's rings looming huge in the foreground and our tiny blue dot just barely visible in the far distance. I exhort you to find it online and just give it a moment of consideration.

Cassini has twice had her mission extended but on 15 September in the year of publication of this book (2017) she will commit suicide. Cassini flies too far away from the sun to use solar arrays and is therefore powered by plutonium. In a bid to avoid any danger of biological and/or nuclear contamination of potentially inhabitable moons she must sacrifice herself in the lower atmosphere of Saturn. I will raise a quiet glass that day to Cassini and to Huygens who both laboured so long in a cold and dark place to tell us so much.

17
RIDES

AS THE NEW MILLENNIUM APPROACHED and we all hunkered down for the end of the world as we knew it – actually Y2K was just going to be the end of our computers, but that was pretty much the same thing – it was time for reflection. It did somehow appear that time was accelerating and I barely had time to enjoy one magical experience before being thrown into the next. We were early adopters of the internet with a website of our own and it brought us a wide variety of new work.

Keeping a flying logbook was a wonderful thing to do and has proven time and again to be the catalyst to remembering jobs and incidents that might otherwise have faded. But sometimes a job featured no flying at all, such as when a chance phone call led to me being on a train to the coast in order to become the poster boy for Ford. I also had an advance cheque in my pocket larger than any since we'd started the company. An advertising agency had discovered, right at the eleventh hour, that they couldn't

feature a professional helicopter pilot in a commercial unless the actor really was one. 'Does anybody know a helicopter pilot?' was apparently shouted across their office to where a friend and cameraman just happened to be visiting and responded with, 'Give JerryG a call.'

It was a fascinating experience to go on a shoot, not as the film pilot (as in 'Hey mate, great to see you again, how've you been doing?') but as the talent (as in 'Go into makeup, sit there and don't bother me until we call you'). The resultant TV commercial and print campaign for the Ford Escort was entitled 'Jerry Picks His Mates Up In His' and ran for over a year. I might have preferred a GT40 but who cares if there's bread on the table?

Adam Rodgers then recruited me for a part in the movie *Proteus*. The final shot in the film is a close-up of my eye, looking mysterious enough to suggest that I may be a reincarnation of the supernatural monster that has just burned down an oil rig. The excessive width of my pupils in that shot is not a testament to my acting skills, but a result of having taken off at night from an oil rig set that featured flame, smoke and five fire hoses spraying my windscreen. This was another of those moments when I politely declined to do a retake. I had been involved at the planning stage, something I was by now insistent upon, so I couldn't complain that I didn't have the warning, but I hadn't taken on board the full implications of all that had been discussed. My prime concern had been the proximity and strength of the flame that the special effects guy would be using, all of which went entirely according to plan. Strong lights are fine and water hoses are fine as long as they're not pointed in the direction of the engine intake. But put them all together and the effect of the various light sources on a million water droplets sliding down the windscreen was akin to what I imagine a bad acid trip might be like. I pulled in full power, left the burning deck like a cork out of a bottle and flew by the seat of my pants for the first few seconds until my eyes had adjusted to a beautiful starlit sky over the London Docklands.

We filmed many times for the long running TV series *The Bill*, and I shot air-to-air on a military helicopter carrying a shipping container within which, according to the delightful drama *Henri*, sat a little girl on a hay bale, playing an accordion. Another chance phone call led to an engaging conversation with Richard (Lord) Attenborough for over an hour as I flew him to his film set. He has to be one of the most generous and lovely individuals I've ever had the privilege of meeting. I was, however, mortified when he checked the framing of one of his shots that day and loudly called out, in front of a crew of around a hundred and fifty, 'Jerry, come and see what you think of this.' I was, after all, only his taxi driver for the day. I can't remember which film he was working on at the time, nor whether I found something erudite to say; all I remember is the falling stardust.

We made our first corporate film for a golf course and country club and I was on location with the *Time Team* crew (led by Tony Robinson of *Black Adder* fame) when they uncovered the remains of a Saxon woman who was still holding her dead baby in her arms. I directed my first music video for British heart-throb Michael Ball. His track 'From Here To Eternity' included a Scottish bagpipe player and I was pretty proud of my script that required three helicopters to film it on Lundy Island. The use of a lighthouse had apparently trumped the other fifteen scripts that were all set around castles. My lasting memory of that exercise is of having to send the artist and the Sony management team back by ship instead of helicopter when fog set in after the very successful shoot. Just as Sara, who accompanied them, was being transferred from one ship to another by a jackstay hoist (a bouncing and undignified metal basket pulled along a wire) in a storm, her mobile phone rang. She answered with, 'I may have to call you back, I'm on location.'

My fascination with the many ways in which our brains can be tricked led me to a lifelong friendship with Peter Parks, a man whose skills and knowledge in the area of 3D filming is second to none. If you can clear your way across Peter's always-cluttered workshop, piled high with books, film cans and his own beautiful artwork, you may get as far as the mantelpiece on which sits not one but two well-deserved Oscars for technical achievement. Peter has taught me many little tricks over the years about how we perceive the world around us. Here's one you can try at home: Find a grouping of overhead power or telephone lines. Now stand about 30 metres horizontally away from and shield your eyes from seeing the poles at either end. Try to discern which line is closest to you. Can't do it? Now turn your head 90 degrees to the side and you'll know exactly which line is the closest. This is because our eyes are horizontally displaced and we therefore only see 3D laterally, not vertically. Sadly I never got to work in 3D film because the human eye can only perceive 3D out to about 400 feet, so it doesn't work very well with filming from a helicopter.

Despite the work being brought to us from various agencies outside our own company, there was a parallel initiative going on, led and run by Sara as she grew into the role of producer. We had married on New Year's Eve five years before the millennium, and when people asked how I managed to work with my spouse my answer was always, 'How do you not?' Our first foray into motion ride films with the Showscan project led us into raising funds to make five ride films of our own. The paradigm of self-financed productions was a new one for us and was risky. It relied upon existing operators of small motion bases to like and to license our films. Since each film was no more than five minutes long, the throughput of audiences at theme parks around the world who licensed our films was huge and I used to claim, with validity, that more people had seen our productions than most of the Hollywood blockbusters of the time. In making these films we gained enormous experience in which subjects work well on a motion base, how to programme the movement, and how to film in such a way as to enhance the movement capabilities of specific bases.

We started with a ride in a Harrier jump jet over southern England, then strayed further and further afield, first with a dynamic helicopter flight along the bottom of the towering Gorges du Verdon, which I knew like the back of my hand from shooting so many car commercials there. Next we spent a week filming from the point of view of a snowmobile driver along icy tree-lined tracks in the mountains of Colorado. We discovered that all the tricks we'd learned in using the motion of a helicopter applied to any moving vehicle, so we went on to cars, motorbikes and even an army tank. Each one was a learning curve in itself and each gave us more and more confidence. My favourite is still the mock car race we staged using a full-size 35mm Arriflex camera on a radio-controlled racer. All the other RC cars performed enthusiastically around us and, even though we never tried to hide it, only the most observant of our audiences realised they were experiencing the perspective of a Lilliputian race car driver.

There followed a commission to produce a revised version of the Harrier flight, which would start and end at Europa Park in the south of Germany. Once again we were pushing back boundaries by being the first production company to use the extendable Techno-Crane, a wonderful invention that enabled us to simulate flight below 100 feet through the theme park. We almost always swapped to a different camera operator for each of these rides as every project was different and often benefited from a fresh pair of eyes. In this way we were able to work with Terry Doe (*Colorado Wipeout* and *The Gorges*), Sam James (*Hot Wheels*), who was one of the first professional camera women and went on to work on

Wallace and Gromit with Aardman Animations, and Steve Brooke Smith (*The Nightrider*), who had been our assistant in Kuwait.

When the Commonwealth Institute, a charitable trust based in Kensington, London, commissioned us to generate a ride film for them and to specify the motion base to use, we felt qualified in all respects. Their remit was to display collections of artefacts from the nations of the Commonwealth and to educate Londoners about those nations. We didn't have the budget for the Showscan format, but we decided that if we used the Megamount we could fit a Vista-vision camera to the nose of a local Longranger and achieve an immersive effect on the curved screen we'd chosen.

The content of the ride-film was something we worked very closely on with the institute's director, Dr John Stevenson. We knew how to achieve the entertainment factor, and John had a clear idea of the story he wanted told from within the Malaysian landscape about how the nation had come into being. Once we'd signed off the content, we set off to Kuala Lumpur to investigate the available helicopters, see the landscapes for ourselves and negotiate the high-level permissions we would need. The imposing Petronas Towers were just reaching completion, and in our hearts we wanted to end our short story of a modern-day girl piloting her traditional father from his fishing village to the big city by flying between the towers.

My instinct in our first meeting with the ministers and generals from whom we were seeking approval was to hang back, gain their confidence and ask about the Twin Towers idea at some future meeting. Sara, on the other hand, set the tone for the meeting by gracefully taking the chair at the head of the table and cracking straight on with a wide number of requests. Before the high-ranking officials had time to get over the shock of that little manoeuvre she had scored enough positive approvals on all the minor issues to give her the confidence to go for the big one. Slapping her palm face down on the big mahogany conference table she boldly pronounced, 'So, the other thing we'd like to do is to illustrate your stunning new towers so that the whole world can admire them.'

The glances that passed from one to another around the table were a clear indication that they had never been asked this before, had no protocol for it, and no one wanted to be the one to turn down the opportunity to showcase their country overseas. After a little coughing and muttering one general shrugged and said he had no objection, after which the others unanimously followed suit. I came out of the meeting in something of a daze myself.

Just a couple of months later I found myself, together with Adam Rodgers as cameraman, hammering towards the nearly finished building at 100 knots. When your rotors are half the size of the gap you're about to fly through, I can promise that the space gets smaller as you approach it. With a whoop of joy we passed through, turned sharp left and descended to illustrate Kuala Lumpur from just a few feet above the main street, before landing in the middle of Merdeka square, right in front of the Malaysian parliament building. It was a wonderful conclusion to our journey across rivers, plantations, forests, fishing villages and mosques.

Having specified a beautiful new design of motion base from US firm McFadden, I was at last able to enjoy the wonders of digital programming, working first with McFadden's motion programmers at their base in Long Beach, California, and then refining the programming back at the institute in London. Wave form monitors displayed the movement instructions given to each of the rams that controlled the base, so with the flourish of a laptop mouse the intensity and movement of each sequence could be finely adjusted. Mick, Sara and I had to take it in turns to take the five-minute ride and comment on changes because, until we'd finished the process, the out-of-sync relationship between picture and motion required a very strong stomach indeed.

Her Majesty the Queen opened the exhibit but propriety led John Stevenson to arrange for her to view a group of children taking the ride rather than experiencing it herself. They all screamed and waved their arms about in a display that convinced us (and presumably Her Majesty) that we'd done a job worth doing. It was our first taste of using motion to combine entertainment with education, but it was not to be our last.

With a music video and several motion-ride films under my belt as director, I already felt very comfortable in the job. There had been no fanfare to herald the new title. It had been a natural progression from the days of showing a director what could be achieved with a helicopter, to directing the aerial sequences myself, and finally on to directing entire projects from concept to completion. I enjoyed it, I felt born to it and I was ready to begin pushing back a few boundaries.

18

SPACE – PART TWO

WE TAKE SO MUCH FOR GRANTED so quickly. I was more than happy to wait for all the whirring and the clicking down the telephone line just to be able to watch tiny little thumbnail videos of shuttle launches from Kennedy Space Centre. When they started broadcasting live from the International Space Station (ISS) I was in seventh heaven and sat glued to the screen for long hours.

I guess all daughters go through a surly phase in their early teens. Mine was no different. She glanced idly at the docking procedure I was watching and commented disparagingly. She was even less impressed when I marched her out into the garden, but as I pointed out the fledgling ISS coming up over the horizon she became interested, animated, then enthused, asking many questions. I have to harness this, I thought.

As luck would have it, the next institution to call for innovative edu-tainment (horrible word, but generally used) ideas was the London Science Museum. I put to them an ambitious proposal for explaining about science conducted in space, intended for young and old alike. Ultimately the museum opted for a less ambitious, off-the-shelf solution, but Sara doesn't give up easily. She had just become a founder member of the European chapter for the Themed Entertainment Association, which had been running effectively for many years in the USA. One contact led to another until she triumphantly hit success with a commission elsewhere not only to incorporate all my original ideas but to add some expansions as well. Teenage son, Sam, and daughter, Tips, accompanied Sara and me on a reconnaissance mission to the Kennedy Space Center in the Easter holidays. I took many photographs to emphasise the design detail I wanted to replicate in the theming of each of the areas in our exhibit.

The commissioner was Manuel Toharia, director of the City of Arts and Science (CAC) in Valencia, Spain, and I will always be grateful to him for the ride of a lifetime, which we called *Space Academy*. His right-hand man, to whom we reported for all things technical regarding the design and installation, was Domingo Escutia. Together they ran a wonderful institution in a building designed by Calatrava, a man of exquisite vision. From 2001 to 2002 we collaborated with Farmer Studios in Leicester, UK, to create an entire thirty-minute experience featuring a static display, an introductory video, a lift to the top of the shuttle launch tower, a launch into space and a full-sized mock-up of the laboratory aboard the ISS. The lab revolved around the audience with the theme 'In space there is no way UP'. That simple shift in perspective allowed our audiences to understand the unique value of the science being conducted above our heads as the ISS orbits the Earth every ninety minutes. To this day I love the party trick of checking the time of the next pass (on heavens-above.com), and then pointing it out to dinner guests as it flies overhead.

We employed every trick in the book to fool audiences into being convinced that they were experiencing the scenarios we illustrated.

Even something as simple as believing that you're going up in a lift to the shuttle cockpit can be achieved with a tiny sensation of movement through your feet, combined with the confirmatory signs of light passing from top to bottom of the elevator and sounds moving in the same way.

Some years after installation we met Domingo for lunch. He pulled out a handful of photographs and apologetically pushed them across the table.

'*Domingo*,' I shrilled. 'That's *Neil Armstrong* standing in our exhibit.'

'Yes,' he replied. 'I'm sorry I forgot to tell you. He visited last year.'

'You *forgot*! Good grief, whatever did he say?'

'Oh, he said it was the finest sensation you could get without actually going into space.'

I thought I was going to explode with pride.

There were many life-changing experiences along the way to producing this exhibit. First we used the skills of Nick Farmer's team to create a small stand-alone experience for the very young. We wanted to illustrate the relative size and distances between the planets within our solar system, but it had to be all at the same scale. To do this we used a local helicopter to create the backdrop for an animated (computer graphics or CGI) character, Sparky, to fly around known local landmarks. In this way the kids came to understand that if the Moon was only 2 metres away from the exhibit they were in, then Pluto would be the size of a pea and 19 kilometres away at a monastery they would already have driven to with their parents. A robotic professor, complete with dramatic lighting and special effects, explained the story while the youngsters felt they were participating in the action as a rocket launched from the professor's desk vibrated and moved their seats. We called our exhibit *Space Cadet School*.

For the main *Space Academy* we first travelled to the European Space Agency (ESA) in Noordwijk, Holland, to film Spain's only native astronaut, Pedro Duque, as he narrated to camera the introductory script I had written. When our production secretary Marcia Woddy had first joined us a year or two earlier, the position of makeup artist and liaison to an astronaut had not featured highly on the job description, but an eleventh-hour hospitalisation of Sara meant that Marcia had to take over many of the diverse tasks Sara habitually fulfils. We shot each segment with a different backdrop among the many full-sized training mock-ups that ESA use to train their astronauts. Pedro had been into space on the same shuttle as Senator John Glenn, the first American to orbit the Earth, who returned to space in 1998 at the age of seventy-seven. Working with Pedro, for me, was a bit like interviewing the Archangel Gabriel while trying desperately not to keep asking about what God's like. Pedro is a great linguist, which was just as well as our contract called for us to deliver everything we did in three languages: English, Spanish and Catalan. At the end of each take in the unfamiliar Catalan, Pedro would ask me if the take was OK and I could only respond with, 'I have no idea.'

Henry Marcuzzi was our DoP in Noordwijk, as he had been in Valencia for the *Space Cadet School* shoot and also in the UK for the ground sequences on our Showscan project. Purely by chance I rarely flew with Henry, but his eye for light was extraordinary, making him our first choice for ground shooting every time. It's a great sadness that Henry was taken by motor neurone disease at a young age, but in his last weeks he gave me a gift of insight which I treasure. We had wanted to spend some hours together and chose to visit the museum at the Royal Greenwich Observatory. We laughed and laughed at the absurdities of life, as we had always done. If you've never tried pushing somebody around a building (particularly a museum) in a wheelchair, I highly recommend you try it. The experience was an eye-opener for me not just in terms of basic access but in how a seated person is able, or not, to appreciate the exhibits. I still miss Henry terribly and occasionally share a good joke with him in my head, and I have often had cause to thank him for the final insight he bestowed.

To ensure our theming and graphics were true to reality we had to repeat our trip to Kennedy Space Centre, Florida, for another week of work. When you take the public tour of the facility, fabulous though it is, the closest you can get to the launch pad is the observation tower about 2 miles distant. However, NASA's outreach programme allows for the occasional film crew to visit and record. We had been working closely for over a year before our visit, so, having been assigned our host, we were welcomed with open arms. Orbiter *Atlantis* (as the shuttles are more properly called) had launched only a few days before our arrival and the launch pad was therefore more accessible to us than it might otherwise have been.

It was hard to get down to doing the work we had come for when every direction held another awe-inspiring sight. The trench into which the launch flame is channelled is constructed from red brick, but it's hard to tell that because the brick has melted and run down the sides of the trench. Holes in the far fence attest to the damage that even small stones can do when kicked up by the enormous thrust at the moment of launch. At the top of the tower we took a large-format photograph of the entire complex, for use in a simulation of being an astronaut and walking out along the arm that leads to the cockpit. At the end of that arm lies the White Room, a small cubicle in which no sound is ever recorded as the astronauts spend their last few thoughtful minutes with their technicians. The room has a door at each end; one door leads to Earth, and the other to the stars. A member of our film crew turned to Sara and said, 'Thank you for bringing me here.' It was an emotional moment for our little company and required a group hug.

We recorded sounds, we shot video, we took photographs and we marvelled at the ingenuity of man that had made this grand adventure into space possible. We also took IPIX photographs, the very first form of 360-degree imaging, which had just become commercially available. On our last scheduled day at the facility we asked our host where might be a good place around the perimeter to watch the return of *Atlantis*, as we'd planned a day off for the experience.

'You'd better come with me,' he responded.

'Oh, thank you very much. Where do you watch it from?'

His answer froze me to the spot. 'On the runway.'

The return of an Orbiter is considerably more dramatic than you might imagine from a news telecast. Having begun to slow across the Pacific Ocean it then passes across Texas and Louisiana (the two states onto which the debris of *Columbia* later fell) before flying at right angles over the runway at Kennedy. At that point it's still well above airliner height and is still doing 25 times the speed of sound. The sonic boom felt on the ground is therefore dramatic in itself. Only about three minutes later it can be seen on the final sweeping turn towards the landing, but of course it's not powered at that point and so is almost silent. As the wheels of Atlantis gave a little squeak of protest at finding tarmac once more, I had tears in my eyes at the enormity of having witnessed such a feat of modern aviation at first hand.

The final installation of our creation into its home in Valencia continued right into the middle of the night before the opening ceremony, which took place in front of Pedro Duque and Spanish royalty. Sara's transformation from overalls with a tool belt into elegance fit for royalty was a miraculous thing to witness, as were her rather good attempts at the Spanish language, which she'd been practising in the kitchen over the previous two years. We were both very proud of our creation, and I'm pleased to say it's still operating successfully at the time of writing, fifteen years later.

This wasn't to be the end of our involvement with NASA. We were later commissioned to build the ISS laboratory portion of *Space Academy* for the Powerhouse Museum in Sydney in 2007. All our previous engineering drawings were pressed back into service and our build incorporated a theme with much more clutter in the lab, in keeping with the reality on the space station after several years of continuous habitation. The Powerhouse called their version *Zero G*. Apart from building the hardware, we needed to refresh the associated soundtrack and the introduction film. For that we needed Australia's only serving astronaut, Andy Thomas, who, as luck would have it, was working at the Johnson Space Centre (JSC) in Houston at the time, a facility I had never previously visited.

JSC might not have the glamour of rocket flames and noise but it's where all the serious work is done and where NASA's astronauts have their homes and offices. Andy was gracious by email during the scriptwriting phase and then, like all astronauts, a consummate professional when it came to delivering his lines. Andy served aboard four shuttle missions, the last of which was the return-to-service flight following the loss of *Columbia*. We had the added bonus that Andy's wife Shannon Walker was also in Houston for the shoot. At that time Shannon had not flown into space but she later served aboard the ISS as flight engineer on Expedition 25, which was both sent and retrieved using the Russian Soyuz capsule. Shannon cracked me up during the interview process when she mentioned in passing that she and Andy travelled quite a bit. A circumnavigation of the globe every ninety minutes for many months does indeed qualify for that expression.

NASA had tight restrictions on the size of crew they would allow us to bring into Johnson and the amount of time they would

allow Andy and Shannon to be allocated to our project; it was only a PR exercise for them, after all, hardly a mission-critical task. Sara assumed her multiple roles as NASA and astronaut liaison, hair and makeup artist and producer. We took our Australian DoP Warwick Field to light and film the sequence, and hired a local Houston-based sound recordist Sara had sourced. As well as writing and directing the script, I also manned the autocue and acted as an assistant to Warwick. We had a two-hour window of opportunity in which to work with the two astronauts, during which my script called for Mission Control as a backdrop. The speed with which Warwick arranged, tested, shot and then struck his lights was remarkable, while Sara mopped Andy's brows, arranged his hair and simultaneously worked with the NASA liaison officers. I directed Shannon and Andy, viewed their performance on my monitor and coached them through the script. I'm pleased with the results and with the fact that, nearly ten years after installation, *Zero G* is still operating daily at Sydney's Powerhouse Museum.

As with so much of our work, the simple experience of finding ourselves in unique locations and circumstances was half the fun. The shuttle flights are all done and dusted now, with each remaining member of the fleet assigned to eternal duties in museums, but at the time of our shoot there were three mission-control rooms at JSC. One was for the shuttle when on orbit, one was for the space station and the third was, and is, a national monument, being the place where all the adventures of the Mercury, Gemini and Apollo era were played out. For me, the guys who manned those missions were the bravest of them all, and a surprising number of them were from a naval flying background. Probably my favourite of the autobiographies that line my bookshelves is that of Gene Kranz, the quintessential NASA flight director. Gene's book is entitled *Failure Is Not An Option*, a reference to his extraordinary role in the ultimately safe recovery of the crew of the otherwise doomed

Apollo 13. To be invited to sit in his seat in Mission Control Houston was an honour beyond measure.

One thing brought us all up short during our tour. Our guide, who had been with NASA since those early days, asked us to guess what was the most frequent question she was asked by kids who visited the historic Mission Control Room. We all took a turn at guessing and we were all wrong.

'It's "What's that?"' she said, pointing at the rotary-dial telephone that sits on every desk in Mission Control.

Our most recent NASA visit was to their Jet Propulsion Laboratory (JPL) in California where the unmanned Mars missions are designed, tested, constructed and controlled from. That project of ours has yet to come to fruition so I'd better leave that story for another day. In the meantime I continue to be thrilled with the leaps and bounds being made by Elon Musk through his company SpaceX and count myself very lucky to be living in a time when we can watch those achievements in live HD on a crystal clear broadband signal. The significance of now being able to launch into space, deploy a satellite and then return to Earth all in less than ten minutes is remarkable. The additional fact that his Falcon 9 rocket returns to a robot vessel out in the ocean and lands both vertically and upright, virtually ready for its next launch, is nothing short of miraculous. The whole project is a game changer beyond measure and I'm looking forward to the renaissance in space travel it undoubtedly heralds.

19

FULL NORTH, FULL SOUTH

I CONTINUED TO GET THE OPPORTUNITY to work on the movies of others, despite the long periods spent concentrating on our own productions for motion simulation and space exhibits. These contracts usually required only one or two days of flying work, but of course their high-profile nature added to our CV.

True Blue was an enjoyable film about the annual Oxford and Cambridge University Boat Race. For this, achieving an entirely vertical shot looking down on the rowers as their oars dipped into the water gave me a real challenge. I say 'challenge' because you can see neither the camera nor the boat from the cockpit when flying directly above. You must look at the video monitor on the dashboard and convert the vertical movements you're seeing on the screen into horizontal helicopter adjustments; it takes a bit of doing. The end result was pleasing; it looked like the progress of an insect across a pond, and made it onto the poster for the film.

Taylor Hackford, husband of Helen Mirren, produced *Greenwich Mean Time*, written by their nephew Simon Mirren. My recollection of that is of a long, tiring, cold and wet couple of days spent filming wild teenagers cavorting along a beach on the Isle of Man, but I guess it can't always be about sunshine and spaceships.

2001 brought me *Black Hawk Down* completely out of the blue and right at the last minute. As with *View To A Kill*, nearly two decades earlier, I had Marc Wolff and his flying partner of many years, Dave Paris, to thank for the opportunity. *Black Hawk Down* was a truly enormous aerial undertaking. Like many of Ridley Scott's productions, the entire film was being shot on a scale that defied belief. Rabat, the capital of Morocco, was chosen to represent Mogadishu, the capital of Somalia, where the real-life events had taken place and which was too dangerous to use as a location. Rabat lies on the Atlantic coast about 150 miles to the south of the Straits of Gibraltar. The city is cut into two distinct halves by the Bou Regreg river which runs east–west and additionally divides the 'haves' in the south from the 'have-nots' in the north. The southern half is charmingly influenced by its long French association, whereas the working-class Sidi Moussa district to the north is rambling and run-down.

Each day Sidi Moussa became a chaotic dance of armoured vehicles, helicopters and simulated gunfire. Each morning the local residents were invited to leave or stay at home for the day, but they couldn't change their minds halfway through. The only exception to this was when a local woman went into early labour and had to be taken to hospital. A whistle blew, the ambulance came and went, then another whistle allowed the street fighting to resume, with many second-unit teams filming simultaneously.

When I arrived on location, Marc Wolff, as aerial unit director, was unusually stressed. The US Department of Defense had offered a squadron of Blackhawk helicopters, and a further squadron of

Little Bird light observation and assault helicopters, used by their special forces – all of which should have arrived from the USA but for some reason hadn't. The best thing he could do was to rustle up a gaggle of Vietnam-era Hueys from their assorted civilian operators across Europe. Ridley Scott was not a happy man, so neither was anybody else.

The problem became more complicated when the Blackhawks and Little Birds were released to travel but needed two monstrous C5 Galaxy cargo-lifters to carry them across the Atlantic. The Galaxies were nearing the end of their service life and only 30 per cent of those that began taxiing ever made it as far as takeoff, for one technical reason or another. For three days we were stop-and-go. One of the Hueys had made it all the way to Rabat but the rest were on hold partway through their flights south across Europe. Eventually a huge cheer went up across the city as both Galaxies appeared in the skies above us and turned languidly towards the local military runway. Within only a couple of hours their precious cargoes had been unloaded, reunited with their rotor blades and flown onto the film set. We could at last begin work.

The job was exciting, hectic and challenging. Most of the best film pilots of the era had been gathered together under Marc's umbrella for the first time ever and many of us only knew each other by reputation, or by having watched each other's films. There was a wonderful mix of national stereotypes with self-effacing Brits, confident Americans and a quietly efficient and highly competent German, but we were all somewhat humbled by the scale of the project and cheerfully took on whatever job Marc gave us for the day. My roles were threefold: flying the only Huey as a cameraship with an enormous Wescam gyro camera on the side, flying the same aircraft as an action machine appearing on somebody else's camera, and taking turns at coordinating operations from the ground. Working with more of the world's

best aerial camera operators was another bonus of the job, particularly Mike Kelem in the back of my Huey and John Marzano in the helicopter alongside us.

During one of my stints in the cameraship role I had two Little Birds beneath me in a static hover; one flown by legendary aerobatics pilot Dennis Kenyon (who is still performing today, well into his eighties) and the other flown by Bobby Zee, one of our American cousins. We repeated the shot on two consecutive days. On the first day a party of local lads had to be escorted away from where they were throwing rocks at Bobby's lower hover position. When we returned on the second day, so did the local fusiliers, only by this time they had fashioned a catapult out of a tyre inner-tube with which they promptly fired a melon-sized rock at Bobby's tail rotor, bringing him straight out of the sky. The consequent crash landing was executed superbly and Bobby did well to keep his helicopter upright as he cushioned it onto the rocky clifftop beside the Atlantic. It could so easily have ended very badly. It was sometimes hard to remember whether we were shooting a pretend war or participating in a real one.

It was a wonderful film to participate in and was released to wide acclaim, earning an Oscar for the soundtrack. By this point in my career I was simultaneously riding two horses: being a director on our own productions and continuing as a film-pilot-for-hire. Of course, each fed the other. I was a better film pilot through understanding the directorial responsibility from end to end and I was certainly becoming a better director as the result of being exposed to masters of the trade such as Sir Ridley. On the rare occasions when I was required to report to him directly, or even had a tenuous excuse to be in his general environs, I would loiter longer than strictly necessary, like Peter Sellers behind a pot plant as Inspector Clouseau in *The Pink Panther*, hoping to pick up a few clues. Sir Ridley is an exceptionally gifted storyboard artist and would frequently use the lunch break to sketch out a few fresh ideas. When he handed the results to his first assistant director and suggested that it might be nice to weave them into the afternoon's proceedings, it was comical to watch the waves of implication spread out to the lower ranks as each department hastily tweaked their own activities to accommodate the new requirements.

I loved the film flying as we captured waves of Blackhawks assaulting the streets beneath us and I was vaguely aware of being simultaneously captured on film myself in the role of the Command and Control helicopter. When it came time to take my turn at coordinating the aerial ballet from the ground, I was right at home. Military experience, film-pilot experience and directing experience all flowed seamlessly together to qualify me as the man for the job. I was happy as a pig in poo on a sunny afternoon.

Mindhunters was another big movie for me, but in a different sense. Finnish director Renny Harlin chose a number of locations in Holland, most within sight of the European Space Agency complex at Noordwijk, so I knew my way around the area. He kept the crew light and nimble, which was just as well because we spent three days chasing sunlight that vanished as we arrived, or sheltering from the wind and the rain. I had collected a Bell 212 (effectively a civilian Huey but with two engines) from a German operator and flew it across to Holland to meet up with my old mate Mark Barry-Jackson (BJ), who had brought a Twin Squirrel over from the UK with a Wescam system mounted to it. We called the 212 the 'yes' machine because it did whatever you asked of it. I particularly appreciated its capabilities on the day I had to lift vertically out of a courtyard in the middle of The Hague with two pilots and eight actors aboard. The film was an ensemble piece but it was quite a high-profile ensemble, all of whom had different roles to play. In no particular order there was Val Kilmer, Christian Slater, LL

Cool J, Patricia Velasquez (the beautiful queen from *The Mummy*), Kathryn Morris (*Cold Case*), Eoin Bailey (*ER*), Clifton Collins Jr, and English actor Will Kemp.

The normal way of working on a film is to set up for a shot, complete it, then move on to the next. However, after three days of continuous downpour, we had a list of about twenty sequences we'd failed to achieve. When the weather finally cleared, the only chance of saving the day was to go immediately from one sequence to the next and grab as much as we could before the sun set and the actors had to move on to other obligations. With any pilot other than BJ in formation, I wouldn't have chanced it. It required total concentration and perfect communication. For example, I would call 'Beach arrival shot' and BJ would instinctively know the direction I would be landing in and would position himself alongside me accordingly. I didn't have time to confirm it with him because in the meantime, apart from flying the helicopter, I would be calling back into my cabin with something like, 'Val, Patricia and Christian, in twenty seconds we'll be landing on a beach. Exit in that order. Christian slide the door closed behind you. Keep your heads down and begin to explore the island as soon as I've lifted. The other chopper will be filming you . . . Go!' With which I would land, then take off as soon as the three actors had left, being certain to avoid BJ on my way up as he would be concentrating on the actors now on the beach.

The moment BJ had finished that shot I would call him into position alongside me again to film LL Cool J (whom I had already repositioned in the cabin) looking out of the window pensively. And so we went on, capturing shot after shot after shot and abandoning the hapless actors in whatever portion of Holland we'd dropped them. As the milky sun began to kiss the orange horizon we lined up for BJ to shoot the end sequence of the film. As he called 'Cut' the sun disappeared and both our fuel warning lights came on at the same time. It had been a total blast, an exercise in continuous organised chaos, but we'd ticked every shot on the list that we'd missed in the preceding three days. BJ and I high-fived and left it at that.

One of the great opportunities I've had as a film pilot was to go, nearly, to the North Pole. We had just finished the opening of *Space Academy* in Valencia when Tim Desbois called to say that there was another Ford commercial he needed a film pilot for and he thought I might be the man. The shorts I was wearing in Valencia weren't going to be exactly ideal for the task so Mick and I flew Valencia–London (grabbed some clothes), London–Oslo, Oslo–Tromsø (I had no idea that Norway was over 1,000 miles long), Tromsø–Hammerfest. Hammerfest lies well inside the Arctic Circle, very close to the Russian border and to the port of Murmansk, from which a massive ice breaker appeared around the desolate but ice-free headland the next morning.

Ford's advertising agency in New York had devised a script for the launch of their new and powerful F250 pickup truck which would imply it had the strength to tow an icebreaker through pack ice. I guess that such a thing would be created in computer graphics these days but at that time the best answer was to go close to the North Pole and actually do it. As this was the world of advertising we took two cars, plus a helicopter which had been flown up from Oslo for me, plus endless creative Americans, one of whom was dressed in shorts and steadfastly remained that way for a week. We set off to cross as much of the 1,500 miles between us and the North Pole as the summer ice floes would allow: an estimated journey of some three days. I had assumed a diet of boiled cabbage but had reckoned without the priorities of a New York advertising agency, whose full-size shipping container, lashed to the side of the flight deck, turned out to contain the raw ingredients that would be needed by the Manhattan chef they'd brought along. We soon settled down to the

sort of long lunches that require an equally long siesta to get over; there was little else to do.

On the third such afternoon I was just in the middle of a particularly confusing dream about the heat of Spain and the cold of Norway when I was woken by the racket Mick made as he threw the metal cabin door against the grey cabin wall, exclaiming, 'You have to come outside, it's soooooo exciting.'

The little dance he performed before again slamming the door to my sparse cabin persuaded me that it was worth putting on my ski suit and venturing out into the cold breeze. The steel grey sea no longer stretched to the horizon; we were now ploughing our way between, and over, vast sheets of solid ice and snow. I say 'over' because, contrary to my ignorant assumptions, an icebreaker doesn't have a sharp bow to cut through ice, but a blunt and rounded bow to ride up over the top of the thick covering and break it by virtue of the ship's own weight.

Mick beckoned me over to his position at the bow where an excited posse was pointing at the snow-covered ice passing beneath. The size of the fresh footprints made us wonder for a moment what monster animal might have created them, before we were quickly rewarded with the sight of an extremely large female polar bear supervising her two ravenous cubs in a bloody lunch party of their own. The enormous specimens you see captive in your local zoo are pygmies compared to their wild brethren. There is a culture among film people that it's extremely uncool to be impressed by anything. We've all been there, seen that and shot this, so there's nothing left to get excited about. Except that when you're nearing the North Pole and the sun is refusing to set on the white monster bears that are hardly bothering to look up from their feast of seal entrails, it is possible to get very excited indeed. Even the jaded Bronx camera assistant was jumping up and down in his ludicrous attire of shorts and sweatshirt.

Preparations for the shoot began. To gain a better understanding of how the Russian captain wanted the helicopter to operate from his flight deck, I resorted to the multilingual capabilities of his junior navigational officer on the bridge. I was particularly struck by the map he was using, which showed concentric circles radiating out from the pole towards the barely visible northern tips of Greenland, Canada, Alaska and Russia. It was a fascinating lesson in perspective. We really were at the top of the world.

From there the whole operation went downhill. Our big and hairy Soviet-era mariner drove his vessel into the first pristine ice pack we found and then manoeuvred it around many times until he had completely destroyed the visual clarity of the shot we were after. Once this had been achieved on four separate occasions our director was almost crying in despair. As it was 10pm, time for a change of watch, I noted that my new friend the navigation officer was about to replace his bombastic captain in charge of the ship, which was just as well as the latter had begun to set about the vodka bottle. Switching into my Royal Navy role, I suggested to our director that everybody get some sleep while I stay up through the night to try to find the spot we needed in conjunction with the navigator. Night is, of course, a misnomer when the sun merely dips towards, but not through, the horizon at midnight before beginning its climb back to an equally milky midday positon. The effect of this solar behaviour was to turn the enormous blocks of ice we were crunching our way across into shining turquoise jewels, whose intense colour could never be replicated artificially. Mick stayed up with me, peering intently at the radar screen for signs of a big enough ice floe for our purposes. By breakfast time we were able to report to the film crew management that we were firmly positioned in the ice at a perfect spot with a long straight channel of water delineating our track behind us.

A car was lowered to the ice cap by crane and we all listened intently to the safety briefing, without which we would not be allowed down the ship's side ladder. We had to sign our name and take a tag so that everybody could be accounted for in the event of a sudden klaxon call to abandon the ice. The armed guards that were then posted around the ship's railings left us in no doubt that the danger posed by the large white local inhabitants, in a landscape that was also entirely white, was very real. Once down on the ice it was easy to appreciate how the eternal process of melt and freeze had resulted in multiple lumps of ice above the surface, each about the height of a man. Without disciplined caution, it would be so easy for a polar bear to creep up unannounced and select the charcuterie of the day from the sumptuous platter that a southern film crew presented.

With the car in position and a long tow rope attached to the bow of our vessel, the ground team began shooting the short segments that would lead in to the aerial master shot. I made my way up the long climb to the bridge to request the captain's permission to start the helicopter. As I arrived in his lofty nest he was gesticulating loudly towards a polar bear ambling its way to the ship from the blind side of the crew. The first mate pulled the overhead cord to the deep bass foghorn, which blared its uncompromising warning. The bear stopped in its tracks and, as the dreadful noise continued, sat down on its hind legs. Despite the number of times I've been accused of making this up, I continue to assert the truth: it slid down onto its front haunches and put both of its gigantic paws over its ears.

At this juncture the film crew had all abandoned their gear and hurried up the steep ladder to the safety of the ship. This was completed at about the same time as two burly Russian sailors frightened the life out me by appearing on the bridge with fire axes, climbing out onto the wing and beating the foghorn to death. The gesticulation from the captain needed no translation: the thing had stuck in the on position and was starting to unhinge his already fragile character. The distorted metal lump that used to be a horn clattered finally to the metal deck in silence. At this point the distant polar bear tentatively lifted its paws from its ears, hauled itself into a standing position, sniffed the air and turned with a single backward glance that exuded disgust before ambling off to who-knew-where.

Finally we were able to get airborne and shoot a relatively straightforward orbiting shot that revealed the storyline of the car pulling the icebreaker through an endless white landscape. As with so much of my work, it would ultimately only occupy around five seconds of the finished commercial, but it was an essential five seconds without which the story would not have succeeded. The one bit of my job I'd executed rather too well was the beaching of the icebreaker, which, as it turned out, was then stuck fast. Judicious applications of full power and full rudder throughout the rest of the day eventually saw us free of the ice and on our way down south with little except another three days of culinary opulence to look forward to.

Despite the wonderfully magical experience of a trip to the top of the planet, Sara and I rolled the dice in the opposite direction when we emigrated to Australia just a few months later in December 2002. Our move was brought about by a successful foray we had taken some years previously into the world of generating stock shots. Back in 1993 there was already a well-established market for photographs that had been speculatively generated and placed within a library for possible future use. The photographers earned a royalty each time one of their shots was used while the magazine or newspaper saved the often enormous cost of despatching a photographer for a single shot. Chief among such libraries worldwide was The Image Bank, a wholly owned subsidiary of Kodak with local franchisees around the globe. London owner Dana Cass was visionary in seeing the potential for a similar paradigm in moving imagery.

Around the same period in the early 1990s we had been contracted by a client for a morning shoot along the Thames on 16mm film. It was a shot that started on Tower Bridge and ended on Parliament, with its clock Big Ben. We'd executed that shot to illustrate 'This is London' more than a dozen times previously but still took time to compliment the director on his unique creative vision. Once we'd waved him goodbye at Battersea Heliport we reloaded the camera with an extra roll of film we'd brought along and made the same move, but this time with retained ownership. Thus we had instigated shot #1 in a library that would eventually grow over the years to more than 3,500 short film clips. It quickly became clear that trying to administer sales from our own library was never going to work, and so Sara's proposal to Dana Cass was warmly welcomed on both sides of the deal.

Throughout the 1990s we always included a clause in any contract that we would retain the rights to footage we shot. In this way we'd been able to submit shots to The Image Bank such as our flight between the twin Petronas Towers in Malaysia which we saw re-purposed in edits that didn't conflict with the original client's production. When The Image Bank was later bought out by Getty Images, our monthly royalty cheque was often ploughed back into producing more stock shots, either by specific excursions across Europe or by always having a spare roll of film with us when a job took us to a new location. Initially our content was largely oriented towards generic imagery of capital cities and iconic landmarks, but the industry soon became much more sophisticated and the editors at Getty fed back to us their needs for concept shoots to illustrate 'isolation', 'communication', 'silver surfers' and so on.

A brief visit to Australia for the wedding of my brother-in-law convinced us that the country was ripe for a stock shot expedition and so we raised funding and moved, for the first six months of 2003, to the country that would become our adopted home. During the period that we were researching potential locations, we were invited to a dinner, where I happened to sit next to a delightful companion for the evening, Jen Clarke. Jen and her husband Tim are farmers in the Western District of the State of Victoria, whose family roots are easily traced back to the first British settlers on the land. Once Jen had told me of the perfectly shaped extinct volcano on their property, we devised a route across much of southern Australia that would take us to their farm and beyond.

After a decade of shooting for Getty Images we had a pretty good idea of what sort of shots had the potential for high earnings. We began our trip over Melbourne city where images of shipping, glass-sided office blocks, air travel and traffic congestion soon accumulated. By the time we set off to the west we were relaxed: the country was giving us exactly the sort of clips we needed, all generated on 35mm and in glorious light captured through the skillful hands of Warwick Field. Warwick already had a fine CV of aerial work on movies such as *The Dish* and we were pleased to have found him. In the air we clicked like brothers, with all the immediacy of silent communication that I'd had in the UK with Simon Werry and Adam Rodgers.

Sara's detailed research and planning meant that we had a plethora of shots to try for, but always with the flexibility to capture the unexpected. One of my favourites came as we were filming a nose-mounted shot across extensive sand dunes when three emus suddenly flushed from the long coastal grasses and set off with their fat wiggling bottoms in a photo-bomb over which we had no control. It was good to be working in a country that offered such rich pickings but without the visual clutter we had often encountered in Europe. At the Clarkes' farm we allowed ourselves to branch out into more ground shooting than we had normally embraced, and the location was quite typical in as much as the results of shooting the volcano rim, our original purpose for going that way, didn't work out in

quite the way we'd expected. That paled to insignificance alongside the wonderful ground imagery we were generating of quintessential Australian agriculture and the Clarkes' young children, Will and Sophie, both of whom were natural actors. One shot of Sophie leading her pony past a beautiful stone barn went on to earn more than any other shot in our library, and, according to her parents, funded the first years of her education.

Mick Wright had flown out to join us from the UK to look after our locally-hired Jetranger but even his resilience was stretched by the swarms of flies that invaded us at every step of our progress up through south Australia and into the more remote regions of northern Victoria. We shot kangaroos and wild donkeys, coalmines and steelworks, forests and deserts in an orgy of sumptuous visuals. By the time we handed back the keys of the helicopter we had more than doubled the size of our library and had fallen head over heels in love with Australia. In due course we would buy land, build a house and regard the country as the home from which we would operate forever more. I had a very strong sense that this was the country where I was supposed to be and it's a feeling I've never lost.

TO THE OLYMPICS ONCE MORE

MIDWAY THROUGH 2002, BEFORE LEAVING for Australia, Sara began to believe that we might be ideally placed to bid for some helicopter work on the Athens Summer Olympics, scheduled for 2004. Together we generated bid documents but were ultimately beaten to the post by a consortium of companies from Greece and other European countries. After a few months the incumbents realised they'd bitten off more than they could chew and their contract was rescinded. Despite Sara's reminders that we were still available, the contract was then awarded to another consortium, until one day in early 2004 she received an email out of the blue, asking whether we might be able to supply three helicopters to cover the sailing competitions taking place on the waters outside the ancient port of Piraeus. So began another of life's journeys.

We partnered with our old friend David Voy, who had been my civilian flight examiner for many years and whose company, Starspeed, had gained such prestige over the years that it operated the majority of helicopter flights for British royalty. Their motto, 'You can buy excellence', was no idle boast. David, together with Mick, began to look into the many practical issues we would face while Sara pressed on in her relationship with Athens Olympic Broadcasting (AOB) and I began to bring myself up to date with the modern ways of live television sports broadcasting. To cut a very long story short, Sara's persistence, in partnership with David, paid off with the award of a contract to supply all ten helicopters, along with their crews and ancillary equipment, that would be needed to cover all the outside races and sailing as well as the opening and closing ceremonies. In an extraordinary juxtaposition and coincidence, the Olympic torch, on its worldwide tour before the games, changed hands in the car park beneath our Melbourne apartment only twelve hours after we'd received the signed contract. It felt like a fine omen and was an emotional moment for us.

With only six months to go before the flame would reach Athens, our task was looking like a mountain that might be too high to climb; we would normally have allocated two years to the preparation. Thankfully the previous Olympics in Sydney had raised the bar on broadcasting excellence, an achievement personified in the shape of Michael Hartman, who was in operational charge of all the technical aspects for Greece. Michael had already been living in Athens for some time and our daily phone conversations often lasted for several hours as he brought me up to speed on the requirements, the different ways in which each sport was to be broadcast, and the local peculiarities. Sara and I would work for twelve hours from Melbourne, then hand the lead to David and Mick in the UK, who would hand it back to us another twelve hours later. In this way we were able to achieve a genuine 24/7 process of preparation. As summer set in across Europe we departed to Athens, ready to hit the ground running.

When you've looked at your home, contemplated cleaning it and sighed at the scale of the task, you can begin to understand how we exhaled at our first sight of our operating base. Continuing the comparison, imagine that someone has chopped up every item of furniture in your house and left the detritus strewn across every square metre of the floor. The first reaction is to question the sanity of someone who would do such a thing, but then comes a point at which you've just got to roll up your sleeves and begin shovelling. In our case the area we needed to shovel measured a square kilometre and was covered in bits of airliner. When the new international airport was opened 15 kilometres to the east of the city, the old airport on the seafront to the south was closed and abandoned, but a number of old airliners, too far gone to ever fly again, remained. These venerable wrecks included a 747 which had been the private transport of Aristotle Onassis, famous for being the owner of the largest shipping fleet in the world and for his marriage to JFK's widow Jackie before his death in 1975. Thankfully the big old Jumbo was still sitting on her wheels, but most of the other airframes had been attacked by a massive earthmover with large hydraulic jaws. On completion of this bizarre exercise, the driver of the machine had gone home, leaving sharp metal objects for almost as far as the eye could see, plus about a thousand airliner seats.

Over the course of the next few months we were to discover that making a horrible mess of things and failing to clear up behind you was entirely in keeping with the Greek approach to just about anything. Most building construction sites were half-completed, often many years earlier, then abandoned. At one stage on a long drive through the city we began to wonder whether the Greeks thought that the Parthenon, with its rubble strewn around it, had been a template and perhaps hadn't realised that it had taken 2,500 years to deteriorate to that point. Apparently there were financial incentives in place which worked towards everybody half finishing a building and never completing it, the logic of which escaped us. Eating the usual very late supper one evening, we asked ourselves how it was possible that a great civilisation such as this could go from dominating vast swathes of the Mediterranean map and beyond for over eight hundred years, inventing small and useful things along the way such as civilisation and philosophy, then deteriorate to this disaster where picking up a cup of coffee and playing a game of cards exhausted them to such a state they had to go home and lie down for a siesta. We began wondering whether successive empires had all done the same thing but in ever-accelerating cycles up to the present day. If that's the case and you live in Washington, then hold onto your hat because you'll probably be living in a Greece-like society by around next Tuesday.

The metal rubbish across our helipad varied in size from entire jet engines to individual bolts. We have an expression in aviation: FOD, which stands for Foreign Object Damage. This is what happens when a helicopter comes into land, blows dust and debris all over the place, then sucks a small piece of metal into its own engine which dramatically blows up and causes a couple of hundred thousand dollars' worth of damage. To avoid this happening, there is a favoured technique known as a FOD PLOD, in which a line of people walk slowly across a helicopter landing area with their heads bowed down looking at the grass, concrete or tarmac and collecting any piece of metal, no matter how small. Even a washer can cause catastrophic damage so it's a procedure we take pretty seriously. However, before we could even think about embarking on a FOD PLOD, we had to find and employ a bulldozer to push what had once been four or five airliners into the corner, followed by two large mechanical road sweepers to collect as much of the small stuff as possible. With that completed we could begin to paint circular landing markings for each of our ten helicopters, plus a couple of extra spots for carrying out refuelling with the engines and rotors still turning. It might seem like overkill to bother painting spots for temporary operations but it ensures that each machine is far enough away from the rotor diameter of its neighbour when both are running. It also enables good organisation of the helicopters when they're returning from a day's work and need to be parked in the order in which they will be used the following day. When you begin to account for ten pilots, each of whom ideally need to know before their takeoff which spot they will be returning to, you can begin to get a sense of the level of preparation and planning that had to go into each day of operations.

We had included the erection of a small hangar in our budget. It didn't have to be any more complicated than six steel uprights on an existing hard concrete base, four walls and a ceiling. Next to this we already had a good double-sized Portakabin that would serve as our offices and briefing room. The hangar might at first seem like a bit of a luxury but the reality was that all our ten helicopters were going to need a two-day service at some point during their stay, and the Greek summer sun would be merciless on our poor engineers if we'd tried to execute those maintenance periods outside on the apron. There would also be an initial need to fit five sets of camera mounts plus four sets of communication relay packages, take them all off at the end, plus rotate them from one helicopter to another as each went in for its service during the period of the games. Apart from the sun, another practical consideration is that during a service many panels are removed and a good number of small parts are often dismantled and laid out on a bench. The last place you want to be doing this is next to other helicopters that are coming and going. For many good reasons, therefore, the rules stipulate the two-day service must be done within a hangar and the otherwise ideally located base didn't have one before our arrival.

The maintenance on all aircraft is carried out on a cycle of either flying hours or calendar days, whichever comes first. On a well-used helicopter there is a simple one-day inspection after 50 hours, a two-day dismantling after 100 hours and at least a week of work with two attendant engineers after 300 hours. By the time our machines had arrived from the UK, flown all their tasks and returned home, they would each have flown more than 100 hours so we had to schedule downtime for each of them, in addition to any care they might need in the event of unscheduled failures.

So we built a hangar. More accurately, we contracted local workers to build a hangar for us and were both surprised and delighted with the speed at which it went up. After a long day of sweaty meetings in central Athens and a hastily grabbed meal, Sara and I drove back to our hotel via the hangar, which we'd been advised was finished. The workers had indeed left the site and had also left about 3,000 tiny rivet shafts lying on the ground, all of which would need another FOD PLOD in the morning. But what really left us scratching our heads was the point at which the hangar met the ground. At one end the wall neatly joined the concrete floor as one might expect, but by the time it had reached the other end it had divorced itself from the ground until there was at least a 12-inch gap. Without a spirit level it was impossible to tell whether we were looking at a flaw in the levels of the old concrete apron, which didn't seem likely, or an amateur effort at the easiest piece of construction in history, on which I would have placed a large bet.

We asked the construction foreman to return the next morning for his cheque and took the opportunity to express our surprise at the odd geometry.

'Oh yes,' he said with a completely straight face. 'We always do it like that in Greece, in order to let the water out.'

I guess we could have made an issue out of it but frankly we had bigger problems to address so we sent him on his way with his payment. We did allow ourselves a moment to reflect on whether the Parthenon had indeed been originally 'finished' with rubble lying all around it.

We had chosen to use entirely British-based helicopters. Given more preparation time we might have considered some machines that were a little closer, but the advantages of contracting choppers that all came under one set of rules, could all be inspected by Mick, and each of which came with an old and trusted friend at the controls, outweighed the cost of the three-day flight to Greece from the UK. In the weeks preceding their departure it fell to me to try to build a group of disparate aviators into a coherent team, despite me being at arm's length in Australia then Greece. If I'd waited until everything was decided and in place before beginning to describe the tasks our boys would be undertaking it would have been too late. I therefore adopted the technique of sending a comprehensive nightly email, almost in the form of a blog. In this way our team not only appreciated the scale and detail of each task but they also understood the compromises that had to be made along the way and therefore felt fully invested, even before seeing the place. It was deeply satisfying to see them begin to interact among themselves by email, swapping advice, offering help and occasionally suggesting amendments to our modus operandi.

Sara and I thought we were pretty well sorted by the time we received word that our 'squadron' had set off. Even getting to Greece was a major undertaking, one that we'd left Mick and the pilots to organise. Ten helicopters form a long queue for refuelling and therefore had to split into three groups, each refuelling and accommodating at different airfields en route. On the last day before their arrival in Athens we had completed an operations manual that ran to a very full ring-binder for each of our team to study on their arrival. We gleefully presented it to our Greek military liaison officer, a charming, knowledgeable and helpful

fighter pilot with a long name but known to all as Colonel Panos. The colonel explained in careful English that he hugely appreciated us taking the trouble to let him have a copy of our manual, but that in so doing we had turned it into an official document that therefore also needed to be submitted in the Greek language. What a wonderful thing the website Babelfish turned out to be during that interminable night as I meticulously copied and pasted every single paragraph into the online translation engine. I have absolutely no idea what the end product read like, but I'm pretty sure that nobody ever put it to the test.

Bang on time our ten-ship squadron appeared over the horizon, having joined back together at the Greek airspace border and in turn having been joined by Colonel Panos in a military helicopter of his own. Despite all our careful preparations, their entire radio band was then comprehensively jammed by Greek dancing music (we never did discover where from), causing our nice tight formation to judiciously open out from each other and follow the colonel to the airport like a flock of confused ducklings.

The accommodation we'd chosen was ideal and never let us down during the period of our stay. It was basic and clean and had a recent claim to fame as the place where Crown Prince Frederik of Denmark stayed during his Olympic sailing competition training, just before his marriage to the beautiful Australian Princess Mary. The hotel's three advantages to us were that it was only a five-minute drive away from the base of our flying operations, the size was exactly right for us to billet our entire team as if it were our own country house, and it featured a wonderful swimming pool. Since each of our crew would need their own room for a stay of this length there was no disadvantage to us in inviting them to bring their wives and girlfriends to stay occasionally. Pilots and engineers get very used to a default position of hanging around in a grubby and often stiflingly hot crewroom reading five-year-old magazines until suddenly required to perform at their best. I think they all thought they'd died and gone to heaven when we announced that their default position would be by a swimming pool, often with their girls in tow. Of course they each had a schedule to follow but the advantage of this accommodation was that when things suddenly changed we knew we had a resource of manpower that was not only ready to go but also happy, refreshed and keen. The evening barbecue at a long table beside the pool became something of a tradition, and was usually where we handed out the briefing updates for the following day. I noticed that this country-club atmosphere also engendered a remarkable culture of teamwork. An evening conversation over a beer would often begin with, 'We've been thinking, boss, and we reckon we might be able to improve things by . . .'

In this spirit we negotiated our way through the many pitfalls of preparation until we felt entirely ready to go on the day of the opening ceremony. I had to come to terms with having promoted myself out of my natural environment, so it was with mixed feelings that I watched the glamorous excesses of the ceremony on the operations room monitor and not through the window of a helicopter. Nevertheless I was immensely proud of the visual results that our team transmitted around the globe, as I would continue to be throughout the period of the games.

Sport broadcasting is such a different game to the movies and commercials that had been my bread and butter up to this point. Apart from the sheer volume of material being generated, it's all shot, and of course transmitted, live to air. Most helicopter pilots have done some form of sports work, but having up to eight helicopters airborne at one time, all involved in capturing or relaying live television pictures, was a whole new ballgame for me. This especially struck home during the opening ceremony. I could plan, I could preach, I could mentor and I could monitor, but there wasn't a damn thing I could do in real time to change events as they

happened. This was a reversal of everything in my career up to that point and I just had to get over it and get on with it.

A coterie of three of our choppers and their crews was autonomously assigned to the sailing regattas that continued throughout the event, so apart from a general oversight I didn't have to get too involved in that area of our team responsibility. Sara excelled in her specialisation of liaison with clients, while our daughter Tiffany ruled over the pilots' paperwork submissions with a rod of iron. The marathon was a typical example of my own part-of-ship where two cameraships and three choppers relaying imagery from the bikes on the ground had to be coordinated in an airborne dance, and within the parameters of safety, fuel requirements and pilot fatigue limits. From the ancient town of Marathon, from which the event takes its name, the route took our helicopters directly through the climb-out lane of the airliners departing the international airport. Much advance negotiation had led to the camera choppers remaining below 500 feet, while the relay ships climbed much higher than helicopters really like to fly, in order to give the Jumbo jets room to depart beneath them. Once again the ability to keep a three-dimensional map in my head came in handy as I simultaneously gave mentoring advice about the images being created and kept an eye out for operational flexibilities. Somebody above my pay grade had made the decision to employ and impose upon us a group of cameramen who only spoke Spanish. I'm sure it made sense to someone, but not to me.

Our engineering department performed flawlessly. Our helicopters were rotated through our makeshift hangar in double-quick time and in all cases were eventually handed back to their owners in as good a condition as they arrived, or even better. In one case a chopper that had always run rather hot was found to have had the oil cooler fan fitted back to front at the time of manufacture, more than ten years previously. On the sole occasion that one of our machines failed to start, I was only alerted to the problem by the stream of volunteers from all departments rushing out to help. By the time I'd rid myself of three radio frequencies and two telephones, the recalcitrant machine had been pushed into the hangar, replaced by another, the camera equipment swapped over and the replacement helicopter was already airborne.

It took me some weeks to see the funny side of being arrested for 'misappropriating government property' when we needed a sheet of metal and I found just the right thing in the enormous pile of airliner rubbish that we'd bulldozed to one side during the preparation of our helipad some months earlier. Two bored policemen had apparently observed me doing that and had decided to make it their highest priority of the day. There were other little incidents here and there that would fill a book on their own but by the end of the closing ceremony we all knew we'd done a good job in the face of much adversity.

Earlier in the games I had allowed myself only one lie-in beyond dawn, and it was on the morning when only a single helicopter was scheduled to film the rowing, but what a mistake that turned out to be. Great Britain were due to achieve a gold medal and the flying task was relatively easy, but as I opened my eyes I sat bolt upright in the realisation that I'd omitted to organise the fuel that I'd promised at the remote military airfield near the rowing venue to the north-east of the city. Thankfully the pilot, Richard Banham, exhibited considerable fortitude in landing at the military field unannounced on a Sunday morning and had then gone knocking on doors until he found someone who not only spoke English but also knew where the fuel manager lived. I next allowed myself to sleep around the time we were crossing Italy on our way back to England. It had been a long, tiring, but very satisfying six months.

Of course there is always one small memory that lingers way beyond its significance to the task, and in this case it involved my

daughter Tiffany. As we took off from Athens and joined up for one final formation fly-past, Tiffany let go an ear-piercing scream into the headset of the pilot she was sharing a cockpit with. A large rat had decided it didn't want to live in Greece any longer and had hitched a ride out. Even by the time we landed for fuel around three hours down the track, there had been no accord reached between the three occupants of that particular helicopter, and so the entire squadron joined on the airfield tarmac for one last team effort and extracted the stowaway.

21

KATRINA

AROUND THE TIME WE FINISHED IN Athens I was beginning to wonder whether to hang up my flying gloves. I'd reached the age of fifty without damaging myself; many old friends and contemporaries had not been so lucky. I'd had a good run at some very special jobs, been blessed with capturing every conceivable lighting effect the heavens could offer, and flown lower and closer than most pilots ever achieve in a career. I was also beginning to feel that I might have rolled the dice often enough, and that if I blindly carried on I might not stay so lucky. Then along came the Cineflex in 2005.

The Cineflex camera system is enclosed in a neat weatherproof ball, carries the very latest cameras and is stabilised to an extent that I never thought I would see within my lifetime. I'd always shied away from owning the big gyro-stabilised systems such as the Wescam and the FLIR because their reliability was suspect. Imagine spending half a million dollars on a car and finding that it only

worked half the time, provided there was an engineer accompanying it on every occasion. But the Cineflex was new-generation, had an outstanding reputation for reliability and enclosed a beautiful Sony HDC 1500 camera that recorded in the brand new high-definition tape format. Of course Moore's law, which observes that the processing power of an integrated circuit has doubled every year since they were invented, has since resulted in cameras with eight times the number of pixels recorded to solid state hard drives, but in 2005 the Cineflex left the competition for dead.

We took the plunge, borrowed an eye-watering amount of money and set off to Los Angeles to learn about, play with and ultimately take delivery of our brand new baby, #21 off the production line. Gyro-stabilisation is a black art whereby a tiny electronic box senses the movement of the helicopter and imparts an equal and opposite movement into the camera. In this way the lens remains firmly fixed on the subject even in the face of enormous air turbulence or, more likely, pilot incompetence. This has been the holy grail of aerial filming for a very long time but the stumbling block was always the delay between the gyro sensing the movement and correcting for it. John Coyle, the designer of the Cineflex, had somehow overcome this problem and produced, quite literally in his garage, a wondrous system. From 12,000 feet up and 12 miles away, a Cineflex can hold a person in centre frame and record exactly what they are doing, even if the helicopter is being thrown around the sky.

I have since heard some very experienced film pilots claim that the advantage lies in how much easier it makes their job, but to me that misses the point. With stability of that magnitude, the creative possibilities offered to the aerial team become almost endless.

Mick had flown in from the UK and Warwick had accompanied Sara and me from Australia. We started by lashing the system to the rear tray of a pick-up truck and equipping the 'cockpit' of

the truck with all the monitors, recorders and power supplies we would eventually be using in a helicopter. In this way we could experiment, learn and gain experience without the pressure of cost that a chopper implies. We whooped with joy at the imagery we were creating. Unfortunately we did get a little carried away. As we left the Hollywood area, we began experimenting with how tight we could zoom in to the airliners coming and going from LAX. The police cruiser that pulled us over was accompanied by around six other similar vehicles, all lit up like Christmas trees. Mick and I exited our front seats and stood against a wall, as instructed, to receive a stern lecture about pointing things at aeroplanes at an airport. Meanwhile Warwick was so totally surrounded by equipment that he couldn't evacuate the vehicle and was lucky not to get his head blown off by the police officer he surprised by eventually emerging with his hands on his head.

With that little misunderstanding laid to rest, we moved on to the helicopter work and I confirmed to myself that I was now back in the game for the foreseeable future. The *huge* zoom capability meant that we could achieve relative movements of the foreground and background beyond our wildest dreams. We could look in towards the centre of downtown Los Angeles and fill the frame with the reflective windows of one skyscraper while making the windows of another pass in front. It was a process of realisation, exploration and joy.

As Mick wrestled with new technical challenges, Warwick found new sensitivities in the fine fingertip controls and I expanded the 3D map in my head to encompass foreground and background subjects that were often separated by many miles, Hurricane Katrina relentlessly bore down on New Orleans. The rolling CNN news coverage gave us a feel for the strength of the storm as we watched reporter Anderson Cooper being blown off his feet right in the middle of the wonderful town where we'd partied during

previous visits. But the one thing not being conveyed at all was a sense of scale and context.

With stock shots in mind, plus an opportunity to learn how to use the Cineflex in the field, we decided we had to be there. This was the mindset at the start, but how different our emotional involvement would turn out to be by the end.

A helicopter was despatched. Sara sought and achieved permission for us to be one of only two helicopters allowed into the restricted zone, but failed to find accommodation anywhere in the southern states, while Warwick, Mick and I packed our brand new Cineflex into the thirteen bespoke flight cases we'd had manufactured locally. Sara additionally confirmed with Getty Images that, yes, they would most certainly support our endeavours while she continuously rang every vehicle hire company she could find. The only vehicle available to us across the whole of the southern United States was in San Diego, just 100 miles south. In a take-it-or-leave-it deal, it was going to cost us $10,000 per week for a very high-tech expanding truck with all the mod-cons. Sara grabbed it with open arms and by dusk that evening we were in San Diego collecting the keys to our *Star Trek* spaceship. So began a road trip of over 2,000 miles towards the devastation that was once New Orleans.

While one of us drove the other two were able to sleep, navigate and explore what would become our home for the next two weeks. The first exploration revealed that we didn't have any bedding and Sara's indignant call to the hire company was received with, 'Your boys are going to New Orleans. Everything will get stolen so we've taken whatever we can out of the truck.'

By the time we joined a long line of military vehicles queuing to cross the Mississippi in Baton Rouge, Sara had taken the red-eye to Getty's offices in New York from where she would shuttle backwards and forwards with tapes under her arm over the coming

shoot period. We found a deserted schoolyard in Slidell, just across Lake Pontchartrain from the equally deserted New Orleans, and whistled up the helicopter to join us.

Our experiences in Louisiana and Mississippi post-Katrina were legion, but the principal highlights that are seared into my soul are these:

- An entire, vital, modern American city lying under water.
- The complete absence of people, like something from a post-apocalyptic movie.
- Calls over the radio from rescue helicopters who were seeing human bodies being consumed by alligators.
- The day that George W. Bush came to town for a photo call and all relief helicopters were grounded for 24 hours in the interest of *his* safety.
- The smell permeating our chopper, even from 1,500 feet, of oil mixed with sea water, rotting vegetation, sewage and human remains.
- Long freight trains that had been picked up by the wind and tossed into a forest.
- The depot of a freight-forwarding company wherein every single shipping container had been thrown on top of one another, then topped off with the trucks that used to move them.
- More than a hundred school buses parked in neat rows, unused and underwater.
- Aeroplanes blown upside down and parked on top of each other.
- Mud, mud and more layers of toxic mud covering everything.

. . . and so on and so on and so on. In most of the film work I've undertaken we have been able to remain detached and professional, centring our attention on the lens and the framing. In New Orleans we found ourselves often pausing in our work to simply stare out

of the helicopter window and try to wrap our heads around the enormity of the human catastrophe we were witnessing, all brought about by Man's belief that he can ignore and master Nature. I concluded that this particular fallacy had surely been laid to rest forever – but of course it hasn't.

When witnessing and trying to record a disaster on this scale it sometimes takes a small thing at a personal level to bring it home. That moment came for me at Baton Rouge airport one day when I left Warwick supervising the refuel while I sought out a small corner of the public car park to smoke a cigarette. At the other end of the bench from me sat a large black lady whose entire being could be summed up in the word 'Mama'. She was dressed in her Sunday best and could so easily have been sitting in her church. With her flowery hat and her hands folded neatly in the lap of her long and pretty dress, she politely engaged me in conversation. I answered her questions about what an English boy was doing in her neighbourhood and she thanked me – thanked me, for heaven's sake – for doing all I could to make the world aware of what had happened there.

My new friend introduced me to her meek and confused husband, her proud and upright teenage son and her disabled young daughter, each of whom were about to be evacuated to California by the wonderful Angel Flight organisation, through whom corporate jets are donated to humanitarian causes. She had heard of California but had no idea when, or if, her family would come back. She was staying; she just knew that her calling was to rebuild the family home so they had somewhere to come back to. She laughingly asked if she could come on my next flight ('I'm only little, you'll hardly notice me'), just to see if her home was still there.

She had already told me that she came from the ninth ward area of the city. Therefore I already knew that her home wasn't there any

longer. Nor were the shops where she used to get her groceries, nor the church for which she had dressed. In the face of such enormous optimism and human resilience, I just couldn't bring myself to tell her those things.

More than ten years later I still haven't fully got over that encounter with the human face of a disaster of such magnitude, nor was it helped by another face, this time a white one, when we landed back at Slidell for the night. A single café had managed to stay open using gas cookers – there was no electricity. Our otherwise charming middle-aged hostess related to us the story of how her elderly parents had taken to their sailing boat on the night of Katrina, had drifted for ten days and of course she was hugely relieved that they had just been found alive and well. Her parting shot to us that night was, 'Of course it's been terrible for the city but in the end it might not be a bad thing . . . you know . . . with the cleansing an' all.'

22

GAMES

THE CINEFLEX CAMERA SYSTEM PLAYED A big part in our lives for the next ten years. We became sales representatives for the manufacturer in addition to using multiple systems on our own work. A short time before the Olympics in Athens, Sara had spotted that the sports management company IMG had won the bid to be partners in the host broadcasting of the 2006 Asian Games in Doha, Qatar, and she had consequently invited senior producer Mike Wilmot and his technical director Dave Shields to visit our helipad during their fact-finding tour of Athens.

To understand some background to that, it's necessary to pause for a short history lesson. My experience in Sarajevo twenty years earlier had come at a time when the broadcasting of the Olympics had been entirely in the hands of the Americans. The bid for 1984 had gone to ABC Sports (who later became part of ESPN), as it had for every games since 1964, but in 1988 the baton passed

to NBC, who have been the US broadcaster ever since and who now have a contract in that role through to 2032. The tradition was that the incumbent US broadcaster would provide a 'world feed' which the much smaller national rights holders around the world could buy into and thereby avoid much duplicated effort. The host nation usually believed there would be a bonanza of work for them but even in the most developed countries the reality was that the national broadcaster only dealt with their own national programming while ABC sold images to the rest of the world to recoup their bid fee.

Then in 1996 NBC made a big mistake at the Atlanta Olympics by concentrating their cameras almost exclusively on American athletes. Countries like Kenya with world-class athletes would stay awake into the wee hours to watch their sportsmen competing but were lucky to get a glimpse, even if they were leading and on their way to a gold medal. Instead they would be treated to endless footage of the first-placed American, even if he was well down the field, together with spurious documentary background about what he'd had for breakfast and so on. Following that debacle and the associated cries of protest, the International Olympic Committee (IOC) decreed that it should never happen again and set up their own broadcasting arm. At the 2000 Games in Sydney this was known as Sydney Olympic Broadcasting Organisation (SOBO) – presumably they didn't like the idea of it being called SOB – but thereafter it was shortened to AOB for Athens and BOB for Beijing. In each case the higher echelons were taken up by IOC appointees who appointed one company, or sometimes the partnership of a couple of companies, who would be country-agnostic and would comply with strict contractual rules about how much screen time to give to each athlete, dependent only on how they were doing in the competition. In this way a new type of professional broadcaster was born, known as Host Broadcasters, and Mark McCormack's company IMG, which had originally been set up to manage individual sportsmen, was one of these.

On his return to London Mike Wilmot invited us to stop by his Chiswick office, once we'd completed our Athens tasks, to have an exploratory conversation about the things we'd recently learned and about the possibility of working for him in his forthcoming role in Qatar. By November 2004 we were on our way to check out the practicalities that would confront us in Qatar; the start of many such planning visits that exposed us to a whole raft of new geographical and cultural challenges. While this preparation dominated much of our work throughout 2005, apart from our time in the USA during Katrina, we had taken on the parallel task of broadcasting the Commonwealth Games from our hometown of Melbourne in 2006.

It was just as well that we lived in Victoria as it enabled us to keep the costs down on a budget that was very tight indeed. Having lived in Australia for three years by then, we had become used to the few cultural differences over which it's easy to trip. The Australian expression, 'No worries,' used to catch us out; we had initially assumed it meant, 'I've heard you, understood you and will action your request without fuss, post haste,' but in fact it can encompass anything from that end of the scale all the way down to, 'No idea what you were talking about, wasn't really listening, and hope to be off duty when this problem next rears its ugly head.' It all rather depends on who is uttering the phrase.

Our duties on the Commonwealth Games were similar to those we'd performed in Athens and required similar attention to detail, although we would only be using four helicopters. At least the reduced number of machines allowed me to resume my seat in one of them for some of the events, and in particular for the opening and closing ceremonies. The former began with a flight running along the Yarra river, between the huge gas flames

emanating from the Crown Casino, and over a long line of historic couta boats followed by multiple giant floating fish sculptures, all of which conjured up a spectacular procession as we made our way over the Melbourne Cricket Ground (MCG) and used the zoom of the Cineflex to take us right down to the podium where the flame would shortly be arriving. It was a wonderful moment and left me full of excitement for what our hometown could do.

Less impressive was the obstruction we'd received from VicUrban, the authority for urban renewal that blocked every single application we put in for a temporary operating base. Eventually we prevailed upon the kindness of the *Herald Sun* newspaper for use of their small grass area in the Docklands, next to the river.

Conversely the Civil Aviation Safety Authority (CASA) and their counterparts at Airservices Australia, who control all of Australian airspace, could not have been more helpful, friendly and positive in their responses to the many issues that inevitably arose. I was installed as the arbiter of the special airspace established for the event, a responsibility I had never expected to shoulder during my career, and which took up a good deal of my time. In the final analysis it worked out well in the way it protected our own film pilots from being hassled by general aviation traffic. I did have a wry smile on my face towards the end of the opening ceremony when the local police chopper declined my polite advice on changing the position he had chosen to loiter while he waited to escort the Queen's road cavalcade. Once I'd mentioned the height and intensity of fireworks that were due in ten seconds, nine, eight . . . he seemed to take interest and move quite quickly. The only security threat on the opening night came from a farm pilot who had decided the 40-mile exclusion zone didn't apply to him. Thankfully the long sessions I'd had behind closed doors with the Australian Defence Force and their Special Forces Commander paid off. The wayward farm pilot was invited to look out at his wingtips where two F16 fighter pilots waved cheerily back at him. He duly decided that he might choose to exit our airspace after all.

I hugely enjoyed filming many of the sports myself and none more than the Cycle Road Race. This gruelling event took place over five hours within and around the picturesque Botanical Gardens, which provided a splendid backdrop for the images but whose overhanging trees made it hard to maintain line of sight with the leading peloton. I had teamed myself up with Dave Manton, one of the world's great sports cameramen, and together we pushed beyond the boundaries of our abilities to achieve some of the best shots I've ever flown. I brimmed with pride when the broadcast director called me on the radio to say, 'You don't need me, I'm going outside for a cigarette, just keep doing what you do.'

A few weeks later we were on our way to Doha. In a male-dominated society like Qatar, which at this point didn't allow women to drive, it was always going to be an uphill battle for Sara, in overall charge of our aerial unit. She played it sensitively in all her phone conversations and subsequent face-to-face meetings.

For our operating base we choose Losail, which is Qatar's international motor-racing track, first opened in 2004, only two years before our arrival. It was well out of the city of Doha so there was no danger of us disturbing anybody if we had to come and go at unsociable hours or carry out night engine runs for maintenance reasons. The huge tarmac car park was free of any obstructions beyond the large lighting towers that would provide us with ideal illumination for night landings. (For a short time around then Losail held the title of being the largest permanent venue sports lighting project in the world.) There was ready-made office space in multiple Portakabins, good clean bathroom facilities and a great little café. The manager was enormously helpful, there was a good permanent

security organisation and all the staff were already geared up for visiting motorcycle teams coming to test out of season, so we could be easily absorbed into their normal day-to-day activities.

We did need to organise a large clean tank for storing aviation fuel, but this arrived on the day after we'd asked for it and was quickly craned into position. We also needed a small hangar to take one helicopter at a time, but as we wouldn't be doing anything like the volume of maintenance we'd had to cope with in Athens we were able to opt for a pop-up tent. Next we needed fuel to put into our shiny new tank and were introduced to a large man who seemed to be perpetually smiling. We soon discovered that the reason for his smile was that once the symbolic flame had been lit at Khalifa Stadium, atop a brand new circular hotel rising up to the improbable height of 900 feet, it was scheduled to burn 'for eternity', and the man we were dealing with had the contract to supply the gas. This would apparently take five articulated trucks a day. Since Qatar is the world's largest exporter of liquefied natural gas and has enough reserves beneath its gulf waters to supply the entire world's needs for two hundred years, I guess they thought that burning off five truckloads a day was a perfectly acceptable thing to do.

While we prepared our operations base, our colleagues back in the UK were preparing our helicopters: two Bell 206 Jetrangers and two AS350 Squirrels. Once they'd been fully serviced and given a clean bill of health for the next hundred hours of flying, they had to be flown to Luton airport where Mick Wright and Geoff Webster, probably two of the most experienced helicopter engineers in the country, took the blades off and readied the machines for conveyance to Qatar. In pre-planning with IMG we'd established that they were also going to need to bring two huge outside-broadcast trucks from the UK, so it had been decided to charter two Russian Antonov 124 cargo planes.

There are only twenty-six civilian Antonovs in the world, so the ones that are available are working continuously. If you imagine a 747 that's been chopped off at the knees so the belly nearly scratches along the ground, then add about thirty extra wheels, cut off the front so that the whole nose can hinge upwards, and finally give it a gastric problem so that it blows up out of all proportions, then you get some idea of what an Antonov looks like from the outside. Inside is like the interior of a huge roll-on-roll-off car ferry, with ringbolts in the floor and huge chain lashings to firmly secure every item of cargo. It even smells like a ship.

Once our two planes had been loaded with a broadcast truck and two helicopters, Mick Wright phoned us with a brief of what to expect on arrival.

'We'll roll to a stop. They'll exhaust the hydraulic pressure from the front landing gear so that it kneels down like an elephant at the front. The nose will open upwards and a great big ramp will unfold. These guys work three months on, one month off, and are paid based on the number of flights they achieve so don't get in their way because they are in a *serious* hurry. They're all Russian and don't speak a word of English but we've learned to trust the loadmaster foreman so just stand back and let him do his job. It'll frighten the life out of you but I promise it will go OK.'

Mick spoke true words indeed. The whole thing ran like clockwork and the big old Antonovs spat out our precious cargo into the hot Doha night. We had hardly patted our helicopters before the nose doors of the planes had closed and they were taxiing back to the runway, on their way to who knows where.

Every single person involved in preparations for the games was now operating at a fever pitch, but none more so than the team who were erecting a giant video screen that would occupy one entire side of the Khalifa main stadium. It was the biggest video screen ever assembled, and unusually was in the shape of a semi-circle.

To support this monstrosity they had commissioned a number of massive rolled steel joists (RSJs) from the nearest available manufacturing plant – in Macedonia, a straight-line distance of about 2,000 miles. A convoy of these things had left the plant some weeks earlier for the tortuous drive across many countries to reach Qatar, but they fell at the last hurdle when Saudi Arabia refused them transit permission. I have no idea what local dispute caused the problem but there was no way that permission was going to be granted. The expression 'Failure is not an option' is never more true than in the run-up to an event like this. Consequently five more Antonovs were pressed into service and, hey presto, the gigantic RSJs arrived by air and were soon cutting a fine silhouette across the desert landscape.

The first crew briefing is always a bit overwhelming and has to be taken slowly and methodically. You can guarantee that most of the guys will take in only about half of what's said, and so it has to be backed up by a comprehensive operations manual that goes into the finest detail of not only their flying tasks but all the domestic details over which they would otherwise stumble in a foreign land. Preparation of that manual is what occupies every waking hour for a year or two in advance of the event. The process of writing the manual is a way of making sure that you've looked into every dark corner, examined all the what-if scenarios and checked the details over and over and over again. In that respect our experience in Athens was invaluable and I drew heavily on all the forms and templates we'd found to work well. Two years on from Greece I was still having nightmares about the day I'd left Richard Banham without any fuel arrangements, and it was memories like that which drove me to check the operations manual again and again.

I loved the flying, I loved being in the desert and I loved the opportunity to work once again with some of the finest aviators I could have asked for. For Sara it was much harder. Ten minutes before we were due to start our broadcast to the whole of the Middle East and Asia she was phoned by the brigadier who was our most senior liaison officer.

'All of your helicopters must land immediately,' he barked before slamming the phone down.

Sara called us obediently to the ground and waited an appropriate couple of minutes before calling the brigadier back to hear, 'They may fly again now.'

She politely asked why he had required us to land, obviously so that she could avoid anything similar happening in the future.

The answer she received was, 'To prove to you that I can, and to establish that you will.'

He didn't trouble us again for the next two weeks.

My abiding memory of Qatar is once again of the opening ceremony, on which so much money had been lavished. As the minutes ticked down to the sumptuous event my position above the stadium revealed lightning and a huge storm coming down towards us from the north. The forecast had suggested the possibility, but not on the biblical scale I was witnessing. We faced the huge and impossible dilemma of either running back to Losail for cover, in which case we'd blown the ceremony entirely, or finding a night landing site next to the stadium in the space of ten minutes. I handed the decision to Sara on the ground, while I engaged in a small contretemps in the cockpit with our local security officer who had suddenly decided that half the moves we'd rehearsed during the previous week couldn't be used as they were going to reveal the dark patch in which, invisibly, lay the residence of the Qatari royal family. With only one minute to go before I had to avoid the lightning, a huge area of concrete right next to the stadium was lit up by a thousand arc lamps in a tribute to Sara's ingenuity, resourcefulness and speed in a crisis. We landed, the storm and lightning passed over us in just a couple of minutes, the security officer sulked, and I

took off again as the countdown clock on the huge video screen hit zero. Game on.

The other sport in our 'big four' was the World Cup held in South Africa in mid-2010. This was a whole new ballgame (forgive the pun). We had bid to contribute to the previous tournament, four years earlier in Germany, but the position of the venues precluded the use of helicopters as they mostly lay at the end of airport runways. Old friends Skip Margetts and Chris Bohnenn had been doing a number of promotional shoots for Host Broadcasting Services (HBS) through their South African aerial film company Helimedia. HBS had also been our clients in Qatar (split 50/50 with IMG) and had been pleased with how we'd run the aerial unit for the Doha Asian Games, so we naturally fell into a partnership with Helimedia to try to win the World Cup gig. Together we won the contract for the rehearsals for the World Cup, spent eighteen months or more filming South Africa from our helicopters for the advance media promotions, and were eventually awarded the much-longed for aerial broadcast unit opportunity.

The reason it was different to the other three global events we have covered was because of the structure of our work. We had been used to all our helicopters being based together, the crews being briefed together and flying in close proximity before celebrating together on completion of each day's work. In South Africa our seven locally sourced machines would be spread around the country at one of the ten soccer stadiums, often moving large distances. This compressed our management skills into multiple individual phone calls to each of the teams, which on reflection was not a great way to do it; it led to feelings of isolation for the remote teams and stretched my time to breaking point. If I had that time over again, and with the internet access now available, I would use an app like Skype or Periscope to host a daily conference for all concerned.

The second difference was in the shooting role we committed to. Each team would capture as much local beauty as they could in advance of each game; this footage would then be woven in with the live material being captured in the run-up as the opposing soccer teams made their way to the stadium in their national buses. Our role ended once the players had marched onto the field and sung their national anthems.

We were glad to be the first aerial unit to ever support the World Cup and I was immensely pleased with the variety and quality of beauty material – as opposed to the sports material – being generated. In many ways I was basking in reflected glory as many of the people I passed in the International Broadcast Centre congratulated me on the latest shots they'd seen projected. The encouragements that Sara and I had been passing down phone and radio lines had undoubtedly contributed to those successes, but I began to feel as remote from the action as our teams were feeling in the field. Only on later reflection did I also realise how strange it was to be deemed surplus to requirements just as the main sporting tournament kicked off each day.

It's hard to recall South Africa without being overwhelmed with memories of how Sara had spent the entire year of pre-production battling with a particularly virulent form of cancer. I shake my head at how many internal production meetings we held in our home office in between sessions of radiotherapy, chemotherapy and strong doses of morphine. The medics were entirely right in attributing Sara's miraculous survival to her attitude throughout the awful treatments but if they'd known about the organisational work she was doing in between each session they may well have put her in a straightjacket and had me locked up for abuse. Maybe the upcoming event gave her extra focus and determination to beat the awful disease, who knows? I just know how grateful I am that she did.

I'm very glad of the job we did, exceptionally proud of the images our teams captured, and thoroughly enjoyed my one excursion into a cockpit for the opening ceremony as usual, but we were desperately tired by the end of that sporting month. It was the one sporting tournament from which we emerged feeling that we should perhaps have managed things differently. I'd love another go at it, in Russia or maybe even back in Qatar.

23

IMAX

THROUGHOUT OUR GLOBETROTTING WE NEVER forgot to invest a few extra days and dollars back into stock shots for our library. South Africa of course provided some wonderful opportunities, and there were always a few special shots that we mentally put to one side for the IMAX film we hankered to make. We always remembered the impact of the massive screen experience and we shared the underlying assumption that our day would come.

When Sara took a trip to the UK and left me with some spare evenings I began to tinker with assembling a first edit. The impetus came from reading an environmental article which, described the damage that mankind was doing to the Earth. I began to contemplate the proposition that the damage we were inflicting was as nothing compared to the damage She could do to us if we persisted in this mindless ecological vandalism. I had seen that effect with my own eyes in the aftermath of Hurricane Katrina. Out of that thought the

title *The Earth Wins* sprang into my head; about five minutes later I was sitting at our edit desk assembling sequences from South Africa, New Orleans, Europe, Los Angeles, and from the specific flights we'd made over the devastation caused in our home state of Victoria by the Black Saturday fires which had burned more than half the state and taken many lives. By the time Sara returned from her three weeks away I was able to show her, and our long-serving production manager Matt Downey, a completed cut.

Editing for IMAX is very different to editing for smaller screens. The canvas on which the imagery will eventually be experienced is so huge it requires small head movements by the audience to take in everything that's happening from top to bottom and from extreme left to extreme right of screen. The same consideration has to be applied when choosing how much camera movement to allow in a particular shot; if a movement of one inch is perceived across a TV screen it will translate into a movement of many tens of feet across a giant IMAX screen, which can be very unsettling to the audience. Any shot that was anywhere less than perfect therefore had to end up on the metaphorical cutting-room floor. In generating our own shots across the years we had always kept this project in mind, but even then it was surprising how many shots I rejected for reasons of excessive movement.

I *love* to edit to music, in the same way that I've always tried to fly to a pace and a rhythm. Wearing her producer's hat, Sara was gulping for oxygen on hearing the tracks from The Who, The Temper Trap, New Order, Coldplay, Art of Fusion and Yothu Yindi that I'd woven into the fabric of our film; she knew only too well that she was listening to a soundtrack that was going to cost us well into six figures to licence. I hadn't been entirely irresponsible in my choice since we had more than a passing connection with Toby Dundas, drummer of The Temper Trap, and with Rebecca Boulton, an old friend of Sara's who had been the manager of New Order for several decades. Once Sara and Matt had applied their critical and creative minds to my initial ideas, we all began to feel that we had something we could proudly take to market.

As with so many creative undertakings, there comes a point when commercial reality begins to intrude and then to dominate, ultimately becoming the be-all and end-all. This is even more true when that creativity is being brought to market in a medium as expensive as IMAX. Another reality, as with so many of the stories in this book, is that I could write another thousand pages and still not convey the detail and intricacies involved in trying to successfully complete a project on this scale and of this intensity. We learned through listening very carefully to the best minds in the business of large-format film making. We learned by attending global conferences and expos on the subject, always a long flight away. We experimented by taking small portions of our film through the whole end-to-end process of upscaling our images, subtly colouring them, sending them to Hollywood for printing to chemical film, then shipping huge rolls of celluloid back and projecting them – through the generosity of Melbourne IMAX manager Richard Morrison – onto a real IMAX screen. It's a very long journey from the small edit screen to the big projection screen.

We also learned about how to distort our imagery for the domes of planetariums around the world and about how to achieve faithful translations of our script into multiple languages including 'Latam' and Mandarin. Throughout all this Sara was exercising her overall producer's responsibility for content and simultaneously negotiating distribution contracts with as many IMAX theatres around the world as she could. Between starting the project and releasing our film the IMAX name experienced an explosion of popularity and brand recognition through the advent of digital projection and a consequent exponential increase in the number of screens. In theory you might think this would be a big advantage

to us in our search for exhibition outlets, but in fact the reverse turned out to be true. The paradigm that IMAX had operated within for three decades was to exhibit one or two chosen films, always of forty minutes duration, usually with some educational content, throughout the day on a one-hour audience cycle. A bottoms-on-seats contract for a year therefore meant that you could be reasonably certain of a substantial return on your investment, albeit over a long period. I think the correct financial expression for this is having a long tail. The new paradigm of interweaving these more traditional IMAX documentary offerings with the latest and greatest Hollywood action blockbusters meant that our little film was now unexpectedly competing head-to-head with the likes of *Superman*, *Iron Man* and *Gravity* in large format.

The Earth Wins opened to great critical review in Melbourne and in the UK, where we were particularly excited to host Toby Dundas and Joseph Greer of The Temper Trap, Bernard Sumner, Phil Cunningham and Tom Chapman of New Order, plus individual friends such as Formula One driver Mark Webber, film pilot Marc Wolff, co-ordinator Tim Desbois and many of the other people who had contributed so much to the adventures told in earlier stories. Despite the buzz associated with such occasions, it's still the presentations to school parties that I most enjoy. If each of us who care about the planet we walk upon can encourage just a couple of youngsters from the incoming generation to think more about our interaction with our home then maybe we can improve things one child at a time... I hope.

The production of *The Earth Wins* was a great opportunity to put into practice so many of the techniques I'd learned and honed over the years: as a film pilot, as a director and as an editor. The Cineflex camera system enabled us to draw the setting sun forward into a shot of an industrial megalith, to the extent that the two seemed almost interwoven in space and in meaning. Our relationships with various exceptional camera operators allowed us to create groundbreaking sequences such as an airliner passing across the face of the Moon, which most people still believe cannot have been shot from a helicopter, and probably could not have been without the magic hands of DoP Mike Parker. Sara's powers of persuasion got us into locations that most film makers can only dream of. I had to continually dig deep inside myself to be the best film pilot I could possibly be.

I was going to say that my favourite shot in *The Earth Wins* involves the town of Marysville near Melbourne, but the word 'favourite' cannot be the right word for something that depicts death and destruction. Perhaps 'thoughtful' would better describe the implication of a shot that harked back to the day when I had seen that ship ploughing through the fog all those years ago. At that moment I had wanted to share the experience with as many people as I could. Around thirty-five years later the massive IMAX screen allowed me to do just that, as faithfully as if each audience member had been there in the cockpit with me. We began the shot by circling at high level to illustrate the extent of the devastation wrought by the fires of Black Saturday. Those fires had nearly reached our own back door but for 173 less fortunate souls it had taken their lives. As we lazily circled, the shone sun down through a clear blue sky, the likes of which we had not seen through the smoke haze for months, and the blackened forest stretched as far as the eye could see in all directions.

Warwick Field, who would go on to receive the Gold Tripod award from the Australian Society of Cinematographers for *The Earth Wins* – the highest award from the ACS and the only Gold Tripod given in 2014 – was on top form that day and I could feel the helicopter as an extension of myself in a way that only happens on special days. Our intention was to cut the camera and reposition for a medium-level shot of the town that we could see laid out like a map beneath us, but when the air is smooth, the chopper is stable, the camera is performing to perfection and we're both in the zone, it's better to just let it continue. In the knowledge that this shot was ultimately destined for a very big screen I gently rolled the helicopter level and simultaneously initiated a smooth descent. Down, down and down we went, seeing the town grow in the frame and in our windscreen. The expletives we whispered came out as more of a prayer as it slowly dawned on us that we weren't looking at a town in a valley, we were looking at the ghost of where a town used to be. Every single homestead had been torched and destroyed in a firestorm whose intensity we could only guess at. It was almost as if the camera and the helicopter also knew that they had to show their respect for the departed by behaving gently and with dignity. Our shot ended in a perfect hover directly above two houses whose only recognisable feature, the corrugated roofing iron, was lying flat on the ground.

As Chris Martin of Coldplay sings the words 'I will try to fix you' in our film I still find it hard to watch that sequence without a lump in my throat. It's a tough one for any audience to watch because they are experiencing the moment and discovering the reality of the image exactly as I did when we filmed it. In that regard I felt on the first day of the film's release that I'd achieved what I'd set out to do all those decades earlier.

24

DISRUPTION

Man must rise above Earth to the top of the atmosphere and beyond, for only then will he fully understand the world in which he lives.

Socrates (469–399BC)

I CAN'T FOR ONE MOMENT CLAIM TO fully understand the world in which we live as a result of my career above it, but I do believe that it's given me a more privileged perspective than the banker all those years ago who was so puzzled by me he turned on his heel and went to talk to someone else. We are all at the centre of our own little world, and I assume that his world was coloured by the city, by the movement of money around that city and by the continuous flow of information he received from screens, newspapers and like-minded contemporaries. I guess it's no wonder (and certainly not his fault) that he couldn't find a point of engagement with a strange animal whose world was coloured

by the sun, by the ebbs and flows of the natural world and by a continuous flow of information received from above and below. It might seem like a dreadful contradiction to have initiated that flow of natural information by climbing into a modern, hi-tech, gas-guzzling and noisy machine but that just happens to have been my path in life.

When I'm asked whether I still fly I tend to answer with 'Occasionally', but then I count on my fingers and realise the last time I flew a helicopter with a camera attached to it was at the Korean Formula One Grand Prix in October 2012. For two years we provided the live broadcast aerials at all of the Grands Prix around the world and I finally got the chance to fly on one myself. In yet another neat joining of the circle, it was a race at which Mark Webber started on pole. As we hammered around the track at very low level, cutting corners to stay ahead of Mark during his blistering qualifying lap, I felt that I was putting together all my skills and experience into that 1 minute 37.242 seconds in the same way that he was. The camera operator whispered to me as we crossed the start/finish line alongside Webber, 'I think I can hear the sound of sweat coming through your headphones.' He could indeed.

When my first book was published I found myself introducing it by standing up in an auditorium full of people, telling a few stories and trying to draw a wider conclusion here and there from those tales of rising above the Earth. I thoroughly enjoyed those encounters and the audience reactions caused me to look more inwardly to ask what lessons I had truly learned, and perhaps even ask if there was something about myself that I might have learned along the way. I already knew that my job had taken me to more dramatic places each year than most people get to experience in a lifetime, if at all, and I was already extremely grateful for that. But when I began to experiment with talking about broader concepts of perspective, of context, of resilience and of stretching one's own boundaries, I was not prepared for the overwhelmingly positive feedback from audiences who had taken away something that they could relate to and apply to their own job or to their own life.

A chance encounter with a friend who was working for the TEDx organisation led to my first opportunity to stand up in front of an audience that exceeded 1,000 people and take tentative steps towards intentionally conveying something that might be useful to them. I chose the subject of how my brain had speeded up to a seemingly impossibly high rate during a life-threatening incident when my tail rotor had failed; I called my fifteen-minute presentation 'I have been Superman and I think you can be too'. My postulation that we all have inherently extraordinary capabilities within us, if only we could work out how to access them, was well received, despite my internal obsessions with where I was standing, how I was projecting my voice and what was playing on the screen behind me. Despite all the normal fears associated with public speaking, the kick I got from interacting with a live audience was enough to persuade me that Sara's idea of doing more motivational and inspirational speaking gigs might not be such a bad one. She negotiated a contact with the wonderful husband-and-wife team of Winston Broadbent and Nanette Moulton, whose great team at Saxton, the largest speakers' bureau in the southern hemisphere, set me off down an entirely unexpected new career path. In a recent period of nine days I spoke in front of over 4,000 people from five diverse organisations, including the CEO and his senior managers at Optus, the Australian Society of Sonographers, and the entire Australian Fleet Air Arm. If you'd predicted that career path to me twelve months earlier I would have laughed openly in your face, but the journey wouldn't be called life if it was predictable.

I used to think that the word 'disruption' was some sort of corporate-speak for the inconveniences suffered by a large

company when they initiate a change to their logo or to their canteen arrangements. Then it became the buzzword for coping with new technology or new business paradigms, most often illustrated by a reference to the world of taxis and the invasion of Uber. Little did I understand how the word 'disruption' actually refers to the day on which you realise that everything you've based your entire working life on, up to that point, has been turned upside down and must be rethought. Nor for one minute did I imagine that this could be something I would have to face up to in the closing years of my career.

Remotely controlled model helicopters had occasionally made forays into my world as a film pilot from the mid-1990s but they were little more than a novelty back then. As I stood beside my full-size machine, my main interest lay in not losing the use of my knees to their sharp rotor blades as they set off to generate wobbly images in low resolution. We had even become briefly involved in remote piloting ourselves during a project with the young and highly talented aerospace designer William Ives to build and operate immense airships within London's Millennium Dome on the night the Queen came to the midnight party. After a year of continuous indoor flying operations we went on to take William and his team to Qatar for the Doha Asian Games six years later, where they built for us a similar type of innovative flying machine to capture aerial imagery of indoor sports.

Drones were starting a progression into the same area as we went head-down into the creation of our own IMAX film but by the time we emerged back into the sunlight Moore's law had advanced the world of drones to the point where they were having a serious impact upon our day-to-day business. Try as we might there was little we could do to combat the film industry's appetite for the latest and greatest toy in the game, so our operating and financial predictions had to be revised downwards on a weekly basis. Allied to this rush towards miniaturisation, our sales of large gyro-stabilised camera systems disappeared in just the space of a few months. Disruption suddenly meant something tangible, concrete and very frightening indeed.

There followed more painful months of witnessing technically competent drone images appearing in just about every production being broadcast from dawn to dusk, while our poor TV set had to suffer the abuse and profanity I was throwing in its general direction. Sara had to endure similar privations when she tentatively suggested that I might consider learning to operate this new form of flying machine; I simply didn't have the heart to begin competing with kids in reversed baseball caps listening to rap music through their earphones. My main complaint about the footage I was seeing was the disregard for creative images that were sympathetic to the specific production. The stability of the picture from a drone was not in question but I refused to accept that values such as having a beginning, middle and end to a shot had entirely disappeared. Nor could I see the point in a drone pilot either remaining in a static hover or, conversely, rapidly weaving around the sky to prove what a cool dude he was. There seemed to be a lack of appreciation for the subtleties of the art in which I'd been schooled for nearly forty years.

Then came the lightbulb moment, once again initiated from the female half of our team, that if there was a lack of understanding in the new generation of miniature film pilots then there was a need for tuition and mentoring. Within just a few weeks we had designed a residential course, taken on our first students, coached them into results that they hadn't believed possible, and sent them out into the world to ply their craft commercially. It was a seminal moment at which we paused, raised a small glass to ourselves (perhaps more in relief than in celebration) and reflected once again on the vagaries of the journey of life.

Just last week, as I write, we had the enormous privilege of being invited to the Sydney Opera House during the incredible Vivid festival that illuminates so much of the city and results in the roof of the iconic building displaying spectacular projected imagery. It was also the week in which Intel's autonomous squadron of one hundred drones lit up the night sky in a breathtaking dance to music over Sydney Harbour. Our invitation had come from Rebecca Boulton, Bernard Sumner and all of the band New Order, who were in town to play several nights at the Opera House. At the time of the release of *The Earth Wins*, the band had been enormously supportive on our opening night and had gone on to adopt footage from our film to illustrate their track 'Your Silent Face' throughout their world tour of the last two years. I find it hard to convey the enormity of seeing our work projected on such a stage as part of the performance by such a seminal band. Sometimes Sara and I both have to stop and pinch ourselves.

As I write this final paragraph an email has just popped up inviting me to direct a film, shot mainly from drones, in a country we've never previously visited. Who knows if this project will come to fruition or whether we will find the funding for our proposed online masterclasses in film-flying for drone pilots and their camera operators? Either way, I can look back on a fabulously enjoyable career, feel privileged to have experienced it all, and at last understand something of the continuum between what has been, what is and what will be.

Bring it on.

WITH THANKS

I seem to have used up my word allowance in story-telling (how unusual!) so I have to be brief in remembering some special people, many of whom should have had paragraphs or even chapters of their own within the book. My heartfelt thanks:

To Zigi Yates – production co-ordinator extraordinaire who shared such intense times in Melbourne and Qatar and who generously introduced us to Matt as her replacement.

To Matt Downey – without whom, quite literally, the latter chapters of this book would not have come about in the ways they did. His first question to me in 2006 was, 'How do you take your coffee?' then he wrote it down. It was no surprise that by the time he left eight years later he was a highly accomplished producer in his own right. Too many things to thank you for, Mattski.

To Sam and Tips – I'm so proud of you guys and what you've achieved. Thanks for all the creative input along the way, the fresh perspective from younger eyes was always invaluable.

To Mick Wright – for standing back-to-back with us in some long hard struggles. Long may 'HD On The Move' thrive as your personal spin-off from all our times together.

To Rick Wysocki, Chester Merrill, Marjie Weitzel, Dana Cass and all the crews at Getty Images and Corbis Motion – who so lovingly cared for our stock shots.

To CJ – for the Australian impetus, for the helicopter in New Orleans and for carrying the Helifilms name forward into the USA.

To all the highly skilled cinematographers who shared the journey, some of whom are named in the book, but particularly to Warwick Field, Adam Rodgers and Mike Boidy.

To Roger and all of the Dundas family – for much moral and practical support throughout the second part of the journey.

To Dave Wheatland – for the eye-opening film tour of Australia by fixed wing that there wasn't room to tell about.

To everybody who worked with us on *The Earth Wins*, but particularly those who toiled to make it a worthwhile and useful resource for teachers worldwide: Jane Morrison, Phillipa Beeson and all the team at Cool Australia.

To David Voy and all the pilots, engineers and camera crews who worked so tirelessly alongside us through multiple adventures.

To everybody at Bloomsbury, and the teams in their offices worldwide, who've given life to this book, in particular to Kate Cubitt, Adam Kirkman and the team in Sydney, and Janet Murphy, Jonathan Eyers and the team in London. Thank you everyone for the belief.

To Mari Roberts for saying yes once again to working with me as editor. I really love that process with you, Mari.

Most important of all, to Sara Lou; the love of my life. Thank you, my darling, for being the hardest worker I know and for creating all those opportunities that I could never have envisaged in my wildest dreams. I'm so looking forward to the rest of the magical mystery tour together.

Finally to all the good friends and great aviators who didn't make it all the way, in particular Pete Barnes and Henry Marcuzzi. I miss the laughter of you both.